Expert Advice From The Home Depot®

Trimwork 1-2-3®

Meredith® BOOKS

Trimwork 1-2-3®

Senior Editor: John P. Holms
Graphic Designer: Tim Abramowitz
Copy Chief: Terri Fredrickson
Publishing Operations Manager: Karen Schirm
Edit and Design Coordinator: Mary Lee Gavin
Editorial and Design Assistants: Renee E. McAtee, Kairee Mullen
Marketing Product Managers: Aparna Pande, Isaac Petersen, Gina Rickert, Stephen Rogers, Brent Wiersma, Tyler Woods
Book Production Managers: Pam Kvitne, Marjorie J. Schenkelberg, Rick von Holdt, Mark Weaver
Contributing Copy Editor: Don Gulbrandsen
Contributing Proofreaders: Julie Cahalan, Kathy DiNicola, Mason Dolan, Sue Fetters
Illustrator: Joel Wires
Indexer: Don Glassman

Heartwood Books

Writers: Jeff Day, Kenneth Burton Jr., Steve Cory
Photography: Donna Chiarelli, Thomas Wolf
Photo Styling: Pamela G. Simpson
Set Construction: Jeff Day, Ron Day, Hunter's Run Studios
Model Construction: Kenneth Burton Jr.
Model Painting: Donna Chiarelli

Meredith® Books

Executive Director, Editorial: Gregory H. Kayko
Executive Director, Design: Matt Strelecki
Executive Editor/Group Manager: Benjamin W. Allen
Senior Associate Design Director: Tom Wegner

Publisher and Editor in Chief: James D. Blume
Editorial Director: Linda Raglan Cunningham
Executive Director, Marketing: Jeffrey B. Myers
Executive Director, New Business Development: Todd M. Davis
Director, Sales-Home Depot: Robb Morris
Executive Director, Sales: Ken Zagor
Director, Operations: George A. Susral
Director, Production: Douglas M. Johnston
Business Director: Jim Leonard

Vice President and General Manager: Douglas J. Guendel

Meredith Publishing Group

President: Jack Griffin
Senior Vice President: Bob Mate

Meredith Corporation

Chairman and Chief Executive Officer: William T. Kerr
President and Chief Operating Officer: Stephen M. Lacy

In Memoriam: E.T. Meredith III (1933-2003)

The Home Depot®

Marketing Manager: Tom Sattler

Distributed by Meredith Corporation.
Meredith Corporation is not affiliated with The Home Depot®.

Note to the Reader: Due to differing conditions, tools, and individual skills, Meredith Corporation and The Home Depot® assume no responsibility for any damages, injuries suffered, or losses incurred as a result of following the information published in this book. Before beginning any project, review the instructions carefully, and if any doubts or questions remain, consult local experts or authorities. Because codes and regulations vary greatly, you always should check with authorities to ensure that your project complies with all applicable local codes and regulations. Always read and observe all of the safety precautions provided by any tool or equipment manufacturer, and follow all accepted safety procedures.

We are dedicated to providing accurate and helpful do-it-yourself information. We welcome your comments about improving this book and ideas for other books we might offer to home improvement enthusiasts. If you would like to purchase any of our home improvement, cooking, crafts, gardening, or home decorating and design books, check wherever quality books are sold. Or visit us at: meredithbooks.com

Contact us by any of these methods:
Leave a voice message at: 800/678-2093
Write to: Meredith Books, Home Depot Books
   1716 Locust St.
   Des Moines, IA 50309–3023
Send e-mail to: hi123@mdp.com.

Trimwork 1-2-3

Meredith BOOKS

Trimwork 1-2-3®

Table of contents

Chapter 4

TRIMWORK PROJECTS 148

Chapter 5

GENERAL CARPENTRY 182

How to use this book

rimwork and molding are the finishing touches that help define the style of your home. A perfectly installed crown molding or baseboard is also an expression of the pride you take in making your home a comfortable and inviting place to live.

Almost everyone is aware, whether they can express it or not, of the impact that properly integrated trimwork has on the look and feel of a room. The right baseboard, chair rail, or window trim unifies a space and provides both visual stimulation and focus. Trimwork says you care about the details.

It's about style

Deciding to install a little trim to spruce up the living room is not a difficult decision. The challenge for most homeowners is deciding what form the new trimwork will take and choosing from the hundreds of different molding products on the market today. Part of that decision is a matter of style and that's where *Trimwork 1-2-3* begins.

The first chapter of *Trimwork 1-2-3* is simply called **Styles**. In **Styles** you'll find a detailed look at five basic styles—Traditional, Country, Victorian, Arts and Crafts, and Modern—and see how trimwork is used in each style to help define it. Understanding the basic trim elements of a style will help you make decisions.

Tool up

The second chapter is called **Tools and Materials.** This section introduces you to the

▲ From ceiling to floor, trimwork adds detail on many different levels. Note how the bookcase ties into the crown molding that surrounds the room. The wainscoting is installed at the same height as the cabinets below the shelves and the same trim is used on both to emphasize the built-in look.

tools and materials you'll be using to install trim and molding. It provides an overview of how to use and maintain each tool, some tips and tricks straight from experts at The Home Depot®, and clear instructions on how to use each tool safely. On the materials end you'll find information on choices for molding materials and common

molding profiles, along with the nails and screws you'll need to install them.

Install trim

In chapter three, **Finish Carpentry**, you'll get to work. Finish carpenters used to say that they only had to know two things in order to get the job

The right tools help you do a great job

IT'S NOT LIKE THE OLD DAYS

Finish carpentry is definitely a skill that requires practice to master, but cutting a perfect miter is nowhere near as difficult as it was in the days before high-quality finishing tools such as tablesaws, power miter saws, routers, and cordless drills became available to the general public. New tools and associated construction materials along with new technologies have made the job of installing trim and molding accessible to homeowners who have a good understanding of basic carpentry. These days tool centers are like toy stores for adults. If you're thinking of adding a little trimwork to your home, treat yourself to a stroll down the aisles and check out the tools that will help you get the job done right.

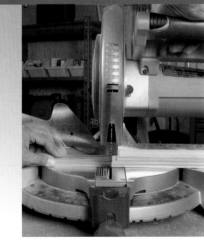

Grow your skills—one project at a time

Back in the days when most tools were powered by a strong arm rather than electricity, finish carpentry was a difficult and demanding skill. Today, however, almost anyone with a little patience and the willingness to follow some instructions can master complex woodworking tasks. *Trimwork 1-2-3* is full of projects that will help homeowners who are ready to take their knowledge of basic carpentry to the next level and grow their carpentry skills as they improve their homes.

done: what is it made of and what is it supposed to look like? On these pages you'll find projects that help you install trim from the ceiling to the floor that use clear step-by-step photography and easy-to-follow instructions. You'll also find tips and tricks such as **Safety Alerts**, **Closer Looks**, and **Work Smarters**, plus how long the job will take, and the tools and materials you'll need to complete it.

To help you make decisions about style, projects also include examples of how the trimwork would appear in each of the five styles we outline in the book.

More projects
In chapter four, **Trimwork Projects**, you'll get the chance to tackle some more advanced trimwork projects such as making a window seat and installing three different styles of wainscoting.

General carpentry
In chapter five, **General Carpentry**, you'll find projects that involve more than trim—you may want to put in a window, a door, wainscoting, raised panel framing, or wood paneling to enhance the style you've chosen to employ.

Woodworking terminology can be confusing so inside you'll also find a glossary of woodworking terms to help clear up some of the confusion.

Finishing thoughts
Finish carpentry is both challenging and satisfying. Take your time, work safely, and, most of all, enjoy learning some new skills and adding beauty to your home.

Acclimate your wood

Seasonal changes and humidity are hard on wood but you'll have much better luck with your installations if you allow your molding and trim (or any wood for that matter) to acclimate to the room it's going in before you install it. General guidelines for acclimation are 24 hours per ¼ inch of thickness of the stock. A little patience now will result in a more successful and durable installation.

◀ In Modern style the absence of traditional trimwork such as crown molding, chair rail, or baseboard does not mean that the same consideration to balance and form isn't as present as it might be in a Victorian or Country home. Imaginative use of geometric shapes created from drywall and natural materials (such as this room's fireplace surround), produces unity and focus in the same way that standard trim does in more traditional styles.

Styles

1 t's a common complaint that one house in the suburbs looks pretty much like another. But homes of any era have always had a similar look and feel. A block of Victorian row houses are nearly as identical as a neighborhood of Arts and Crafts bungalows. Styles exist because certain tastes in architecture gained popularity, became established, and remained predominant in the culture for an extended period of time. There is no single dominant style in North American architecture today; instead we take a more eclectic view, borrowing from popular styles as they excite us and reflect our interests.

What is style?

Historians have found countless ways to define the styles that have contributed to American architecture. Victorian architecture alone has been divided into many different styles. But "Victorian" will do nicely for those of us who simply want our houses to evoke a sense of 19th-century grandeur. We know "Country" has a dozen faces and that rural homes looked different in 1830 than they did in 1930. What matters, if Country is your style, is the simplicity, the honesty, the love of color, and the lines.

Trimwork helps define style

More than almost any other element, the molding and trim on your walls,

Chapter 1 highlights

TRADITIONAL STYLE
Traditional style is elegant yet comfortable, offering a sense of history that is compatible with more modern touches.

8

COUNTRY STYLE
Country style is familiar and unpretentious, a mix of simplicity and practicality that rises out of an interest in our rural past.

12

VICTORIAN STYLE
Victorian style is romance and embellishment on a grand scale—excessive perhaps, but still satisfying and intriguing.

16

ARTS AND CRAFTS STYLE
Arts and Crafts style is grounded in images of nature and celebrates the details in a home by emphasizing their natural origins.

20

MODERN STYLE
Modern styles are based on the structural elements that make up a living space. Clean lines and the geometry created by intersecting shapes are hallmarks of Modern style.

24

windows, doors, and ceilings defines the style of your home. The difficulty most homeowners face is sorting through the mass of molding options and then making choices about trim that will enhance the style they are trying to achieve.

Five common styles to study

To ease the decision-making process we're going to examine five common North American styles: Traditional, Country, Victorian, Arts and Crafts, and Modern. Traditional is the urban cousin of Country: Think Williamsburg. Arts and Crafts was an early-20th-century reaction against Victorian architecture, rejecting ornateness in favor of straight, clean lines and

invoking images of nature. Modern architecture was a reaction to the more ornate styles that predominated the early 20th century. Modernists embraced emerging building technologies by revealing the structural elements of a building that were usually hidden under molding and trim.

Creating your own style

The trimwork and molding of each of the five styles has its own unique and instantly defining signatures. Knowing these signatures will help you create finishing touches that will not only offer continuity throughout your home but also reflect your personal style and taste.

Traditional style

Traditional style is the big-city equivalent of Country. Where Country is simple and sometimes naive, Traditional is high-end and often reflects the work of highly skilled craftsmen. In fact, the term is used loosely to describe two well-developed colonial styles—Georgian and Federal.

The Georgian style was in vogue from the 1690s to the 1830s. The front of a Georgian house was rectangular with a paneled front door in the center. Columns built flat against the house called pilasters usually flanked the door and supported a decorative crown called a pediment. There were five windows across the front of the house upstairs, with four windows and the doorway downstairs.

The Federal style ran from about 1780 to 1840 and shared many features with Georgian. Federal houses were distinct, however, in that they were symmetrical with a central entrance flanked by equal numbers of shuttered windows on either side. The roofline was higher than Georgian, but the roof itself was pitched low or flat and was often decorated with balustrade—rails and banisters that made the roof look like a huge balcony. There was often a fanlight immediately above the door, with narrow windows, called sidelights, on either side of the door. The second floor above the entrance often featured a Palladian window—a double-hung window with an arched window above it and two slightly shorter windows to either side. Dentil molding was a popular crown molding, both inside and out. Woodwork was typically painted.

Traditional architecture may have fallen out of favor during the Victorian era, but from 1910 to about 1950 the country underwent the Colonial Revival period, which borrowed liberally from both Georgian and Federal style homes and reestablished Traditional style as a major influence in American home design.

◄ **While Victorian and Arts and Crafts styles favored natural woodwork in public spaces, trim and molding were richly painted in a Traditional home.**

◄ **Stairways were showpieces with painted balusters and darker banisters made of walnut or mahogany. Walls might be paneled or plain, balusters fancy or simple.**

▲ **Scrolled brackets were sometimes added to the risers below the stair tread for an extra touch of ornamentation.**

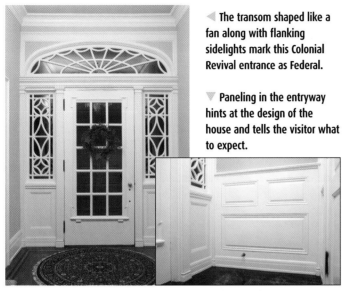

◀ The transom shaped like a fan along with flanking sidelights mark this Colonial Revival entrance as Federal.

▼ Paneling in the entryway hints at the design of the house and tells the visitor what to expect.

◀ Frame and panel trimwork adds texture and depth to the wall behind the staircase and expands on the wainscoting and paneling that covers the recess under the staircase. The natural wood of the banister and the stairs are highlighted by the creamy brown paint on the paneling.

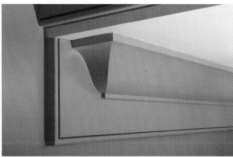

▲ When crown molding comes to an end, it can't just stop without revealing a large space between the molding and the wall. In this classic example of what's called a return, the crown comes to an end, and then turns and runs into the wall. The molding with the bead running along the bottom is actually a separate piece of wood. It's mitered, so that the bead turns up, providing a border for the end of the crown.

▲ When windows interrupted frame and panel wainscoting, the wainscot continued, but the size of the panel was adjusted. Masonry homes, both stone and brick, had walls that were sometimes two feet thick. Sometimes the sides of these thick openings were plastered; other times a frame and panel surround dressed up the wall around the window.

▲ Flat columns called pilasters like this one often flanked entrances to homes.

▲ The furniture may be late Victorian, but the windows are markedly Traditional. The built-up molding that flares at the top of the window is a classic Traditional detail.

■ Fireplaces were a necessity in Colonial homes and a prominent feature in Colonial Revival homes. The dentil molding and fluted central panel were common details.

▲ Elaborate trim begins simply. A window or door treatment like this begins with a flat board that has a molded edge. The board is cut to create the step at the top. The trim along the outside edge is a piece of base cap mitered to wrap around the board below. The seam between the two is covered by a long narrow piece of wood, called backbanding, that forms the outside edge.

◀ Sometimes door trim ended in a cornice. Simple trim along the sides and immediately above the door let the cornice call attention to itself.

◀ Traditional styling often favored repetition and symmetry especially in woodwork. This pocket door was installed in what had been an exterior wall. The carpenter mirrored the frames and panels in the pocket doors themselves to account for the thickness of the wall.

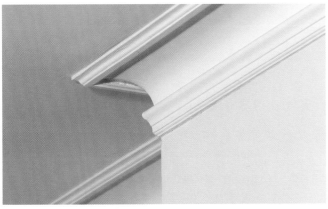

▲ Crown molding doesn't have to stop at the ceiling. Here molding is applied to the ceiling itself after the crown is installed.

▲ The doors and wainscoting that surround this seating nook are a modern interpretation of Colonial raised wooden panels made of MDF (medium density fiberboard). The addition of a cornice to the cabinetry creates a harmonious connection between the units and the window they frame.

◀ This Colonial Revival baseboard is built up from four pieces—shoe molding, ³/₄-inch-thick wood, ½-inch-thick wood, and a ³/₄-inch base cap.

Country style

▲ Wide windowsills, wood paneling, stairs that wrapped around the fireplace, and utensils hanging from exposed beams were typical of early country kitchens. Trim and molding reflect the simple handmade feel of work done by local carpenters with local materials.

The touchstones of Country are simplicity and practicality—comfortable homes that serve equally well when times are good and times are lean. Country does not draw on a historically based architectural style, such as Victorian or Arts and Crafts, but on other centuries, other countries, and an appreciation of the pleasures of rural life.

Country style is highly personal, offering a wide variety of interpretations and allowing for great freedom of expression. Hallmarks are easy to spot: fresh herbs hung to dry, unfinished (or barely finished) wooden furniture, and a simple, warm color palette. You'll find reminders of the Old World in bold folk painting or a long trestle table with caned chairs. Today's Country style showcases the trappings of Americana—from Colonial times through the Industrial Age to the present. The modern trend expresses a lively mix-and-match spirit rather than a historian's zeal for accuracy.

High-end antiques and yard sale treasures mix with ease. Floors are typically wide unfinished, painted, or clear-finished boards. Walls are paneled or plastered. Simple baseboards are painted to contrast with whitewashed surfaces. Wainscoting and chair rails are common, and moldings have a simple profile—often hand-planed 1-inch stock, with single bead ornamentation along the top edge or small beads along both long edges of chair rail.

Windows are often double-hung with six panes in each sash. Doors, a focal point of a Country room, are frame-and-panel; in a more rural vein, they are simply vertical boards backed by Z-shape bracing and hand-wrought hinges and handles. Overhead, exposed beams support the floor above and serve as a place to hang drying herbs or kitchen implements. A massive stone fireplace might be the center of both the kitchen and the sitting room.

▲ The rules of Country design were simple: You put what you needed where you needed it, and decades later people called it style. A door might appear anywhere in a farmhouse; a window might be added wherever it was necessary.

▼ The Shakers stored things on rails with turned pegs, but it wasn't unusual to see rails like this in other country settings. Often a hook or a nail took the place of the turnings that have become known as Shaker pegs.

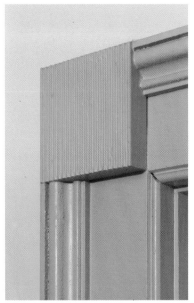

▲ The Country style was not frozen in time, but was continually influenced by other styles. This doorway started out with classic country trim, but was apparently updated when the Victorians introduced rosettes.

▲ The colors of Country, like the furniture and accessories, are rich and warm, inviting guests to be comfortable and at ease. The mantle, although a rustic interpretation of classical symmetry, was made to fit into the existing space. The fact that the columns don't match was of little concern to the builder. The elements of Country trim are carefully chosen, but they fit together as best they can considering the structural limitations of the room.

◀ It doesn't get any more country than this—a pine floor and simple baseboard and chair rail against a white wall. Light colors helped brighten up dark interiors in the days when windows were expensive and light came from candles and kerosene.

▲ Windows were often tucked in the attic next to the chimney. There was very little hidden storage in a country home so this closet would have been a luxury. Note the simple wooden latch and the simply stained trim.

■ The Shaker influence is easily seen in this master bedroom. A picture rail with wooden pegs holds a chair and a colorful quilt that hangs behind the bed. The windowsill is unpainted pine. Note how the picture rail is integrated at the same height as the window trim.

▲ Country trim can exhibit complexity, but even at its most elaborate it never felt obliged to follow the rules. This fireplace mantel was probably crafted out of crown and trim left over from the carpenter's other jobs.

▲ The tradition of farmers working with in pine and other softwoods goes back to Europe where the gentry and the guilds controlled the hardwood forests. Painted or stained, pine remains the wood of choice for trim and molding in the Country style.

▲ The crown moldings; large, deep windows; and elaborate fireplace trim may have been slightly simpler than that found in the city, but other than that, this farmhouse would have been equally at home in a middle-class urban neighborhood. Collections are a big part of Country style; in this living room the ceiling beams hold lanterns, while the rack on the wall displays plates. The plate rail above the cleverly hidden entertainment center shows off a collection of depression glassware.

Victorian style

Queen Victoria ruled from 1837 to 1901—a period during which America elected 19 presidents. The style that bears her name changed greatly during those 64 years, but its heart was always grandness and sometimes excess. It was ushered in by the Industrial Revolution—Victorian furniture and woodwork were the first to be machine-made. And the machines vastly outproduced the cabinetmaker and carpenter, churning out chair rail, crown molding, elaborate baseboard, and gingerbread at little cost. Suddenly the masses could afford decorative effects that were once the province of the rich, and the rich could afford to build on a massive scale.

Oak and chestnut were favorite architectural woods— chestnut had not yet been wiped out by blight. Walnut was a favorite furniture wood. Woodwork in the first floor rooms was often varnished or shellacked. Upstairs or in the kitchen, the woodwork retained its profile, but it was made of more common woods and often painted.

High ceilings were the norm in houses of the well-to-do , and the moldings in those rooms were big because they had to maintain a sense of proportion. Frame-and-panel wainscoting, a painstaking job when done by hand, became easy to make once machinery became available. Although never mass-produced, it was still affordable and popular—mostly in oak, a wood that is virtually impossible to work by hand.

◀ Towers were a classic feature of Victorian homes, even if it meant building curved windows and curved baseboard. It was extra work, but builders were good at it. In some homes even the radiators were curved.

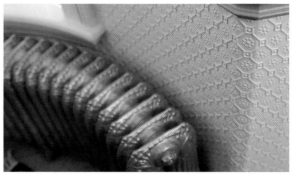

▲ To bend baseboard around a curve, Victorian carpenters cut grooves every few inches in the back of the baseboard. The grooves, called kerfs, made the wood flexible enough to bend. Here the kerfs were cut too deeply and are visible in the front of the board as light lines with flat spots in between.

▲ Late in the Victorian era, the British invented Lincrusta, a thick, heavy wallpaper with raised patterns that imitated the carved stonework like that seen in the mantel (right). Lincrusta is named for one of its chief ingredients, linseed oil.

■ Victorians still relied on the fireplace for heat, and the hearth became a showpiece—fluted columns with capitals, dentil molding, and applied carvings were typical additions to what at heart was just a plain fireplace and mantel.

◀ Plumbing came indoors during the Victorian period, and it did so with a flourish—with patterned tiles, pedestal sink, and frame-and-panel wainscoting in this case.

▲ Victorians may have loved gingerbread in their architecture, but their furniture was often massive, reflecting in part the virgin forests that had only begun to be cut.

1

▲ Pocket doors throughout this house let the owners close off a room, or open up the whole house, depending on the occasion.

■ The trim around this door is made by applying the base cap used in the baseboard to a simple flat frame around the door. Improved production methods allowed designers to create countless variations of the standard six-panel door. Victorian pattern books were filled with countless designs.

▼ Victorian homes often featured an elaborate stairway. In homes of the well-to-do there was usually a second smaller, hidden stairway for the servants.

▲ Elaborate frame-and-panel wainscot like this was made in the shop and brought to the home as one piece.

▲ Victorian homeowners and architects were committed to excessive architectural details. Ornamentation was elaborate and complex. Note all the elements in the entry above. White paneling, deep red walls, walnut columns with no structural purpose, stained glass, and heavy teak doors with large brass hinges and hardware all combine to make a complex but intriguing statement.

▲ Cornices were often elaborate. This one is made of a frieze applied to the wall, with crown molding applied over it.

◀ During one period of Victorian design, Greco-Roman details like the trim and molding shown were commonly used around an elaborate fireplace such as this one. The cornice across the top is made with dentil molding; the beaded columns end in a capital that was preassembled and installed on site.

◀ Everything about the Victorians was grand, though not everything was as grand as this. Crown molding like this might be made of cast plaster, carved wood, or as was the case in this steel magnate's house, cast iron.

▶ Victorian rooms had high ceilings that required ornate crown molding treatments to maintain a sense of scale. In this dining room the crown molding sits on a soffit, which has no architectural purpose other than to accent the molding with a shadow line. The trim on the fireplace echoes the details in the crown above.

Arts and Crafts style

T he Arts and Crafts style was a reaction to what many considered the excesses of Victorian design. Instead of swirls, whirligigs, and gingerbread, Arts and Crafts practitioners preached simplicity and practicality feeling, as Gustav Stickley said that, "the furnishing of a farmhouse kitchen may have an artistic value far beyond those of a costly drawing room."

Stickley was a founder of the American Arts and Crafts Movement and ran one of the two original factories making what has became known as Mission furniture. His magazine, *The Craftsman*, published drawings of Arts and Crafts homes, commented on the arts, and advised readers how to build

Mission furniture. Arts and Crafts quickly became a popular style. As a result, there were eventually hundreds of factories making Mission furniture and countless carpenters building Arts and Crafts bungalows.

Arts and Crafts woodwork was simple, straight, and square. The structure was left for all to see—beams often replaced crown molding in rooms; exposed joinery was popular in furniture. Woodwork was almost always oak. Wainscoting grew taller covering almost two-thirds of the wall. Chair rails disappeared in favor of a plate rail on top of the wainscot. Diamond-shaped panes were popular in windows.

▲ An Arts and Crafts room often used structure as ornament—here oversize joists and the floorboards above are open to view instead of hidden behind a more traditional plastered ceiling. Oak was the predominant wood for both furniture and molding. The simplicity of the trimwork is showcased by brightly colored walls, patterned cushions, and thickly braided floor rugs.

◀ Chair rails moved higher on the wall and became narrow shelves to display slender items such as plates. Combined with the baseboard and simple crown molding, the room feels low and comfortable, even though the ceiling is at a standard height.

▶ Baseboards were often simply 4- or 5-inch oak boards nailed along the wall. Here a recess is cut along the top of the baseboard, and the detail is carried into the door trim. Instead of mitering the pieces, the builder notched the edge of the baseboard and tucked the recess of the door trim behind it to create a simple but elegant butt joint.

◀ Because of their efficient use of space and ability to open up or close off sections of the house, pocket doors survived the Victorian age and were widely used in Arts and Crafts homes. In the transition they became less ornamented and detailed, and the panels were often horizontal instead of vertical. Simplicity of design is again evident in the rectangular geometry of the staircase.

◀ One Arts and Crafts door treatment simply butted the pieces of trim together. The side pieces extended above the head piece for an inch or so, creating ornament out of simple structure.

■ The structure of this plate rail becomes ornamental as well as practical because the details, such as the shelf supports (called korbels), are far more than what would be necessary to hold up the shelf.

▲ This baseboard was probably considered elaborate for a style such as Arts and Crafts that frowned on curves, but was the original trim in this Arts and Crafts bungalow. Styles are guidelines that are always open to interpretation by individual craftspeople.

■ In a typical Arts and Crafts treatment for doors and windows, everything met at right angles and showed a minimum of ornament.

▲ The severe lines of Mission furniture complemented the simplicity of trim and molding. White walls with minimal decoration and white lace curtains keep the focus on the wooden elements in the room, including the oak window trim and the maple floor, along with the dark oak library table and the Mission rocker. Color is added in the form of fabric, rugs, plants, and flowers.

▲ Hand-worked or mass-produced, roughly hammered hardware is a hallmark of the Arts and Crafts style.

Modern style

Form follows function.

With those three words architect Louis Sullivan launched Modern (sometimes called Contemporary) architecture. Decorative styles, he said, were dead. Modern materials made it possible for the shape of something to be determined by its purpose—the way a bird's wing is shaped to allow flight. Moldings, which had no function, were unnecessary; flat doors were favored over traditional six-panel doors.

Incredibly, Sullivan formulated his dictum in 1896, but by the 1920s the Modern style had settled on the concepts popular in modern architecture today: Details and floor plans should be regular, but not symmetrical. Usable space was more important than massive buildings. Construction details favored technical solutions over decoration. Materials used reached beyond the traditional into machine-made; hardware became sleek and shaped to suit its function.

In home construction, Modernist theories resulted in homes like those shown here. Floor plans are open; materials used include cloth on the walls, wire-reinforced glass, and glass block. Rooms have an inherent rhythm established by doors, intersecting walls, or changes in the ceiling height. The absence of moldings required rethinking how to make visual connections in open spaces, and the evolution of new technologies in wall construction, including drywall, challenged old ideas about the function of trim.

▲ At one end of this room a patio door is set off by a drywall facade and a lowered ceiling. The lowered ceiling leads to a fireplace on the opposite wall.

◄ Classic and Modern styles go hand-in-hand in this dining room. Lights are mounted in the lowered ceiling above the table, which also houses the heating and cooling vents. The table and chairs are a modern interpretation of the Arts and Crafts Movement.

The geometric shapes created by cleanly intersecting walls and openings actually serve the same function as more ornate styles of trim and molding did in earlier eras.

► Modern style demands spaces that are both functional and pleasing. A pass-through between the kitchen and dining room—with cabinetry underneath—allows separate spaces to flow easily into one another and avoids the sense of isolation that can come from closed doors. It also functions as a transitional area for sending food from the kitchen to the table.

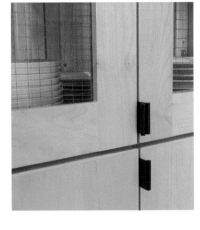

◄ Windows often show a Japanese influence by using imitation shoji screens.

◄ Modern hardware and cabinetry are sleek and simple. The wire-reinforced glass is part of the common practice of borrowing materials from industrial design.

▲ The openings in this wall reinforce the home's open floor plan and create regularity and rhythm in an asymmetrical space.

◀ Straight lines, with black, white, and earth tones, are hallmarks of Modern architecture. With no molding to highlight the recess in the wall, a change in color keeps the detail from disappearing in a sea of white. Passage out of the room is through a door that opens up like a large keyhole in the wall.

▲ Stereo equipment that would break the clean white lines of the room is hidden in a built-in closet.

▲ Stairways can't resist the urge to show off, no matter what the style is.

▲ Use of metal door jambs eliminates the need for trim and lets the architect create a rhythm with light and horizontal and vertical lines.

◀ This baseboard is recessed behind the wall surface and continues around the corner to become door trim. New materials make it possible to rethink old ideas.

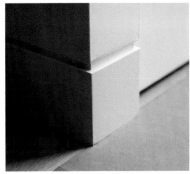

▲ This baseboard is in the same plane as the wall surface with a reveal separating the two and allowing for a change from plasterboard to more durable wood.

▲ Lights mounted on a ceiling slightly lower than the main ceiling create the modern equivalent of crown molding.

▲ Wall-hung cabinets that appear to float in the air appear again and again, sometimes as storage space below the TV, sometimes as a sideboard, sometimes even as a dresser.

▲ Glass blocks mounted vertically and framed by multilayered drywall and stone create a modern version of a sidelight window.

Tools and materials

Carpenters who are old enough to be grandparents remember the days before battery-powered drills, miter saws, and power nailers. They remember installing trim and molding with a backsaw and miter box, a circular saw, and a hammer, and they'll be the first to tell you that it was a little tougher to build things back then.

Advances in tools and technology

Advances in tools and technology have taken some of the mystery out of finish carpentry. Power miter saws, for instance, have made it possible to make a clean, precise cut that carpenters in the old days would have marveled at. Handheld routers have made it possible to do what once required a shaper or a series of hand planes.

It's still a skill

Technology may have made woodworking easier but the finest tools in the world won't make you an expert the minute you take them out of the box. This chapter looks at the tools you'll use to install trim and molding

Chapter 2 highlights

HAMMERS
There's a special hammer for almost any job. Choosing the right one will make it easier.

30

CHISELS
Chisels are essential woodworking tools and properly sharpened they are easy to use.

32

LEVELS
Levels keep your trimwork both plumb and square. Have a level by your side at all times.

34

SQUARES
Whether carpenter or combination, a square is essential for keeping a carpenter on the straight and narrow.

36

DRILLS
Drills have become hammers with motors for many carpentry applications. Choosing corded or cordless depends on the job.

38

SANDERS
A finish carpentry job isn't done until it's been finished with a sander.

40

POWER MITER SAWS
Power miter saws revolutionized the woodworking industry; they are essential tools in any workshop.

41

TABLE SAWS
The table saw is the carpenter's workhorse. If you had to choose one tool for your workshop it should be a table saw.

44

CIRCULAR SAWS
Circular saws make quick work of rough cutting, and with a little practice can do some precision work as well.

51

JIGSAWS
Jigsaws are versatile cutting tools that can handle anything from square cuts to detailed scroll work.

54

ROUTERS
Create your own trim and molding with this multiuse power tool.

55

MOLDING
Trim and molding isn't just wood anymore. New engineered products are available that are durable and easy to use.

61

FASTENERS
The right hardware will make any installation easier. Learn how to choose the right nails, screws, bolts, and anchors for the job.

65

WORKING SPACES
A well-thought-out working space makes every woodworking job easier. It doesn't take much and you'll appreciate the results.

69

and how to use them safely. It explains the most commonly used materials and hardware and how they are applied in installations.

Learning to use the power tools in this chapter will provide you with unlimited options for innovative and unusual trim and molding.

But it's important to remember that power tools can be dangerous if used improperly. Read the manufacturer's instructions and recommendations carefully, use common sense, work in a safe environment, and practice until you're comfortable using a new tool.

Hammers

2

TOOLS AND MATERIALS

Always wear safety glasses when driving nails. The hammer can chip off pieces of metal that can fly into your eye.

When you buy a hammer, consider three things: the weight, the shape of the head, and the handle. For most finishing projects—the bulk of those in this book—you'll want a 16-ounce head with a claw for pulling nails. Many carpenters prefer wooden handles because they transmit less shock to the arm and elbow. Other material—fiberglass, graphite, and steel—are somewhat lighter or stronger, and have grips to protect you from the shock. Framing hammers—used for nailing 2×4s together—are heavier, usually 20 to 22 ounces and have a straighter claw, called a rip claw, that is better suited for pulling large nails.

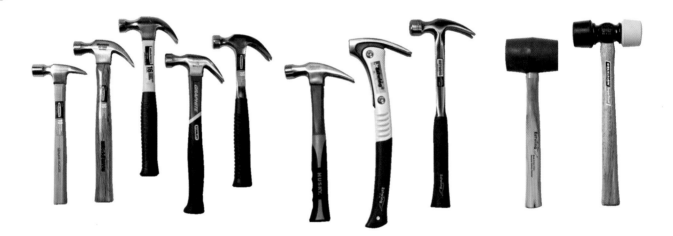

FINISHING HAMMERS

Choose the hammer you'll use for finish carpentry from the ones in this group. On the left is a 10-ounce finishing hammer, used primarily for cabinetmaking. Next to it are four 16-ounce claw hammers, the all-round choice for installing trim and doing other finish carpentry. The handles from left to right are wood, fiberglass, graphite, and steel.

FRAMING OR RIP HAMMERS

The straighter claws on these hammers are designed to pull heavy-duty nails; the heavy heads are designed to drive them. From left to right are a 20-ounce rip hammer with a fiberglass handle; a weight-forward hammer with a continuous claw to make driving nails and pulling them easier; and a 28-ounce steel-handle framing hammer. The milled or "waffle" face on this hammer is designed to grab, hold, and direct a nail when driving it. Since it also leaves a pattern when striking the wood, waffle faces are fine for framing, but not for finish carpentry.

CONVINCERS

When two pieces don't go together quite the way they should, smacking them with your framing hammer is a good way to ruin them. Reach for a rubber mallet (left) instead, which provides both heft and bounce. Since the rubber will leave marks, a second type of convincer has both a black head and a white nonmarring head (right).

Driving nails into small moldings or within an inch or so of the end of the board will cause the wood to split. Drill pilot holes to keep wood from splitting when you drive nails through them. The best bit is a nail itself, one the same size as you'll be driving. Slip the nail in the drill as if it were a bit; drill the hole, and then drive a fresh nail into the hole.

Drive finishing nails so the head is just above the surface of the wood. Drive it below the surface with a nail set, and then fill the hole with putty that you can paint or stain to match the surrounding wood. Nail sets come in different sizes. Use one whose tip is about the same size as the nail you're driving.

Drive nails into concrete with a powder-actuated hammer. Small charges—the size and shape of .22 caliber shells—force the nail through the wood and into the concrete.

WARNING: The "powder" in powder-actuated hammers is a charge of gunpowder equal to that in a .22 caliber shell. Wear hearing protection and safety glasses. Some materials, such as stone, will shatter from the impact. Follow the directions carefully.

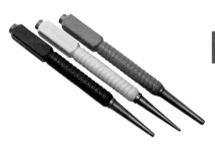

Pneumatic nailers—The hammer reinvented

It may not seem like a big deal, but nailing slows things down a lot, particularly if you're installing a room full of trim or framing a wall. Lately, power nailers—which speed things up and increase accuracy—have dropped dramatically in price. They come in combo packages that usually include an air compressor, a brad nailer, a finish nailer, and an air hose. With a nailer you can hold the piece with one hand and nail it exactly where you positioned it with a squeeze of the trigger. There are three types of nailers you'll use in general carpentry: brad, finish, and framing. A brad nailer drives nails up to about 1¼ inches long and is good in cabinet work. A finish nailer drives nails up to 2½ inches long and is the all-round favorite for installing trim. A framing nailer is designed for building walls and general framing. The old-fashioned hammer still has a few advantages, however; it doesn't cost anything to run, and it's a lot quieter in operation.

The claw of a hammer won't always get into a tight space to pull a nail. Nippers, shown above, will grab the shortest nail in the tightest places, so many carpenters reach for them whenever they have a nail to pull.

Chisels

Unsharpened chisel

An unsharpened chisel is covered by countless little lines left by grinding it at the factory. In order to get a sharp edge, you need to polish away the lines.

Sharpened chisel

The cutting edge of sharp chisel is mirror-smooth both front and back. The edge comes to a razor point and isn't rounded over. You can shave with a properly sharpened chisel.

You can perform two different operations with the chisel—chopping and shearing. Both require a steady hand and a gentle touch.

Chopping

When you chop with a chisel, you hold it vertically, put the cutting edge into the wood, and strike it with a hammer or mallet. Use a mallet that's softer than what you're hitting, or you'll damage the chisel's handle.

When chopping, position the chisel so the bevel either faces or faces away from the wood you're removing. What you do depends on the situation. If the bevel of the chisel faces the wood you're removing, the slope of the bevel can push the chisel backwards so that you end up cutting into the wood you want to remain. In this case, you might want to make the cut with the bevel facing the wood you're not removing. If, however, the cut is on the edge of a recess (like a hinge mortise) that's already been cut, it's often impossible to balance the chisel on the edge of the cut unless the back faces the good wood. When this happens, the layer of wood you're removing is so thin that it usually doesn't push the chisel backwards. In short: experiment. Do what feels right in a given situation.

Shearing

When you shear, you're creating a smooth surface by holding the chisel flat on the wood, bevel up, and pushing forward with your hand. You'll get an even smoother cut if you gently move the chisel from side to side as you push forward, keeping it flat all the while.

Heel
Bevel
Point

📖 WORK SMARTER

STAY SHARP

Even the best chisels and plane blades don't work well right out of the package unless you sharpen them. A truly sharp edge is as smooth and shiny as a mirror so that it can slice—rather than gnaw—its way through a piece of wood. Grinding is the first stage of sharpening—not because you want to grind the edge, but because you want to remove metal near the edge that gets in the way of the second stage, hand sharpening. You can use any number of specialty stones for hand sharpening, but sandpaper placed on a flat surface works just as well, costs less, and is often faster. The first hand sharpening requires several grits, but once you have the blade in shape, subsequent sharpenings may require only the finer grits.

Getting a razor sharp edge

GRINDING. For the first sharpening phase you are using the curve of the wheel to remove metal about midway between the point and the heel of the bevel, creating a slight arc in the bevel. Some grinders, like this one, have a fixed tool rest; others have a tool rest that you can set to control the angle at which the blade meets the wheel. On an adjustable tool rest, set the rest so that the widest possible portion of the blade rests on the wheel while the grinder is turned off. On a fixed rest, look to gauge the proper angle, which you can change slightly, if necessary, once you've turned the wheel on. Tighten the tool rest before grinding. Grind in a series of passes, grinding for a second or two, and then dipping the tool in water so that the edge doesn't overheat, turn black, and soften the metal. Repeat, dipping the chisel constantly until you've ground the arc of the wheel into the bevel leaving about 1/16 inch at the point and heel.

HAND SHARPENING. To sharpen your chisel, apply a piece of 120-grit sandpaper to a flat granite tile using spray adhesive. Sand the back of the chisel—keeping it perfectly flat on the sandpaper—until you've sanded out the manufacturing marks. Then hold the chisel with the cutting edge flat on the paper, and sand out the grinder marks there. Lock your arm and elbow so the angle doesn't change as you sand, and sand only on the push stroke so you don't rock the chisel as you go. Peel off the sandpaper, and repeat with 180, 220, and 400 grit. Sharpening with finer grits gives you a sharper chisel, but isn't necessary for most carpentry.

FINAL TOUCH. When you've sharpened with each of the grits, make a final few passes on the finest grit with the chisel at a slightly sharper angle. Start by lifting the back of the handle about 1/2 inch to the position shown as the fainter image in the photo. Keep the angle constant as you sharpen by locking your elbows and moving from your knees. Push the chisel forward across the paper several times, but don't pull, as changing directions usually causes you to round over the point. Lift the chisel off the sandpaper instead, keeping your elbows and wrists locked, and bring the chisel back to where you started to begin a new pass. After about 10 passes, you will have created a small, polished band, called a micro-bevel, that's literally as sharp as a razor.

Levels

Buildings, doorways, windows—almost anything you build—need to be level (flat with no slope) and plumb (straight up and down). The level and plumb line are age-old tools for checking level and plumb. The water level, a lesser-known tool for finding two points level with each other, is making a comeback based on the addition of an electronic sensor. Laser levels have revolutionized the art of marking a level line along the wall for frame and panel or wainscoting.

THE PLUMB BOB
To find a point directly above or below another, use a plumb bob. As shown above, drop the line and plumb bob from the beam and mark where cabinets will begin on the floor.

THE CARPENTER'S LEVEL
An object is plumb if you put the level against it and the bubble centers between the lines in the end vial, as shown in the inset. If it's out of plumb, move one end away from the wall until the bubble centers. The distance between the object and the end of the level is the amount the object is out of plumb. Set the level flat on an object to tell if it's level. If it isn't, lifting the end will tell you how far out of level it is.

THE WATER LEVEL

A water level is good for finding two points that are level with each other but a long way apart or on different walls.

THE LINE LEVEL

Hook a line level over a mason's line to turn the line into a giant level. Remove the level and snap the line to draw a level line on the wall.

⊘ SAFETY ALERT

USING LASER LEVELS
While it is perfectly safe to look at the line created by the laser, you should not look directly into the laser itself.

THE LASER LEVEL

A laser level gives you a long, level line with the push of a button. The laser, on the stand in the right of the picture, spins rapidly to draw a line all the way around the room—useful when hanging cabinets or installing crown molding. Models vary—some are self-leveling, while others like this one have to be adjusted so that the line they draw is level. Prices on laser levels have fallen in recent years and now vary widely. You can find a variety of laser levels in the tool department of most home centers. Commercial laser levels are available at most rental stores.

Squares

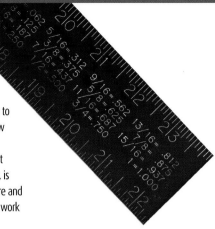

S quare openings and square corners are the keys to successful construction: An out-of-square window won't open correctly. A door in an out-of-square opening will have uneven gaps around it at best; at worst it won't fit. The best way to check for square, not surprisingly, is usually with a square. Sometimes, however, a tape measure and a couple of simple principles left over from geometry class work just as well.

WORK SMARTER

ACCURATE MARKING
Pencils are great markers for general carpentry, but for really precise marks use a utility knife with a sharp blade or a marking knife made especially for the job. Your cut lines will be more accurate and your joints will fit far more tightly.

How square is your square?

The world is not perfect, and no square is perfectly square. To see how square your square is, put the short arm of the square against a flat edge, like the edge on a sheet of plywood. Draw a line along the longer arm. Then, flip the square over so the short arm points in the other direction. Slide the square so the long arm aligns with a point on the line you drew, and draw a new line. Any space between the two lines is equal to twice the error of your square. A gap at the bottom of the two lines means the true angle of the square is less than 90 degrees. A gap at the top indicates the angle of the square is greater than 90 degrees.

Framing squares, unlike other squares, can be adjusted. If the square is less than 90 degrees, hit the inside corner of the square with a ball peen hammer as shown here. This makes the inside the corner slightly larger, forcing the arm out. If it's more than 90 degrees, peen the outside corner.

DIVERGENT LINES
Draw overlapping lines with your square—one line with the arm pointing left, and another with the arm pointing right. If the lines diverge the square is out of alignment.

SQUARE IT UP
You can align an out-of-square framing square by hitting it carefully in the right spot with a hammer.

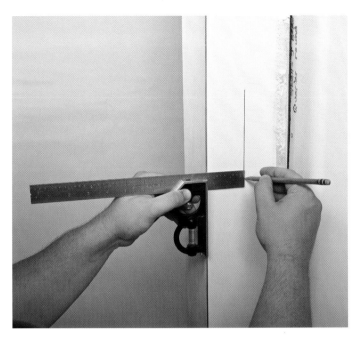

DRAWING A LINE WITH A COMBINATION SQUARE

A combination square is good for checking corners in cabinets and small spaces. Guide the head along an edge and put a pencil against the ruler to draw a line parallel to the edge. You can create 90- or 45-degree angles with a combination square.

CARPENTER'S SQUARE

This square, also called a speed square or quick square, has largely replaced the combination square on the job site. Use it to check corners for square, to lay out lines, or as a guide for your circular saw.

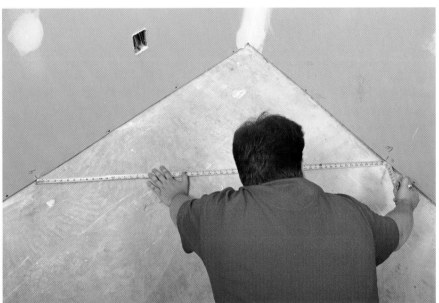

MEASURING DIAGONALS

To check to see if an opening is square, measure the diagonals. If all four corners are 90 degrees, the diagonals will be equal. This is true for all openings that have four sides, whether they are square or rectangular.

CHECKING WITH THE 3-4-5 TRIANGLE

To check a corner for square, measure 3 feet along one wall and 4 feet along the other. If the diagonal between them is 5 feet, the corner is square. The same holds true for any multiple or 3, 4, and 5. If for example, you measure 6 feet along one wall and 8 feet along another, the corner will be square if the diagonal is 10 feet long.

Drills

⊘ SAFETY ALERT

USING DRILLS

Protect your eyes. Always wear safety glasses when operating a drill. Bits of wood or metal thrown by the drill can injure the eye.

Until recently, the ideal of the drill world was the ⅜-inch, plug-in, reversible, variable speed drill. Cordless drills—a godsend to carpenters who had to drag extension cords all over a job site—have made big inroads, and some of them are nearly as powerful as their plug-in ancestors. They're handy for the homeowner, too,

especially in older houses where plugs are few and far between or which may not have grounded (three-hole) outlets. Cordless drills come in 9-, 12-,14.4-, 15.6-, 18-, and 24-volt models. The higher the voltage, the more powerful the drill. With the right attachments drills also double as screwdrivers.

HAMMER DRILL

A hammer drill pounds into the surface as it drills. Use it with a masonry bit for drilling into concrete, brick, and tile.

CORDLESS DRILL

Cordless drills go anywhere and reach just about anything. The most powerful have 18- to 24-volt batteries; the lower voltage drills still do the job, but without quite as much conviction. The lower voltage drills are lighter, though, an advantage if you'll be using them to drill or drive for an extended period.

CORDED DRILL

Corded drills give you continuous, consistent power as long as you can plug them in. A reversible, variable speed drill that takes bits up to ⅜ inch (called a ⅜ VSR) is the standard workhorse. A trigger that adjusts the speed gradually is easier to drive screws with than one that jumps quickly to its highest speed.

COMBINATION BITS

◀ The action of the threads of the screw actually pushes the pieces you're screwing together apart during the last few turns. Avoid this by predrilling with a combination bit. Combination bits, like the one shown here, countersink the head, and provide a clearance hole in the top piece and a pilot hole in the second, all in a single pass. Used in conjunction with the quick-change system shown below, a single drill becomes a multitasking power tool.

ADJUSTABLE DEPTH SCREW SETTER

▶ If you're using your drill to hang drywall, get an adjustable depth screw setter, which you can set to drive the screw into the drywall without damaging it. If you're driving screws through other materials, a magnetic bit helps hold the screw while you get it started.

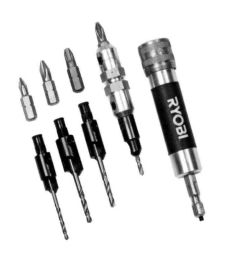

QUICK-CHANGE KITS

▲ This kit lets you change quickly from a combination drill bit to a screwdriver bit. The combination bit drills a pilot hole for the screw, a seat for the head, and a counterbore for setting the screw below the surface if desired. Moving the brass-colored collar releases the assembly next to it, which you remount to expose the screwdriver. Shown are (right to left) the quick-change holder, the assembly that holds the bits, and screwdrivers and bits of various sizes.

ACCESSORY KITS

▲ Accessory kits like this let you change quickly from drilling to driving. Counterclockwise, starting at the lower left are drill bits that pop in and out of the two holders next to them. The first holder is magnetic and is designed primarily for short screw bits. Although it will also hold the drill bits, it becomes long and ungainly when using them. The second, shorter holder is a quick-change holder. Bits shown include slot head, Phillips, and longer versions of each. Shown (top left) are nut drivers and shanks that hold standard-drive socket sets.

Sanders

Sanders are your friends when it comes to custom fitting a miter joint.

Grit

The coarseness of sandpaper is measured by the size of its abrasive particles, called grit.

Coarseness is measured by the number of particles of a given size that it takes to fill a given area. If it takes 80 particles to fill the area, the paper is considered coarse. If it takes 220 particles to fill the same area, the grit is considered fine. When sanding wood you'll start with 80 grit; then move to 120, 180, and 220, with each grit removing the marks left by the previous grit. Grits finer than 220 are meant for sanding lacquers and varnishes.

Machine tracks

All three types of sanders leave telltale marks on the wood you sand. A belt sander leaves heavy parallel tracks. An orbital sander leaves small circular swirls often called jitterbugs. A random-orbit sander leaves fainter elliptical marks almost like a series of cursive Ls. Staining in particular calls attention to the marks, but a light hand sanding once you're done with the machine makes them disappear. Sand through the normal progression with the pad sander—80, 120, 180, 220—and then give the piece a quick hand sanding with 220. If you're going to paint, rather than stain or varnish, the wood, you can stop at 120-or 180-grit, and then follow up by sanding by hand with the same grit.

Belt sander

Unlike a finishing sander, a belt sander isn't designed to give you a surface ready for finishing. It's a workhorse, designed to remove wood quickly. You'll use it for removing rough marks left by the saw, removing a step between adjoining boards, or correcting framing that is out of plumb, out of place, or too large. How much work the sander does, and how quickly, depends on the belt. Manufacturers recommend a 36-grit belt for heavy-duty stock or paint removal. A 50- or 60-grit belt is designed for moderate stock removal, 80 and 100 grit are for light stock removal, and 120- to 150-grit belts are for finish prep.

Even the finest belt takes off wood a lot more quickly than you expect. Until you get the hang of the tool, start with a light grit, and then try successively heavier grits until you've got a belt that's doing the job the way you want it to. Stop at 80 for a surface you want to finish, and then use a palm sander, starting where you left off—at 80 grit.

Palm sanders

Palm sanders are the tool of choice when preparing wood for finishing. An orbital pad sander holds a quarter to a half sheet of sandpaper, and vibrates in small circles to remove wood. A random-orbit sander (right) spins gently as it orbits, and usually takes a circular piece of sandpaper. Either will do the job—orbital sanders are a bit less expensive, but random-orbit sanders remove wood more quickly, and leave less noticeable marks.

How to sand

Start belt and palm sanders away from the work surface, let them come to full speed before you start sanding, and sand in the general direction of the grain. You should also let an orbital sander come to full speed before you put it on the surface, but the orbital action lets you sand with or across the grain. Start a random-orbital sander on the surface, because the random motion can make it hard to control when it first starts up. Sand with or across the grain. Let the sander do the work: Pushing down on it will slow the motion and increase the size of the tracks it leaves. When hand sanding, sand in the general direction of the grain so that you don't leave cross-grain marks that are hard to remove.

⊘ SAFETY ALERT

USING SANDERS

Always wear a dust mask and ear protection when sanding. Long-term exposure to sawdust can damage your lungs. If sanding paint, assume that at least one of the coats is lead-based, and wear a mask especially designed to filter out lead. Wash and clean up before eating. Do not wear jewelry, rings, or loose clothing when operating a sander.

Power miter saws

Power miter saws are designed to cut precise angles in molding, trim work, rafters, and in general carpentry. They can be set to any angle and have stops that make it simple to set the saw to angles you'll cut most often. The cuts are precise, clean, and quick, and miter saws have become as important to the professional carpenter as the circular saw, hammer, and drill. It's a simple tool to operate, but there are a few things that are immediately obvious:

■ Although saws are adjusted at the factory, vibration during transport can knock the saw out of alignment. Check to see if the cut is square and the bevel accurate before your first project.

■ A board clamped at both ends will pinch the blade during the cut, possibly throwing it violently away from the saw. Clamp only on one side of the blade.

■ There are two types of miter saws. Basic miter saws cut a miter—the angled cut you see when you look at the top of the board—and only a miter. Compound miter saws will cut either a miter, a bevel (the angle you see looking at the edge of the board), or both.

■ Most carpentry—including crown molding—doesn't require a compound miter. A compound miter saw comes in handy, however, when cutting angles on the ends of wide boards, when cutting rafters, or when making custom frames.

■ The geometry of a compound miter means that the angle of the miter and bevel are set to something other than the final result. If you're cutting a 45-degree miter that also has a 45-degree bevel, for example, you would set the miter gauge to 35.26 degrees and the bevel gauge to 30 degrees. Check the saw's manual for the proper setting, and plan on making make plenty of test cuts.

■ Cutting slowly reduces splintering.

■ Always bolt or clamp the saw to a stable surface.

⊘ SAFETY ALERT

USING POWER MITER SAWS
Like all saws, the miter saw is potentially dangerous. Keep your hands well clear of the blade, and wait for the blade to stop spinning before you remove any scraps. Small pieces can fly out of the back of the saw, and bounce back, so remove any scraps before making a cut. Do not wear rings or other jewelry, or loose clothing. Wear hearing protection, safety glasses, and a dust mask when making cuts.

2

TOOLS AND MATERIALS

Making a cut

The miter saw cuts precise angles that would be difficult to get with other saws. While you can set it to any angle, there are also preset stops for the most common angles. Loosen the handle, depress the lock plate, and swing the miter table until it snaps into the desired setting. Retighten the handle before making the cut. To cut a bevel or make a compound cut, loosen the bevel lock knob, set it to the desired angle, and tighten.

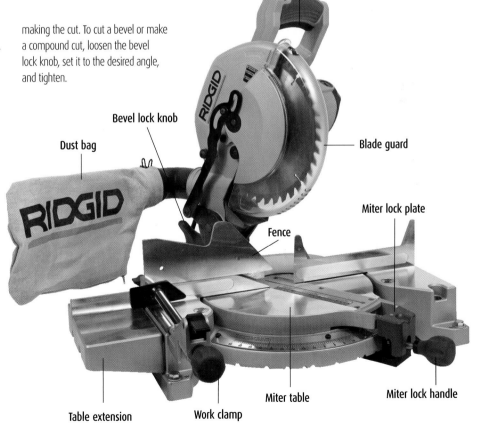

Switch trigger

Bevel lock knob

Blade guard

Dust bag

Miter lock plate

Fence

Miter lock handle

Table extension

Work clamp

Miter table

2

Checking the miter for accuracy

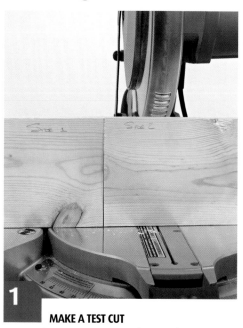

1

MAKE A TEST CUT

No square is as accurate as an actual cut. Cut the widest board the saw can handle. Put the pieces on the saw table. Flip one over and look for a gap in the seam. (Any gap will be twice the error in the saw.) If you see a gap, make the adjustments that follow to correct the problem.

2

LOOSEN THE FENCE

Unplug the saw and loosen the bolts that hold the fence in place. On this saw you first remove the fence extension by loosening a knob and a setscrew before loosening the four bolts that hold the fence in place.

Making accurate cuts

Laser indicators on some saws help you see where the cut will be. If you don't have a laser, start the cut on the waste side of the line. Turn on the saw and ease the running blade into the board and make a cut. If the cut misses the layout line, raise the blade, move the board, and try again.

3

MAKE ADJUSTMENTS

Move one end of the fence and put a square against it, so that the square touches the blade without flexing it. If necessary, turn the blade by hand so that no teeth touch the square. If there's a gap, move the square away from the blade, adjust the fence, and check again with the square. When the gap disappears, tighten the fence bolts, make a sample cut, and repeat the process as necessary. Adjust the pointer so it reads zero, using the eraser end of a pencil if the pointer is hard to reach.

Adjusting the extension table

If your saw has an extension table, like the one to the left of this saw, make sure the fence is flush with the fence on the rest of the saw. If it isn't, loosen the bolts that hold it in place, and slide it into position. To be on the safe side, you can even set it so there's a slight gap between the extension table fence and the straightedge—the main fence provides plenty of support for making an accurate cut.

Changing the blade

1

MOVE ANY PARTS THAT ARE IN THE WAY

Unplug the saw and move the blade guard out of the way.
On many saws the guard mechanism partially covers the bolt that holds the blade in place. Loosen and move the part out of the way as recommended by the manufacturer. On this saw you loosen a screw and then slide the mechanism up and towards the rear.

2

LOCK AND LOOSEN

Press the spindle lock to lock the blade in place. Turn the bolt *clockwise*—opposite the normal direction—to loosen and remove it. Remove the outer blade washer and the blade. Leave the inner blade washer in place. Wipe a drop of oil on the surfaces of the blade washers that touch the blade.

Cutting warped stock safely

Place warped stock so it curves away from the fence or away from the table. If you don't, the board will pinch the blade at the end of the cut, and could throw the board violently across the room.

3

PUT ON THE BLADE AND TIGHTEN

Put the blade on the saw so that the teeth point down.
Putting the blade on with the teeth facing in the other direction can result in serious injury. Put the outer blade washer in place. Turn the bolt counterclockwise until it is snug, plus another ⅛ to ¼ turn. Reassemble the saw.

Checking the bevel for accuracy

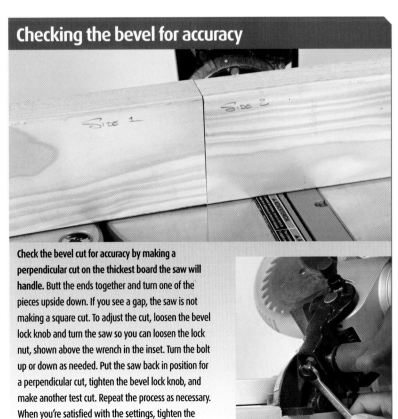

Check the bevel cut for accuracy by making a perpendicular cut on the thickest board the saw will handle. Butt the ends together and turn one of the pieces upside down. If you see a gap, the saw is not making a square cut. To adjust the cut, loosen the bevel lock knob and turn the saw so you can loosen the lock nut, shown above the wrench in the inset. Turn the bolt up or down as needed. Put the saw back in position for a perpendicular cut, tighten the bevel lock knob, and make another test cut. Repeat the process as necessary. When you're satisfied with the settings, tighten the lock nut against the saw housing. Adjust the pointer as needed.

Table saws

- Always use either the miter gauge or rip fence. Never make cuts without some sort of guide.
- A piece that gets caught between the rip fence and blade will kick back—fly back at you with violent force. Never stand directly behind the blade.
- Never use the rip fence and miter gauge at the same time.
- Use the guards that come with the saw; wear safety glasses, hearing protection, and a dust mask.

You can use other saws for many of the cuts you make with a table saw but the table saw will do most of them better. It cuts straighter lines, larger pieces, smaller pieces, and it makes smoother cuts.
- Cutting perpendicular to the grain is called crosscutting. Cutting parallel to the grain is called ripping. A combination blade will do both.
- A saw is named for the diameter of the blade it uses. Ten-inch saws, shown here, will cut through a board about 3 inches thick.
- Portable saws, like the ones shown here, are designed to be lugged from job site to job site.

Carpenters use them for both general carpentry and trim work. They cut through softwoods easily, but may strain on thicker boards and hardwoods like oak or walnut.
- Stationary saws cost more but are more powerful. They weigh more and vibrate less. Because of the power and weight, they'll handle bigger boards with more ease and will also make finer cuts more precisely.
- Expect to fine-tune all the settings when you first get your saw. The saw works best and is safer when properly set up.
- Some saws have built-in features, such as router tables or a sliding table that moves past the blade and works like a giant miter gauge when crosscutting.

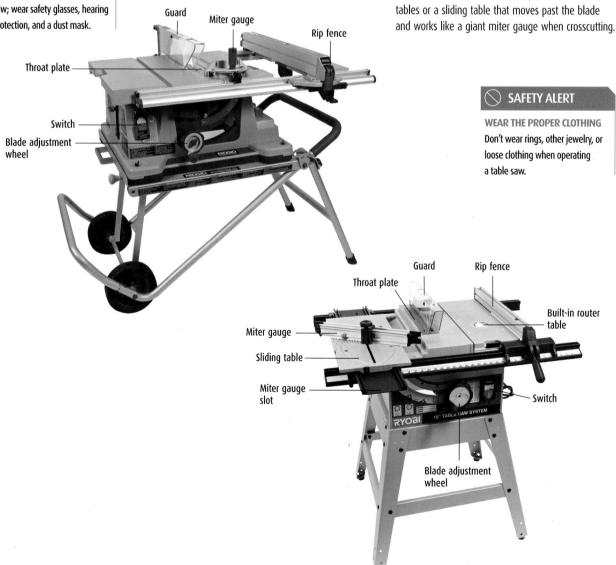

Checking table alignment

When you first get your saw, plan on checking all the settings to make sure they are accurate. The easiest way to check is to make some sample cuts and check their accuracy. All cuts, however, depend in one way or another on the blade and the miter gauge slot being parallel. Before you make any test cuts, check to make sure the blade and slot are parallel. Start by measuring the distance from the slot to a tooth on the blade—once when the tooth is at the back of the blade opening and once after you've turned the blade so the tooth is at the front. If the measurements aren't equal, adjust as directed by the manufacturer.

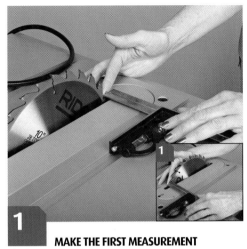

1

MAKE THE FIRST MEASUREMENT

Make a mark on a tooth, and spin it by hand to the other side of the blade opening. Set your combination square so that the end of the ruler just touches the marked tooth. You may have to hold the blade to keep it from spinning out of position, but don't flex it toward the ruler. Rotate the blade forward, and check to see if the measurement is the same at the front of the opening.

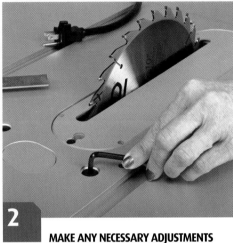

2

MAKE ANY NECESSARY ADJUSTMENTS

If the measurements aren't equal, adjust the way the blade sits in the table. On this saw, you loosen a hex-head alignment screw, push the blade into position, and then tighten the screw.

Making sure the rip fence is parallel to the blade

Safe and accurate rip cuts depend on the rip fence being parallel to the blade. To check the alignment, first make sure the miter gauge slot is parallel to the saw, as described above. Then slide the fence over to the miter gauge slot and lock it in place. If the fence aligns with the entire length of the slot, everything is fine. If the two diverge at either end, adjust the fence, which usually involves loosening a few bolts and shifting the fence into alignment.

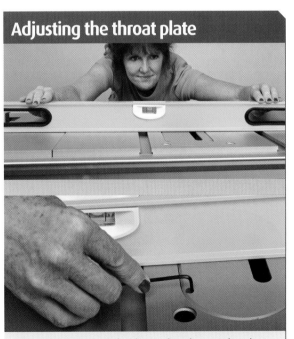

Adjusting the throat plate

Make sure the throat plate isn't sticking up above the saw surface where it can catch the leading edge of a board as you cut. Use a level as a straightedge. Check for light between the level and the saw table, and between the level and the throat plate. Adjust the height by turning the setscrews in the throat plate.

2

TOOLS AND MATERIALS

Table saw blades

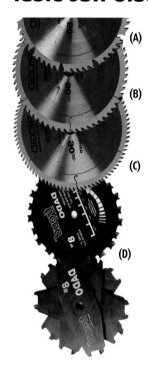

(A)
(B)
(C)
(D)

Choosing a blade

The 10-inch blade **(A)** is a combination table saw blade, designed for both crosscutting and cutting with the grain (ripping.) The 60-tooth blade **(B)** is for smooth, polished crosscuts on the miter saw or table saw, but could scorch the wood when ripping. The 90-tooth blade **(C)** has special teeth designed to minimize chipping when cutting veneered plywoods. (All three are titanium coated.) The black blades **(D)** are a complete dado set for cutting wide grooves in lumber on the table saw. When buying a blade, look for thin, lasercut slots that reduce vibration.

Circular saw blades

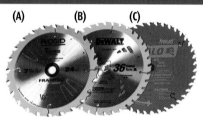

(A)   (B)   (C)

Saw blades come in various sizes, colors, and with a range of teeth. Each has a protective coating that protects the blade from overheating, gumming up, and rust. The gold is titanium, the yellow is special nonslip coating, and the red is Teflon. The big difference is the number of teeth. The more teeth, the finer the cut. The titanium-coated blade **(A)** has 24 teeth for cutting framing lumber. The yellow-toothed blade **(B)** has 36 teeth for finishing cuts in woods that will be exposed, such as doorjambs. The red blade **(C)** has 40 teeth for cutting plywood. For more information on circular saws see page 51.

For more information on circular saws see page 51.

SAFETY ALERT

UNPLUG THE SAW

Always unplug the saw before changing the blade.

Changing the blade

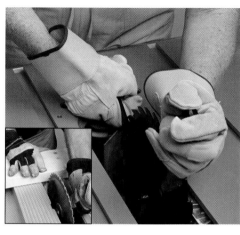

Loosening the blade

Unplug the saw before changing the blade. To loosen the blade, first unplug the saw, then stand on the operator's side of the machine. Put a wrench on the arbor nut and grab the blade while wearing work gloves. Hold the blade and pull the wrench forward to loosen the nut. To tighten the blade, hold the blade and push the wrench backward. If the nut is too tight, you can loosen it by jamming the blade with a piece of wood, as shown in the inset, and pulling the wrench forward. Don't make a habit of it, however. Jamming the blade to loosen or tighten it can bend the blade enough to affect the cut.

Making sure the cut is square

To get a perfectly square crosscut, the blade must be perpendicular to the table and the miter gauge must be perpendicular to the blade. To see if the blade is perpendicular to the table, mark a thick board with a single line on one side and a double line on the other. Cut the board and then flip one of the pieces over. Look at the edge of the boards to see if the vertical seam is tight, as shown above. If there are gaps adjust the angle of the blade, and test again.

To make sure the miter gauge is square with the blade, mark a board as before and make a test cut. Flip one of the cutoffs, and hold them both against a straight edge such as the miter guage. Look along the top of the board—if the seam is tight, as shown above, the miter guage is square with the blade. If there is a widening gap between the boards, the cut isn't square. Reset the miter gauge and test again.

Crosscutting

Cutting perpendicular to the grain is called crosscutting. The key to getting the cut you want is the miter gauge, which travels in a groove on the tabletop. When properly aligned, you can set the gauge to cut a 90-degree angle, and anything up to 60 degrees on either side of 90 (depending on the saw). Before you start making cuts, however, it pays to check the alignment of the miter gauge as described below.

For reasons lost in history, miter gauges are set up so that a 90-degree cut reads 0 degrees on the miter gauge scale. A cut one degree to either side—a 91- or an 89- degree cut—reads as 1 degree; a cut 2 degrees off square reads 2 degrees, and so on. The only time the setting actually

reflects the angle you're cutting is at 45 degrees.

A combination blade is fine for most carpentry; if you're making furniture or doing fine trimwork and aren't happy with the results your blade is giving you, have it sharpened.

If you're still not happy, you may want to buy a separate crosscut blade, which will give you a smoother cut.

Feed the wood slowly to get the smoothest surface; use the guards when cutting, and keep your hands well away from the blade.

Slippery little devil

If you have trouble with pieces slipping sideways a little during a cross cut, keep the piece in place by gluing a piece of 180-grit or finer sandpaper to the back of the miter gauge with some spray adhesive. (See Safety Alert below.)

⊘ SAFETY ALERT

USE THE FENCE PROPERLY
Don't cut pieces more than 6 inches long with the sandpaper method, outlined above. Always position the block so the stock doesn't touch the blade and the stop block at the same time. Cutting longer pieces, putting the block in the wrong place, or using the fence as a stop can cause the saw to throw the cutoff back at you violently.

Cutting pieces to the same size

If you have to cut several boards to the same size, start by screwing a fence to the miter gauge and cutting one end of each board square. Then clamp a stop block to the fence, and make the cuts with the square end resting against the block. The distance between the blade and the block is equal to the desired length of the piece you're cutting.

Cutting small pieces to size

If you're cutting a piece 6 inches long or less, you can use a stop block attached to the rip fence as a guide. Put a block at least 3 inches long against the rip fence, and clamp it firmly in place in front of the blade. For safety, the piece you're cutting can't touch the block during the actual cut. Put the stock you're cutting against the miter gauge, snug it up against the block, and make the cut. Turn off the saw, and remove the piece from between the fence and blade. Repeat until you have all the pieces you need.

Cutting to a line

When you're cutting something to length without a stop block, draw a line on the wood to show where you'll make the cut. Start the cut on the waste side of the line, but don't cut too deeply. Slide the board along the miter gauge until the spinning blade just touches the line, and then complete the cut.

⊘ SAFETY ALERT

NOT A DEPTH STOP
Never use the rip fence as a depth stop without using a stop block.

Ripping

Cutting along the grain is called ripping. The rip is made using a guide called a rip fence. Ripping is a simpler operation than crosscutting—there are no angles to set on a miter gauge—but it can bring your fingers closer to the blade. If your fingers are too close for comfort, use a push stick like the one shown below, or make your own following the pattern.

Most rip fences have a ruler glued to the front rail, which gives you a pretty accurate readout of the size piece you'll be cutting, but you should check for accuracy with your tape measure to be sure.

A roller stand as shown at right helps you support long lengths of stock while ripping.

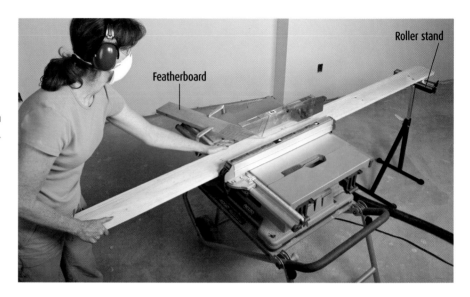

Featherboard

Roller stand

Hold boards in place with featherboards

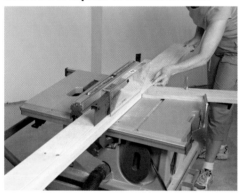

Long boards tend to move away from the fence during a cut. Hold them in place with featherboards—a board into which you've cut several fingers. Put the board in place and put the featherboard against it. Push against the board and flex the fingers so they bend slightly away from the direction of cut, and clamp the board in place.

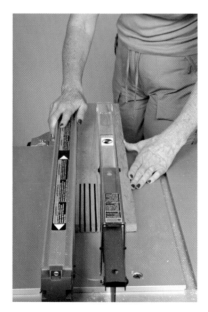

Make your featherboard from a piece of wood 24 inches long and about 8 inches wide. Make a series of cuts 5½ inches long and about 5⁄16 inch apart on the end of the board. Crosscut across the fingers, setting the miter gauge to cut along a line drawn from the corner of the board to a point ½ inch from the corner on the other edge.

⊘ SAFETY ALERT

■ Never cut a piece of stock on a table saw without using a guide. Use the rip fence when ripping and the miter gauge when crosscutting. Pushing wood into the blade without the support of a guide can cause serious injury.

■ Never rip a board to make a piece less than 1 inch wide. Always make sure the board is thick enough that it won't slip under the fence when cutting. Never stand a board on edge to make a rip cut.

Use a push stick

Commercial push sticks as shown at left are fine, but you can also make your own. Lay out a ½-inch grid on a 2×6×14-inch block and trace this pattern. Cut a curve as shown to make the push stick easier to grip. This push stick is wider than commercial models and holds stock better. When making narrow rips, you feed the push stick right across the blade. Make at least two so you'll have one for each hand.

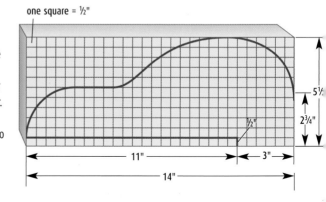

one square = ½"

11"

3"

14"

5½"

2¾"

½"

Cutting a groove along a board

A dado head is a blade or a set of blades used for cutting grooves in wood to create a solid joint for other pieces, such as fixed shelves for a bookcase. It takes its name from old-fashioned wood terminology: A dado is a groove cut across the grain; a rabbet is a groove cut on the edge; a plow is a groove along the length of a board.

There are two kinds of dado heads—stacking and adjustable. A stacked head is a set of blades that combine to get the width you want. An adjustable dado is a single blade held in place by tapered plates. Turning the plates causes the blade to wobble as it cuts, and the wobble results in a groove. Adjusting the amount of wobble changes the width of the groove. The groove left by an adjustable dado is slightly deeper in the middle than at the edges so professionals prefer a stacked head.

Typically, a groove is about half as deep as a board is thick—you'd cut a groove ⅜ inch deep in stock that is ¾ inch thick. Cut deeper and you run the risk of weakening the board. Cut shallower, and the groove isn't likely to provide enough support for the piece that fits in it.

Installing a stacked dado head

When installing a stacked head, put the blades on a piece of wood to keep the teeth from breaking. Put on one of the outer blades, which looks like a regular saw blade, and then put on one or more of the partial blades, called chippers. Add chippers until the width is about ⅛ inch narrower than the cut you want, and then put on the other outer blade. Add the arbor washer and nut, and tighten normally. If after a test cut the groove is too narrow, add spacers, shown in the photo, to bring the cut to the right width. (With some dado sets, you'll make your own spacers out of paper or playing cards.) Special order a dado throat plate to put in the opening in the saw.

Cutting a groove along a board

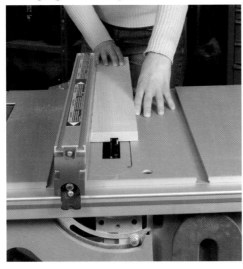

Using the dado head means removing the guards, which would prevent you from making the cut. If you're cutting a groove along the length of a board (a plow), guide the board against the fence. The blade is buried in the wood for most of the cut, but mark where it will be when it comes out the end of the board, and keep your hands well away from the mark when making the cut.

Cutting a groove along the edge of a board

Cutting a groove across a board

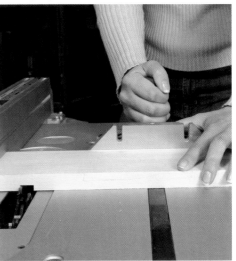

When you're cutting a groove across a board, you get to break the cardinal rule of crosscutting: You can use the miter gauge to guide the cut while using the rip fence as a stop to control the location of the groove. This is safe because it's a groove rather than a full crosscut, so there's no loose piece that could bind between the fence and blade and fly back at you with tremendous speed and force.

Protect the rip fence with a wooden auxiliary fence when cutting a groove along the edge. Bolt or screw the auxiliary fence to the rip fence, following the directions that come with the saw. When you use the fence for the first time, lower the blade completely, and slide the auxiliary fence over the blade. Measure to make sure the blade will clear the metal fence, turn on the saw, and raise the blade slightly higher than the depth of the cut. Check your settings and guide the stock along the auxiliary fence to cut the groove. To cut a tenon, as shown in the inset, cut adjoining grooves on the end of a board, then turn the board over and repeat. (Tenons, commonly used in doors, fit in grooves or mortises to hold pieces of wood together at right angles.)

Making a crosscut jig

Sometimes a table saw needs help making crosscuts. Long pieces, wide pieces, or heavy pieces can twist as you cut them, with one edge wandering away from the face of the miter gauge while the cut wanders away from 90 degrees. This jig is essentially a huge miter gauge that helps hold the piece in place as it crosses the blade. It travels in two runners instead of one, so it's less likely to be overpowered by a hefty piece of wood, and the long fence gives you a greater surface to guide stock against. The rear fence is a 2×6 that helps keep the jig together once you cut through the plywood. The front fence is slightly different: It's a longer 2×6 with a small batten across the back that makes it easy to screw the fence in place and adjust if necessary. The plywood is ¾-inch birch ply.

You can also use the crosscut jig if you need to cut a lot of pieces to exactly the same size. Clamp a block of wood to the fence as shown in step five. Every time you slip a board against the stop and cut it, it will be exactly the same length as others cut against the stop.

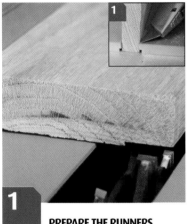

1

PREPARE THE RUNNERS

Start with a piece of oak just wide enough to fit in the miter gauge slots. If the board is too thick, run it over the dado head on the saw, taking off enough to get a good fit. Put the oak in the miter gauge slot, and mark the depth of the slot with a knife.

2

ATTACH THE RUNNERS

Set the rip fence to cut the oak along the knife mark, and use a push stick to cut the runners to size. Put the runners in the miter gauge slot. Put a piece of plywood the size of the saw table over the runners, and align the edges of the plywood with the edges of the saw table. Clamp the plywood to the runners. Drill pilot holes and screw the runners to the plywood.

3

CUT AND ATTACH THE REAR FENCE

Turn the plywood upside down, and screw a 2×6 to the back edge of the plywood.

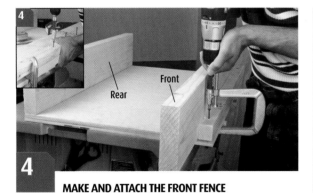

4

MAKE AND ATTACH THE FRONT FENCE

Screw a 1½- × 1½-inch batten to a 4-foot 2×6, as shown in the inset. Stand the front fence up, and use a framing square to position it so it's perpendicular to the edge of the plywood. Clamp the batten to the plywood base. Screw the batten to the plywood with two screws, driving one screw at each end, so that you can adjust the front fence into square later. Turn on the saw and slowly raise the blade through the plywood. Feed the platform across the saw, cutting a slot in the plywood and the fence.

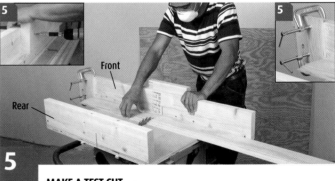

5

MAKE A TEST CUT

Hold a piece of board against the front fence, and feed the jig across the saw to cut it. Check the cut end with your combination square. If the cut is out of square, loosen one of the screws on the batten and pivot the batten slightly. Screw the batten back in place and make another test cut. When the cut you're making is square, drive screws every few inches through the batten. Put an 18-inch piece of 2×6 on top of the batten and screw it to the fence, as shown in the inset (top left), to remind you to keep your fingers away from the blade. Clamp a stop block to the jig, as shown in the inset (top right), for cutting multiple pieces of stock to the same length.

2 TOOLS AND MATERIALS

Circular saws

The circular saw is the carpenter's all-around tool. You can use it for crosscutting, ripping, and cutting plywood, hardwood, and softwood. Unlike a table saw or miter saw, however, there are no built-in guides to ensure a straight cut. You'll either need to follow a line you've drawn or, for more accurate cuts, clamp a straightedge to guide the cut.

■ You can adjust both the depth of cut and the angle at which the blade cuts by adjusting levers near the plate of the saw. Always unplug the saw when changing settings.

■ Always draw a line showing the intended path of the cut. Guide the saw along the line using notches in the baseplate. Some saws have a built-in laser that helps you align the cut.

■ Always support your work so that the cutoff doesn't pinch the blade at the end of the cut.

■ Keep the cord out of the line of the saw so you don't cut through it.

■ To minimize splintering, make the cut with the good side of the board facedown.

⊘ SAFETY ALERT

AVOID KICKBACK

Kickback occurs when the blade binds in the cut and causes the saw to jump backwards. Never stand directly behind the saw. Maintain a firm grip, and release the trigger if the blade starts to bind. Let the saw come to a complete stop before removing it from the wood. When you restart the cut, center the saw blade from side to side in the existing cut, and make sure the teeth are not engaged in the wood before starting the saw.

⊘ SAFETY ALERT

PROTECT YOUR HANDS

Protect your hands by making sure the blade guard operates freely and springs back into place when released. Never reach under the wood you're cutting. Let the saw come to a complete stop before removing it from the wood.

LASER GUIDES

Some saws have a built-in laser guide like the one shown here. Lay out the cut in pencil, and keep the laser line aligned with the pencil line as you're cutting.

Adjusting the depth of cut

UNPLUG THE SAW AND LOOSEN THE DEPTH ADJUSTMENT LEVER
Hold the baseplate flat on the surface you're cutting, and raise or lower the saw by its handle. Adjust it so that the blade is exposed by the length of a saw tooth, and then adjust the lever to lock the baseplate in position.

Adjusting the angle of cut

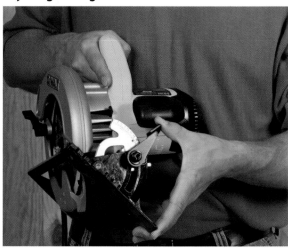

UNPLUG THE SAW AND LOOSEN THE ANGLE ADJUSTMENT LEVER
Pull the baseplate until the indicator arrow aligns with the angle on the protractor scale.

Line guide

ALIGN THE SAW WITH THE LAYOUT LINE
Two notches in the saw baseplate help you align the saw. Use the notch to the right when making 90-degree cuts; use the notch to the left when cutting bevels. The notches are only guides—depending on the blade you use, you may have to line up with one side of the notch or the other. Make a couple of test cuts to see exactly where in the notch the line needs to be.

Starting a cut in the middle of a board

SOMETIMES YOU NEED TO START A CUT IN THE MIDDLE OF THE BOARD
Lay out the cut, and adjust the depth of cut to match the material. Lift the handle on the blade guard to expose the blade. Put the front edge of the saw plate on the layout line and lift the back edge so that the blade is just above the material you're cutting.

Hold the saw by both handles and begin cutting. Gradually lower the back of the saw into the stock using the front of the baseplate as a pivot point. Lower the guard as soon as the blade begins cutting into the material. Wait until the saw is flat on the stock before moving it forward. Let the blade come to a complete stop before removing it from the wood.

 SAFETY ALERT

Pulling the saw backwards will cause the blade to climb out of the cut and cause it to come back at you with considerable force.

Cutting plywood

When cutting plywood, support the cutoff and the main piece so that the stock won't pinch the blade at the end of the cut and jam the saw or cause kickback. Put two 2×4s under the main piece, and two 2×4s under the cutoff so that both pieces remain flat throughout the cut.

Making cuts with a circular saw

Crosscutting with a square

Special squares, like the one shown here, help guide the saw through a short cut. Put the raised edge against the stock and guide the saw along the other edge.

Ripping with the circular saw

Cutting along the length of the board (ripping) is accomplished with the help of a rip attachment or by clamping a board in place as a guide. The rip attachment, shown here, is fine for making narrow cuts. For cutting wider pieces, make a cutoff guide.

Making a ripping cutoff jig

1 **ASSEMBLE THE JIG**
Make the jig from two strips of ¾-inch plywood, each 8 feet long. One piece should be about 5 inches wide; the other should be as wide as the saw base plus 5 inches. Have the home center or lumberyard cut them so you'll get straight cuts, then screw them together so that the edges align.

2 **CUT THE JIG TO WIDTH**
Guide the saw along the fence piece, cutting the wider piece to width in the process.

3 **LAY OUT THE LINE YOU WANT TO CUT**
Place the cut edge of the jig along the line and clamp or screw it in place. Guide the saw along the narrower piece to cut along the line.

Jigsaws

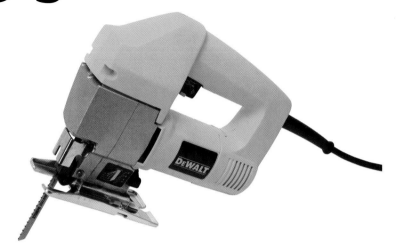

J igsaws cut curves, straight lines, and irregular shapes. The most important rule is to let the blade do the work. If you force the cut, the blade will wander. Jigsaws come with a wide range of options—some even have a device that puffs the sawdust off the cutout line. Speed control is a basic option. Being able to adjust blade speed lets you pick a speed that feels best given the material and the rate at which you feed the saw. Next in importance comes orbital cutting, in which the blade thrusts forward, as well as up and down, for a faster cut. The amount of thrust is adjustable, so if you're cutting through hard materials, you can set it for no orbital action. If you're cutting through soft stock, and speed is more important than accuracy, you can set it for maximum orbit.

Many saws come with a vacuum attachment. A nonmarring overshoe is a soft piece of plastic that slips over the saw's metal footplate to keep it from scratching the surface. An antisplitter insert provides support on either side of the cut.

Make sure the blade guard operates freely and springs back into place when released. Never reach under the wood you're cutting. Let the saw come to a complete stop before removing it from the wood.

Saw blades

What a jigsaw does, and how well it does it, depends primarily on the blade. The key difference between blades is the number of teeth per inch—the more teeth, the finer the cut. A quick sample of available blades includes (top to bottom): a 12-tooth scroll blade for cutting tight curves, a 6-tooth blade for making cuts in particleboard and thicker wood, a 10-tooth blade for general wood cutting, a 10-tooth reverse-tooth blade, a 14-tooth blade for cutting thicker metal, and a 24-tooth blade for cutting thin metal. The reverse-tooth blade has teeth that point down, instead of up, so that the splinters occur on the bottom of the cut, rather than the top. It's particularly useful when cutting through paneling or Formica and other plastic laminates, which chip easily.

Orbital cutting

Many saws have an orbital setting, in which the lower end of the blade thrusts forward while traveling up and down. You can set the amount of thrust or turn it off for cutting metals and making fine cuts in wood. Use the lowest setting for cuts in wood, a middle setting on particleboard and harder woods, and the top setting when speed is more important than accuracy. If you're not sure which setting to use, try them all and use whichever one seems to be working best.

Plunge cuts

You can make interior cuts without drilling pilot holes. Lay out the cut, and then rest the toe of the footplate on the work. It can be hard to know exactly where the cut is going to start, so unplug the saw, pull the blade up to fullest length, and position it about ½ inch away from the layout lines. Turn on the saw, and pivot until the blade reaches the wood. Keep pivoting until the saw is flat on its foot, then cut toward the layout lines. Cut a curve at corners, and then come back and square them up once you've removed most of the waste. Don't try this on metal or when using a scroll blade.

Interior cuts

The jigsaw, of course, excels at curves. But it's also useful for making cutouts. If you have to cut out a piece of paneling around an outlet, for example, transfer the outline of the outlet to the paneling and drill pilot holes in the four corners. Cut from hole to hole to remove the scrap. Use a reverse-tooth blade to minimize surface chipping. Protect the surface from scratching by putting a nonmarring footplate attachment on your saw, if it has one; if not, cover the base of the saw with masking tape.

Routers

In simplest terms, a router is a motor that spins a specialized drill bit at 20,000 rpm. In real terms, it is one of the more versatile tools you'll use. It can cut grooves and joints, rout countless shapes on the edge of a board, and can even make raised panels for doors or wainscoting. This versatility is due to the wide variety of bits—hundreds are available, each one slightly different from the next. Fortunately, you won't need them all. Most woodworkers buy them as they need them and build their collection slowly. Here are a few basic things you'll need to know about routers:

- Router bits have either a ¼-inch or ½-inch shank. You can get most bits on either size shank. If you're doing some heavy-duty routing with a bit that has a ¼-inch shank, take shallow cuts and feed the work slowly, or you may snap the bit in two.
- The shank fits in a nonadjustable chuck called a collet. A router with a ¼-inch collet won't take a ½-inch bit; but most ½-inch collets are removable and can be replaced with a ¼-inch collet, so that you can switch back and forth between ¼- and ½-inch shanks.
- Carbide-tipped bits cut more cleanly than high-speed steel, which tends to char the wood.
- Bits designed to shape the edge of a piece of wood generally have a bearing, called a pilot, in the center of the shaft. Guiding the pilot along the edge of the wood guides the router through its cut without letting it cut too deeply.

- Ball bearing guides are far better than solid steel pilots, which will mar the wood as you cut.
- Bits designed to cut grooves through a piece don't have guides. To guide cuts with these bits, attach a fence to the router, or clamp a fence to the work.

Router bits

Given the various styles of router bits, each of which comes in a variety to sizes, you have literally hundreds of bits to choose from. You'll never need even a fraction of them, and your best bet is to buy a bit when you need it. Here's a typical selection available at your home center.

SAFETY ALERT

USE YOUR ROUTER SAFELY
Follow the manufacturer's instructions carefully and practice safe use until you feel comfortable working with the tool.

(Counterclockwise from bottom left), The first bit is the **flush trimming bit** (A). A bearing on the bottom of the bit rides along one surface, plywood in this case, and trims the surface above it, in this case plastic laminate, so that the two surfaces are flush with each other. A **chamfer bit** (B) is used to rout a decorative edge. The **roundover bit** (C) routs a radius on a piece of stock. The **rabbeting bit** (D) routs a recess along the edge of the board. It's often used to rout a recess to house the back of a cabinet. (Counterclockwise from bottom center), The **dovetail bit** (E) routs a flat-bottom groove with sloping sides and is most often used with a jig to cut dovetail joints in drawers. The

straight bit (F) routs a simple groove, which is often used to house shelves or other parts of a cabinet. The **cove bit** (G) routs a decorative groove on the face of a board. The **ogee bit** (H) routs a decorative groove along the edge of a board. This bit has a ½-inch shank, unlike the other bits on this page, which have ¼-inch shanks. Most bits are available on either shank; the ½-inch shank is more durable, and ¼-inch shanks do occasionally snap off. If you want to use ½-inch shanks, you'll need a router that accepts them; not all do. On the other hand, most, if not all, half-inch routers will also handle ¼-inch shanks. If you're not sure what you're buying, or what you need, ask the sales staff.

Types of routers

There are two broad types of routers: fixed-base and plunge base. Some routers, such as the one shown here, come with a fixed base and a plunge base that are interchangeable, but you can do the work in this book with a fixed-base router.

To adjust the depth of cut in a plunge router, you flip a lever and push down on the router, causing it to travel up and down in its base. Releasing the lever locks the router at the desired depth.

To adjust the depth of cut on a fixed-base router, you generally loosen a lock knob and either turn the base or adjust a knob. Fixed-base routers are a bit easier to make fine adjustments on but are harder to adjust on the go. If you're choosing between one or the other, the plunge router has an advantage if you want to start a cut in the middle of a board. You put the router over the starting point, turn it on, and push the spinning bit into the wood.

Soft-start and speed control

Because the router starts at such a high speed, it will jerk in your hands when you first turn it on. A router with a soft-start feature revs up to full speed a bit more slowly, assuring a smooth start.

Large-diameter bits, like those that make raised panels on doors, suffer from the crack-the-whip syndrome—the outer edge is spinning more quickly than the shaft—and should run more slowly. If you plan to use bits like this, look for a router with electronic speed control that you can adjust to slow the bit down.

Fixed-base router

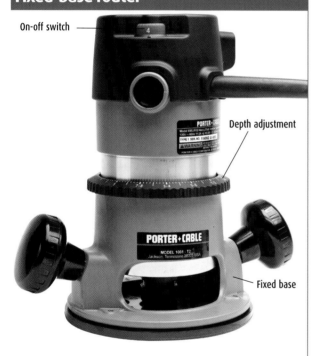

On-off switch

Depth adjustment

Fixed base

A fixed-base router adjusts by sliding up and down in its base. It's easy to adjust and works well for the projects in this book.

Plunge router

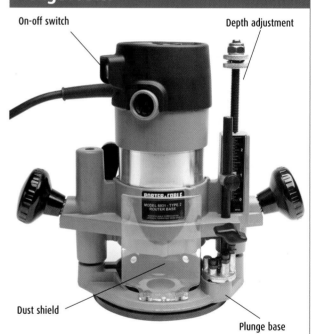

On-off switch

Depth adjustment

Dust shield

Plunge base

A plunge router travels up and down on spring-loaded rods; you can adjust the depth of cut without having to turn off the router. It simplifies starting a cut in the middle of a board, and you can set it to make cuts at a series of different depths.

Using the router

Direction of feed for a handheld router

The bit in a handheld router spins clockwise. Move a handheld router in the opposite direction—counterclockwise—so that the bit doesn't act like a wheel and drive the router across the work at 20,000 rpm. If you're guiding the router along the fence, imagine that it's one side of a rectangle, and move the router as if you were traveling counterclockwise around it.

Easy does it

Running a router along a board at breakneck speeds might get the job done a split second sooner, but the job won't be as good as it would have been if you took your time. Feed the router slowly so that you're just feeling light to moderate resistance as you work. This lets the router use its power and speed to give you the best possible job. Force-feeding stock past the bit means the bit touches the wood fewer times per pass, leaving a rougher surface. It also introduces vibration that leaves lines, called chatter marks, along the routed surface.

Make shallow passes

Resist the urge to make a cut in a single pass. Making deep cuts will do one of three things: Snap the bit off at the shank, overheat the bit and char the wood, or give you an uneven cut. If you're cutting a groove, set up the cut, and then adjust the bit so it's cutting somewhere around ¼ inch deep. Make the cut, lower the bit, and repeat until you've cut a groove the desired depth.

If you're routing the edge of a board with a bit that has a bearing (like the one shown here), set the bit to the final depth of cut and leave it there. When you start routing, hold the router bearing from the edge so that the bit is only cutting about one-third or one-fourth of its final width. Rout the edge, then move the bearing in about half the distance to the edge and repeat. It's impossible to guide the router in a straight line on these first couple of passes, so the edge will be a bit wavy. The final pass, in which you guide the pilot along the edge of the board, will clean up any problems.

Changing bits

Some routers require two wrenches to tighten or loosen the bit—one wrench holds the shaft steady and the other loosens the nut that holds the collet. Others have a shaft that locks in place and use only a single wrench.

If you're loosening the bit, put the router on the bench with the bit pointing to the right. On a two-wrench collet, put a wrench on the nut closest to the router, which is the nut that turns the shaft. Rest the end of the wrench on the work bench or router. Put the other wrench on the other nut with the handle pointing toward you and push down toward the table to loosen the bit. To tighten the bit, turn the router so the bit points left and repeat.

The process is the same on a single-wrench collet, except that you lock the collet in place following the manufacturer's directions instead of applying the first wrench.

Routing end grain

The end of a board will splinter when you rout it, as shown here There are two ways to minimize splinters.

1) If you start on the end of the board, then do the side, the next end, and the remaining side, the board will still splinter, but the damage gets routed away when you move around the stock.

2) To eliminate splintering entirely, clamp a scrap along the edge of the stock you're routing, giving it the support it needs to keep from splintering.

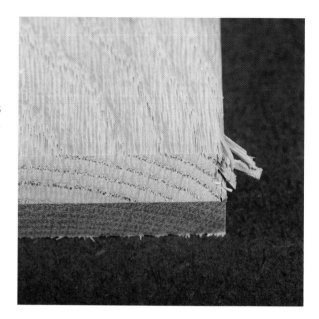

More routing tips

- Use sharp bits. To see if your bit is sharp, look at the edge in the light. If you see a white line instead of two surfaces coming to a point, get the bits sharpened.
- Feed the stock gently— a straining motor makes more noise.
- If you're working on a router table, make sure that both the router and the mounting plate are tightly fastened.
- If you're buying a router, buy one with lots of horsepower, preferably with a speed control. The greater the horsepower, the less noise a router makes.

Guiding the cut along a fence

An unpiloted or straight bit—one that has no bearing on the end to guide it—won't cut in a straight line unless you guide the router against a fence. In some cases you can just clamp a board to the work and guide the router along it. You can also buy a fence attachment that slips into the base and adjusts to position the router properly.

The rotation of the bit can actually help pull the router tight against the fence. Feed the router from right to left if the fence is between you and the router as shown here. Feed in the opposite direction if the router is between you and the fence.

Getting the smoothest edge

Make as many passes as you need to get the final profile, always routing counterclockwise when using a handheld router. Once you've got a smooth profile, make a final pass routing clockwise. This smooths out minor blemishes and helps give you a mirror-smooth finish. The bit will still want to push the stock along at a fast pace, but you can control the speed because you're removing such a small amount of wood.

On difficult pieces of wood—those that splinter or chip—stop routing normally when you've got about 1/16 inch of wood to remove. Make the final pass working clockwise.

Router tables

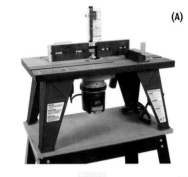

(A)

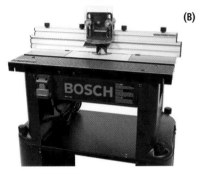

(B)

Mounting a router in a table makes the router even more versatile. To begin with it, is more stable because the work surface is much larger and you won't have to worry about the router tipping when you are cutting a narrow piece of stock. If you're routing a groove on the edge of a board, you can hold it against the table and fence to keep it from wobbling. You can use larger bits, such as those that make raised panels. For routing decorative edges the router table can't be beat—it turns a sometimes unwieldy tool into what is essentially a small shaper.

Router tables can be as simple or as elaborate as you please. Table **A** is a combo kit, sold with a handheld router that you can take out of the table. For a relatively small investment, you get both a router and table. The table is small enough that you can put it on your bench, or on a small work station (not included).

Table **B** is sold without a router so you'll either buy one separately or install your own. It's a heavier table that comes with its own stand, and the fence is longer.

When choosing a table, look for one with a split fence, safety guards, and hold-downs. You'll also want a dust port, so that you can hook your shop vac up to it and remove the incredible amounts of sawdust that routing creates. Both these tables meet the necessary criteria.

Direction of feed on a router table

Mounting a router upside down underneath a table turns the router into a small shaper—an invaluable tool if you're going to make molding for custom trimwork.

The router on a router table is upside down compared to a handheld router. Feed stock from right to left along the fence. If you're guiding a stock against a piloted bit rather than a fence, feed the stock so that it travels clockwise around the bit.

Featherboards

Featherboards help hold the work in place as you rout. You won't need them for most operations, but they're handy if you're routing small pieces or lots of pieces. Some tables come with built-in featherboards, but you can make your own by making a series of parallel cuts in a board on the table saw. Put the featherboard on the table and fence so that it pushes the stock directly against the bit. Clamp it down, and rotate the featherboard to slightly decrease the distance between the featherboard and fence. Tighten the clamp before routing. When properly adjusted the fingers flex slightly when they push against the stock, and you'll be able to feed the board forward but unable to pull it backward.

Adjusting the fence

If you're using a piloted bit, put a straightedge against the fence and move the fence back and forth until the edge just touches the bearing, and then lock it in place. If the fence has sliding faces so that you can adjust the size of the opening, set them so that the opening is slightly larger than the bit.

Cuts on the router table, like those with the router, need to begin shallow and get progressively deeper until you rout the desired profile. Once the fence is set, lower the router so the bit is making a shallow cut, rout each piece, and then raise the bit. Repeat until you've got the finished surface. The amount you raise the bit with each pass depends on the wood and the bit. If you hear the router straining, you're taking off too much in a single pass.

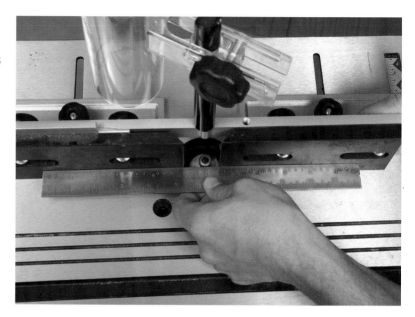

Making a test cut

A router table can look as if it's set up perfectly but be off by just enough to ruin a project. To be safe set everything up and then make a test cut on a piece of scrap to make sure everything is properly positioned.

Miter gauge

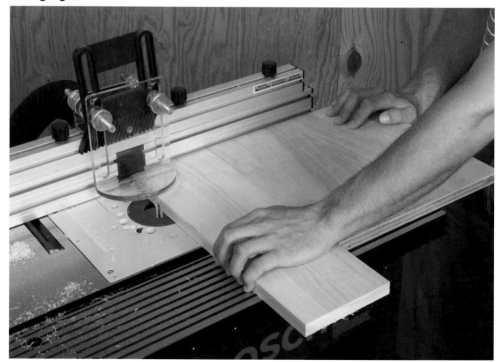

A miter gauge helps hold narrow pieces while you guide them across the bit. A piece of plywood does the same job and provides more support. Set up the cut, guide the plywood along the fence, and rout right into the plywood. It's a cheap, reliable trick—especially if the miter gauge is optional on your table.

Molding

Materials

Moldings are available in a variety of materials. These four chair rails have similar, if not identical, profiles but are made from completely different materials. At left **(A)** is a prefinished polystyrene molding. Polystyrene can be impossible to tell from the wood, but is easier to work. It is not, however, as durable as wood, so use it in places where it won't get a lot of abuse. Hardwood moldings, like this oak chair rail **(B)**, are stock items in some stores and special order elsewhere. They're meant to be varnished—applying a coat of stain first is optional. Stainable pine **(C)** is clear and meant to be varnished, and is usually stained first. It's one of the more expensive moldings, and if you're planning on painting you can save money (and time) by buying a paint-grade molding. You have two choices, the medium-density fiberboard (MDF) molding shown here **(D)** or finger-jointed pine. Both come coated with a white primer and look virtually identical on the rack. The pine, however, is made of short pieces held together with interlocking fingers. MDF is made of finely ground sawdust and a binder. MDF is very smooth, paints well, and cuts easily.

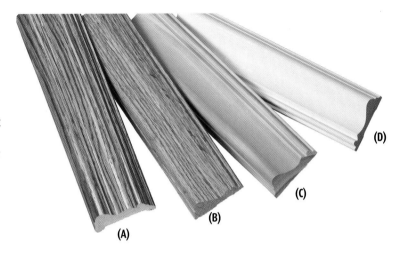

Decorative Molding

All molding is decorative, but some is more decorative than others. The moldings shown here are preassembled. From bottom to top, the bare wood dental molding **(A)** can be stained or painted. The wider, white, dental molding **(B)** is made of MDF. You can screw a prefab piece to the corners to simplify joinery. Regular crown molding **(C)** is flat, and designed to angle between the wall and ceiling.

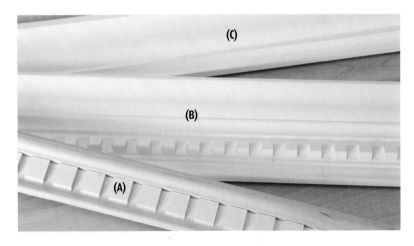

Molding Names

Some molding is named for it function—like the baseboard **(A)** and crown molding **(B)** shown here. Other molding is named for its shape—like the quarter round **(C)** and cove molding **(D)**. You'll also hear builders talking about two families of moldings—"colonial" and "clamshell." Colonial **(E)** consists of similarly shaped door and window molding, (called casing). Clamshell **(F)** includes both casing and baseboard. Colonial is the more ornate of the two families and variations go back to the 17th century. Clamshell molding (also known as sanitary molding) is a more recent development used in both modern and retro designs. There's a variety of molding beyond colonial and clamshell, though none of it has a particular name. Walk through the aisle to see what's available, or ask to see the sample board which shows examples of molding the store carries.

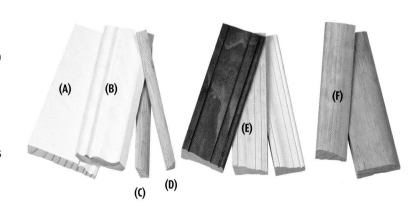

Typical molding profiles

Millwork has many names but, to make it easier, numeric designations have been standardized by the Wood Moulding and Millwork Producers Association—WM followed by a number. There are some 200 standard profiles. Some are larger versions of others; some are unique. There are also hundreds of custom profiles, many of which are sold through home centers, hardware stores, and lumberyards.

Typical softwood moldings are shown here, organized by their intended uses. There are no ironclad rules, however, and if you look around, you're bound to see a picture molding used as a crown, or a shingle/panel molding used to trim a door. Mix and match to get the look you want.

Crown, bed, and cove moldings

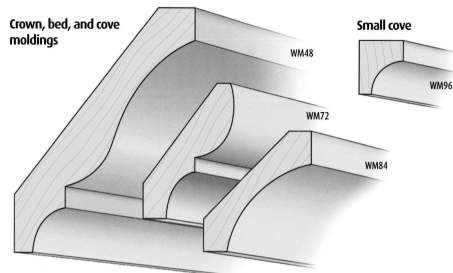

WM48

WM72

WM84

Small cove

WM96

Chair rail

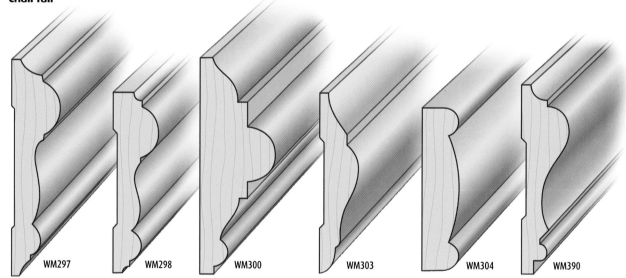

WM297   WM298   WM300   WM303   WM304   WM390

Shingle/panel molding

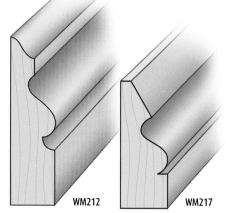

WM212   WM217

Astragal moldings

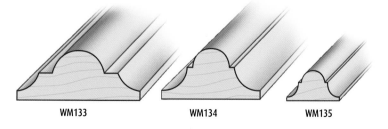

WM133   WM134   WM135

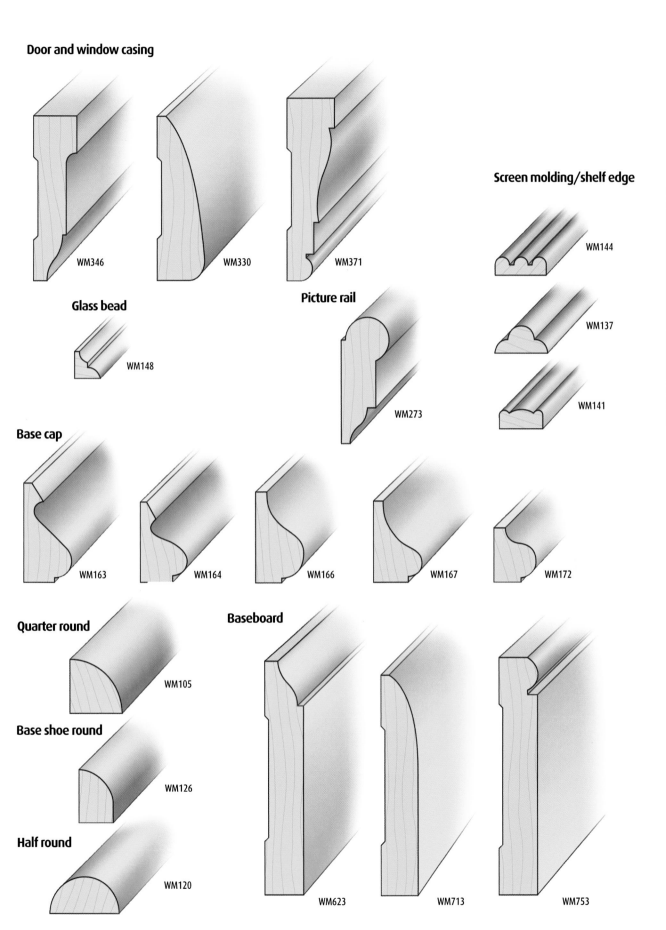

Door and window casing

WM346

WM330

WM371

Screen molding/shelf edge

WM144

WM137

WM141

Glass bead

WM148

Picture rail

WM273

Base cap

WM163

WM164

WM166

WM167

WM172

Quarter round

WM105

Baseboard

Base shoe round

WM126

Half round

WM120

WM623

WM713

WM753

Making custom moldings

Most complicated molding treatments, such as the Traditional window trim at right (see page 123 for more information), are actually built up from several pieces of simpler molding (usually a combination of stock and profiles cut out of 1× stock with a router). You can get as complicated or as simple as you want, and don't be afraid to use a molding intended for one purpose for something entirely different—a wide baseboard upside down around the top of the room is a great base over which you can nail crown molding. Get your ideas from magazines, websites, sample boards at lumberyards, and home centers. Buy a few sample lengths, and give it a trial run. A corner of a drywalled garage or basement makes a great place to test your samples and build your skills until you're ready to start cutting good stock and driving nails into your good walls.

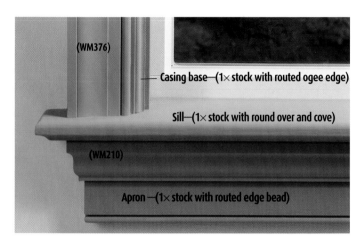

(WM376)

— Casing base—(1× stock with routed ogee edge)

Sill—(1× stock with round over and cove)

(WM210)

Apron —(1× stock with routed edge bead)

(WM448)

(WM623)

Crown molding

When you're building custom molding, it sometimes pays to ignore the rules. This crown molding assembly uses crown molding (**WM448**), but the molding it's nailed to is baseboard (**WM623**), installed upside down. Installing this is a two-part operation. Put the baseboard in place first, upside down and tight against the ceiling. Cope it at inside corners, and miter it at outside corners. Once the baseboard is in place, nail in the crown molding, coping and mitering it in the same places you did the baseboard.

(WM167)

(WM167)

Chair rail

You can buy several different chair rail patterns, but this combination lets you make the molding as wide or narrow as you'd like. Start with a piece of 1×, nailed to the studs at a height that protects the wall from the tops of your chairs. Dress it up by nailing a piece of basecap (**WM167**) along the top and another one along the bottom.

(WM623)

(WM217)

Baseboard

Baseboard (**WM623**) usually has a quarter-round molding across the bottom to cover any gaps caused by an uneven floor. Substitute a molding called a shingle molding (**WM217**) to echo the pattern along the top of the baseboard. For a more substantial look, build up the thickness with a basecap.

(WM371)

Backbanding

Door and window casing

Start simple by trimming the window or door with regular casing—the style shown here is generally referred to as Colonial (**WM371**). Add detail and apparent thickness by nailing back banding around the outside edge, mitering it at the corners.

2

TOOLS AND MATERIALS

Nails

GOOD IDEA

STOCK UP
If you're not sure whether you need a particular fastener, buy a few anyway. It may save you a trip to the store in the middle of the project. If you don't need them, you can either take them back later or keep them on hand for the future.

TOOL SAVVY

A STITCH IN TIME
If you can never find the nail you want, you're no better off than if you didn't have any. Get a plastic organizer case with sections large enough to hold boxes of nails. Put the boxes in the organizer every time you buy new nails. Work on that pile mixed together in the bottom of the drawer a little bit every now and then, and you'll always know what's on hand.

WORK SMARTER

ALL GALVANIZING IS NOT CREATED EQUAL
Electroplated galvanized nails have heads that will almost always rust eventually; hot-dipped galvanized nails will occasionally rust. To ensure against rust stains, use hot-dipped nails, and dab or spray each head with rust-inhibiting paint before applying a final finish.

WORK SMARTER

THE MORE THE MERRIER
In most cases, one nail isn't enough; you should drive two or three nails into each joint.

Virtually every carpentry project is fastened together with nails or screws, sometimes with the aid of an adhesive. Fasteners come in a wide variety of sizes, types, and materials, so you can find the nail or screw that is perfectly suited to your project.

In general, the longer and thicker a fastener, the greater its holding power. If you drive a fastener that is too thick, however, it may split the board, and whatever advantage the extra size gave you is gone.

A penny for your thoughts

Lengths for most framing and finish nails are typically denoted by the term "penny," which is abbreviated with the letter "d" (for denarius, an old Roman coin). The "d" once referred to the price of the nail, so a 12d nail cost more and was larger than an 8d nail. Though there are variations, a 4d nail is usually 1⅜" long; a 6d nail is 1⅞"; an 8d is 2⅜"; a10d is 2⅞"; and a 16d is 3¼". A 20d nail is 4" long. There are no 14d or 18d nails.

Other nails, such as brads, drywall nails, masonry nails, and siding nails, are usually identified by their length.

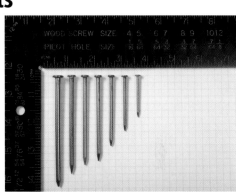

Nails for finish work

Finish nails are often used for trim and cabinet work because they can be rendered virtually invisible. They have small heads, which you usually "set" or drive ⅛ inch or so below the wood surface. Fill the small hole this creates with putty that you can either paint or stain.

(Clockwise from the top), Bright **finish nails** are the most common. Wire **brads** are very small finish nails. **Paneling nails** are coated with a color (usually, tan, brown, or in this case, white), so they blend in with paneling. They have ribs and a slightly more definite head to give them a bit more holding power.

Nails for framing, flooring, and drywall

Framing nails hold more securely than finish nails—they're bigger and have large heads that help hold the board in place. Use them for assembling walls and things that get covered with drywall or trim.

(Counterclockwise from the top right), **Cement- or vinyl-coated sinkers** are used for fastening framing lumber together and are easy to drive. **Spiral shank** nails are also used to hold framing lumber together and have a strong grip. **Ring-shank** nails are more difficult to drive than sinkers but have superior holding power—a good choice for subflooring.

Drywall nails have ring shanks for holding power, as well as concave heads, which makes it easier to dimple them into the drywall without tearing the paper. Expansion and contraction of the studs with changes in moisture can push them back out through the drywall.

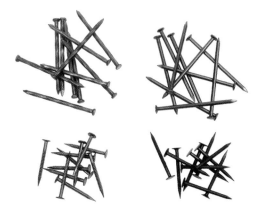

Pilot holes

Drill pilot holes before driving a nail less than 3 inches from the end of a board. In fact, you should drill anywhere where there is even a slight chance of splitting the board. It only takes a few seconds to drill the hole, whereas it will take you plenty of time and money to replace a split board. Even a small split will almost certainly grow larger in time.

You can use a drill bit for the pilot, but the nail makes an even better bit. Put the nail in your drill, tightening the chuck normally. If the nail wobbles when you turn on the drill, either put it deeper in the bit, or clip off the head with a pair of end nippers, or electrician's pliers. Drill normally, and then pull the nail back out while the drill is still spinning. Drive another nail through the resulting hole.

Exterior and masonry nails

Nails that will be exposed to the weather usually have a protective coating. (Left to right), **Galvanized** nails are the most common. Choose hot-dipped rather than electroplated galvanized nails; the dipped nails have little chunks that improve the grip, and their coating is more durable. **Stainless-steel** nails are strong and impervious to weather. They're also expensive. **Siding nails** are coated and colored. They come in either ring-shank or fluted.

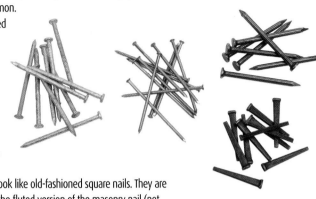

You can nail nails into masonry, too, as long as the joint does not have to be very strong. **Cut masonry nails** (bottom right) look like old-fashioned square nails. They are somewhat blunt and harder to drive than the fluted version of the masonry nail (not shown). Which nail you use is simply a matter of preference.

Nail gun nails

Brads and finish nails for use in a nail gun typically come in what are called clips, because the sides of their heads are flattened and appear to be clipped off. Framing nails come in clips too, but local codes now require that framing nails have heads like those on common nails. As a result, framing nails usually come with round heads, which are strung together by a thin wire or resin, rather than in a clip.

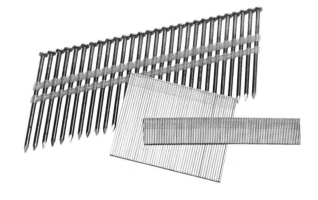

Nail gun nails come in a range of sizes. Unlike other nails they are not named by penny designations but by their length and purpose. Shown here (top to bottom) are **3½-inch round-head framing nails**, **3½-inch clipped finishing nails**, and **1-inch brads**. Each requires a different gun, and you'd need a fourth gun for clipped framing nails.

Different guns take different nails, and you can't assume that a pack of finishing nails will work in your gun, even if it's made by the gun's manufacturer. Framing nails, in particular, are only available in large quantities, so ask for help getting the right nails until you get the hang of it. For information on nail guns, see page 31.

How long is long enough?

Drill pilot holes before driving a nail less than 3 inches from the end of a board. In fact, you should drill anywhere where there is even a slight chance of splitting the board. It only takes a few seconds to drill the hole, whereas it will take you plenty of time and money to replace a split board. Even a small split will almost certainly grow larger in time.

You can use a drill bit for the pilot, but the nail makes an even better bit. Put the nail in your drill, tightening the chuck normally. If the nail wobbles when you turn on the drill, either put it deeper in the bit, or clip off the head with a pair of end nippers, or electrician's pliers. Drill normally, and then pull the nail back out while the drill is still spinning. Drive another nail through the resulting hole.

Screws and bolts

Screws and bolts have two big advantages over nails: They hold better, and you are less likely to damage a board while driving them. Drywall screws are easiest to use. Their sharp point and unique thread mean that you can drive them without drilling a pilot hole first. All other screws and bolts must be driven into a pilot hole. Pilot holes are simple holes somewhat smaller than the screw—ideally they are the same diameter as the screw would be if the threads were missing. You can eyeball this: Hold the butt end of a drill bit in front of the screw. If the drill blocks out sight of the screw shank (the solid section), but you can still see the threads, the bit is the right size.

Bolts, of course, also need to go through a hole. The hole should be the same diameter as the bolt—a ½-inch bolt gets a ½-inch hole.

If you're attaching something to cement, there are several anchors that will do the trick—from screws whose threads grab the concrete, to plastic or metal anchors that expand to grab the edges of hole you drill.

(Clockwise top right), Black **drywall screws**, sometimes called "all-purpose screws," are generally the least expensive. However, they

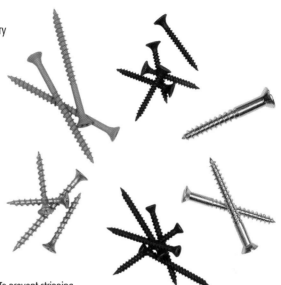

sometimes break or get stripped when driven very tightly, which makes them unsuited to projects that call for a strong hold.

Steel wood screws are softer and harder to break. **Brass wood screws** are attractive and often used when the screw remains visible. Brass is softer than steel, however, and you can strip the head while driving the screw. To prevent stripping, drill a pilot hole and then drive a steel wood screw the same size as the brass screw into it to clear the way. Back out the steel screw and replace it with the brass one.

Trimhead screws are similar to black drywall screws, but have a very small head that can be countersunk and filled like a finish nail, although the hole is larger. They are often square-drive screws.

For exterior work, or where the screw head will get wet, **galvanized screws** offer some protection, but rust is always a possibility. A **deck screw** or a "primeguard" screw has a patented coating that provides much better protection. These screws have a modified Phillips head, and a box of them often includes the bit you'll need to drive them.

Screw heads

When choosing a screw, pay attention both to the type of drive required and the shape of the head. A flathead screw is made to be driven flush with, or sunk slightly below, the surface of the work. Round-head and oval-head screws have a finished appearance, and are meant to show above the surface.

(Clockwise from top left), A **Phillips** head is the easiest to drive, but it is also the easiest to strip. **Slotted** heads make for a surer bit grip, but are hard to drive with a drill, because the bit can slide out of the slot. A **modified Phillips** head is sort of a combination of a square and a Phillips, it's easy to drive, hard to strip, and looks pretty much like a regular Phillips. A **square drive** makes for a sure grip, but is a trifle ugly.

Bolts and lag screws

For serious fastening of big boards, nothing beats a bolt. Start by drilling holes through the boards you're fastening. Get a bolt long enough to pass through both pieces, with at least ½ inch to spare so you can add washers and a nut. A **lag bolt** (left) calls for two washers—one under the head and one under the nut. A **carriage bolt** (center) has a finished head, and requires only one washer. A **lag screw** (right) is almost as strong as a bolt. Drill a pilot hole the recommended size, slip on a washer, and drive the screw using a socket wrench.

Masonry anchors

Masonry screws are the simplest method for attaching something to masonry. You drill a hole in the concrete, and then drive the masonry screw into it. It's quick and strong, and good for attaching electrical boxes or plywood to masonry. If you're attaching a floor plate to a concrete wall, however, you'll need one of the masonry anchors.

Masonry screws **(A)** can be hex-head or Phillips, or both. Hex-head screws are easiest to drive and virtually strip-proof, but they protrude above the board being fastened. Phillips screws, which drive flush, must be driven with care to avoid stripping. The screw manufacturer sells a bit that drills a hole that matches the screw. There are two bit sizes; be sure to purchase the correct masonry bit for the screws you're using.

Plastic anchors **(B)** are the simplest of the anchors, but support very little weight. To install, drill a hole for the plastic sleeve, and then drive the screw into it.

Hammer-set anchors **(C)**, which have a built-in-nail instead of a screw or bolt, are the quickest: Drill a small-diameter hole, poke the anchor in, and drive the nail with a hammer.

Masonry anchors are plastic sleeves or metal slugs that fit in a hole in the concrete; the bolt or nail that goes through them causes the anchor to expand and lock itself in the hole.

Wedge anchors **(D)** work much the same way but have fingerlike wedges that are driven into the concrete when you tighten the nut. They have better holding power than sleeve anchors.

Lag shields **(E)** are stronger than any of the other fasteners but more temperamental. You start by drilling a hole to house the shield and tapping the shield into the hole. Unlike hammer-set and sleeve anchors, however, a lag shield never ends up precisely where you want it—it's too large and ungainly. Lag shields are called two-step anchors as a result. Step one, you put in the anchor. Step two, you drill a hole in whatever you are attaching, positioning it to match the location of the anchor. When you put in the lag bolt, drive it until it's snug. Overtightening can break the anchor loose.

After you drive a sleeve anchor **(F)** into its hole, you tighten the nut to pull the wide end of the anchor into the sleeve. This forces the sleeve to expand, anchoring it in the concrete.

Setting up a home shop

A room becomes a shop the minute you put a table saw in it, and there's an awful lot you can build before you'll need anything more than that.

The shop shown here is well-equipped, the kind of shop a pro might have. The table saw is heavy, more powerful than a job-site saw. It's capable of handling bigger stock and has a larger table to support your work. With a general-purpose combination blade and perhaps a set of dado blades for cutting grooves, you'll be able to do anything from general carpentry to some basic cabinetmaking. On the other hand, the job-site saw will do most of the things a larger saw will do and it has the advantage of being portable. As with any tool the rule is buy the best you can afford and take good care of it.

Good lighting is essential

After the saw, your next most important tool isn't a power tool at all—it's good lighting. Working in a poorly lit shop is dangerous,

depressing, and begging to make mistakes. Fluorescent shop lights are cheap—far cheaper than a table saw. Buy a couple at a time, until you've got enough to light up the room. Be sure to put one directly over every tool and every work space.

More tool talk

Next to the saw, you'll probably use the router most. You'll want it to rout mortises for hinges, to rout grooves for cabinets, and to put decorative edges on stock. Sooner or later you'll want the rest of the tools shown on the bench too—drill, sander, and jigsaw. Buy them as you need them. When you're buying the drill, you can save a couple of dollars and get a more powerful drill if you buy the old-fashioned plug-in style.

There's a miter box in this shop because it's easier to cut molding on a power miter box than it is on a table saw. The cut is cleaner, crisper, more precise, and the molding is less *(continued next page)*

▲ Organizing your tools makes for an efficient and effective workspace. Open steel shelving, which is inexpensive and easy to assemble, offers quick access to hand tools and materials, protects your tools, and keeps things off the floor and out of the way.

2

TOOLS AND MATERIALS

likely to slip sideways during the cut than it is on a table saw. You'll want one if you're doing a lot of trim work and you'll appreciate one if you ever do any furniture work.

The router table is another standby of the shop. If you're making your own moldings, or raising panels, it's almost impossible to do without one. When you buy a router table, compare the various brands because the price range is huge: It's a lot like choosing a table saw. The expensive ones work better, but they all do the job. Get the best you can afford.

Storage is key

Make sure you have adequate storage. There's no point in stumbling all over your tools while you try to work. Inexpensive metal or plastic shelves can hold your power tools when you're not using them. Make a clamp rack by screwing a 2×4 to some blocks that you've screwed to the wall. Put your hand tools—the chisels, planes, screwdrivers, and wrenches that you collect along the way—in a good set of drawers. A mechanic's chest is ideal, but so are old kitchen cabinets, file cabinets, or even an old dresser. The object isn't to have the prettiest shop, or even the best shop: The object is to have a shop that works.

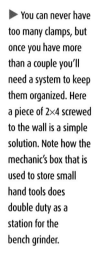

▲ A well-lit saw table top not only makes for more accurate cutting, it is also safer. Fluorescent fixtures are excellent lighting solutions, inexpensive, easy-to-install, and dependable.

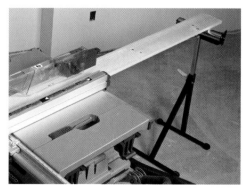

▲ Roller supports or saw horses adjusted to the height of the saw table help you manage long lengths of stock and keep them flat on the table while you're ripping.

▶ Dedicated tables and benches for your large power tools make the job easier. If you don't have the space for an adjustable stand for your miter saw, purchase a ready-to-assemble work station from your home center. Keep the cases the saw blades come in and hang them on the wall near the saw.

▶ You can never have too many clamps, but once you have more than a couple you'll need a system to keep them organized. Here a piece of 2×4 screwed to the wall is a simple solution. Note how the mechanic's box that is used to store small hand tools does double duty as a station for the bench grinder.

▶ A solid workbench is an essential part of any woodworker's shop. You can often find benches like this one in kits at your home center. Note the built-in vise. The assortment of hand power tools (left to right)—a jigsaw, sander, drill, router bits, and a router—are all important parts of a complete workshop.

Job site workshops

f you're like most homeowners your first shop will probably be in the middle of your living room or in a corner of the garage, but you can still create an efficient workspace until you've dedicated some room for a shop. A finish carpenter going out to a job site would probably have all the tools shown here in his truck—just in case. The carpenter would also have spent years collecting the tools he carries. You should buy your tools gradually, too, as the need arises. If you're installing crown molding, get a miter saw. On the other hand, don't bother getting a framing nailer, unless you're building lots of walls.

Probably the most versatile tool on a job site is the power miter saw. You can cut anything from crown molding to 2×4s with it. A miter saw stand, like the one shown here, brings the work up to waist level and has built-in stops for cutting multiple pieces to the same length, as well as supporting the stock while you cut. A shop vac isn't an absolute essential for sucking up the saw's dust, but if you've got one for cleaning up at the end of the job, why not use it as a dust collector during the job?

A circular saw is the workhorse of the framing carpenter. It's good for cutting plywood, cutting bevels, and crosscutting 2×6s, 2×8s, 2×10s, and other stock that the miter saw can't handle. It's probably one of the tools you'll pick up early when you start buying, but on the other hand, if all you do is trim work, you may never need one. As for the table saw, you can live without one on the job site, but most carpenters have a small one somewhere in the back of their truck. It makes life easier when you need to make a 16-foot board ½ inch narrower. A larger saw, like the one shown here, is more powerful, and more accurate than a small saw, and it is still portable. Called a job site saw, this 10-inch model is perfect for most homeowners.

Light it up

You may not think of auxiliary lights as essential until you pull out all the light fixtures in the living room and the sun starts to set. A set of good halogen lights costs little more than you'd pay for a good hammer, so why fumble around in the dark?

Handy tools

Almost everybody who has ever owned a cordless drill wonders how he or she ever got along without it. The drills go anywhere, and with a Phillips bit, they double as a screwdriver. You'll be surprised at how often you reach for it and how much easier it is to use without a cord trailing behind. The jigsaw is something you'll grab less often, but there's no substitute when you've got to make a cutout for a sink or cut paneling for an outlet.

There probably isn't a house built today without a pneumatic nailer. They make framing a wall or installing molding about as effortless as a job can be. The compressors have become affordable; some even come with a finish nailer and brad nailer as part of the deal. With all the attachments available, you'll find endless uses for an air compressor.

Finish carpentry

General carpentry holds your house up—studs, joists, and rafters. You may not see it but you're glad it's there.

Finish carpentry, on the other hand, is what gives a room its "look." A house is a collection of walls before the finish carpenter starts. It always has been, and always will be. Finish carpentry is what finishes a home.

Finish carpentry is about making things look right—cutting the molding so the joints are tight and each part is the right length. Installing

crown molding can look "right" to the eye even if the wall and ceiling aren't exactly square. It's a matter of tricks, practice, and patience.

A little mystery

Some of the techniques of finish carpentry might have you scratching your head until you understand the logic. Does it make sense to miter a piece of molding and hold it in place upside down to mark the exact length? How about making a cut upside down and backwards or drawing lines up

Chapter 3 highlights

BASIC TRIM TECHNIQUES
From coping baseboard joints to installing no miter/no cope, basic techniques apply to any style.

74

INSTALLING CROWN MOLDING
Perfectly installed crown molding is the finishing touch to any room.

87

CROWN MOLDING STYLES
Breaking down the elements of a style into components makes it easy to understand and install.

95

INSTALLING DOOR TRIM
Door trim does double duty; it hides the edges of the hole cut in the wall to install the door while supporting the chosen style.

102

DOOR TRIM STYLES
Each style has its own signature in terms of trim.

106

INSTALLING WINDOW TRIM
Window trim works with door trim and baseboard to unify a room.

116

PICTURE FRAMING A WINDOW
Picture frame trim creates a finished, attractive window.

121

WINDOW TRIM STYLES
Windows are one of the initial points of reference in a room; they instantly define a style.

122

INSTALLING BASEBOARD AND CHAIR RAIL
Baseboard ties a room together and protects the walls from damage.

132

BASEBOARD AND CHAIR RAIL STYLES
A room may not have crown molding or chair rail, but it's almost certain to have baseboard.

138

and away from the corner to lay out the slope of a joint? None of these techniques will make a lot of sense in the beginning, but if you follow the instructions you'll begin to understand why learning the tricks of the trade leads to a great looking room.

Getting the look

The look comes after the tricks, and after the patience. In this chapter it comes after you learn installation basics for each of the major projects—crown molding, chair rail, baseboard, doors, and windows. Once you understand the basics you'll learn how to apply them to your style. You'll see samples for each of the five styles from Chapter One. You'll see how to take the principles of say, framing a window, and then apply them in a Country, Victorian, Traditional, Arts and Crafts, or Modern style.

Basic trim techniques

Trim nailing techniques

What size nail?

The first problem you'll run into when nailing trim in place is choosing the right-sized nail. If you're installing crown molding, chair rail, or baseboard, choose nails that will penetrate at least 1 inch into the framing. Nail into each stud, and nail every 16 inches if nailing into the top plate or floor plate.

When installing door and window molding, drive 8d nails through the outer edge of the molding and into the studs. On the inner edges drive 4d or 6d nails into the jambs. Space the nails roughly 16 inches apart. Drive 4d nails through mitered corners, nailing both halves of the joint together.

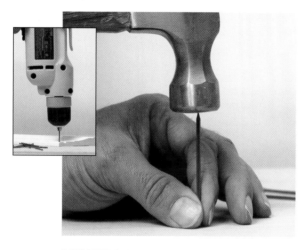

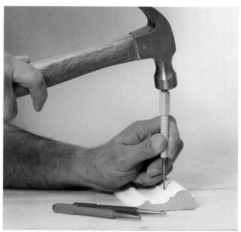

PREDRILLING FOR NAILS

Any nail that is less than 1 inch from the end of a board is almost sure to split the wood. Hardwoods, like oak, are almost certain to bend nails. You can avoid either problem—to a certain extent—by blunting the tip of the nail with a hammer. Your best bet, however, is to drill a pilot hole for the nail with a drill bit the same size as, or slightly smaller than, the diameter of the nail. Most carpenters skip the drill bit, and just pop an unblunted nail in the drill and drill pilots with it.

SETTING THE NAIL

You may not care if you leave a big old hammer mark on your favorite 2×4, but it looks pretty bad on your expensive trim. Drive your nails until they're almost, but not quite, at the surface of the wood. Drive the nails below the surface of the wood with a nail set. Nail sets come in four sizes—get one of each, and use the one that best matches the size of the nail head.

FILLING NAIL HOLES

Setting a nail may drive it below the surface, but it still leaves a hole. Painters fill holes in surfaces they'll paint with glazing putty. Roll a ball of it in your hand, push a pinch of it in the hole with your finger, and then wipe it smooth with your thumb. If you're going to apply varnish or stain, fill the hole with a filler that matches the stain, or use a stainable filler, applying either with a putty knife. There will be a slight difference in color (and sometimes a major difference), but let's face it—everybody knows you nailed the trim in place. The sight of on occasional nail hole isn't going to upset anyone.

Making square and out-of-square cuts

Most of the time you'll want cuts that are square, but there are situations, such as an inside or outside corner of a wall, that are out of square. If that's the case you'll need to make adjustments in the cut to accommodate the problem. Here's how to make both cuts that are square and cuts that are out of square.

Making square cuts to length

1

LAY OUT THE CUT

Guide a pencil along a combination square to mark the entire width of the board where you want the cut to be. Put an X on the waste side of the board so you'll know which side of the line to cut.

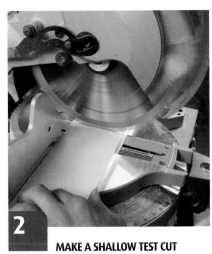

2

MAKE A SHALLOW TEST CUT

Make the cut by lowering the blade about 1/16 inch into the wood on the waste side of the line. Pull the saw back up and check where the cut starts in relation to the line.

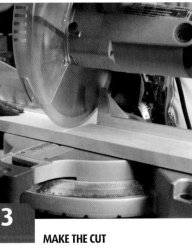

3

MAKE THE CUT

Adjust the position of the wood as needed to align the blade and the line. Retest by lowering the blade again and barely cutting the wood. Make the cut if the test cut aligns with the line.

Making out-of-square cuts to length

1

MEASURE THE ANGLE

Put a T-bevel in the corner to measure the error.

2

SET THE SAW TO MATCH

Set the saw to the angle of the T-bevel and make the cut. For more on using a T-bevel, see page 77.

MAKE SMALL ADJUSTMENTS

It can be hard to make very small adjustments on a miter saw. If a cut only needs to be slightly out of square, shim the board with playing cards, adding cards until you get the cut you want.

Cutting outside miters

The biggest part of putting up molding is holding it in place and driving a nail every 16 inches. It's the few inches around the corners, however, that will require your attention. Inside corners—the kind that out-of-favor children stand in—take a special joint, called a cope joint, see page 82. Outside corners—the kind that stick out into the room—take a regular miter joint.

Miters are most easily cut on a power miter saw. The saw can be set to cut at any angle—set it to 45 degrees for a standard corner. The saw can be set to 45 degrees to the left or 45 degrees to the right. So it's a little confusing at first, but once you get the hang of it, it's automatic.

Most people like to install molding working from the left side of a wall to the right, and these directions assume that you will too. It's hard to get a miter exactly where you want it to be on a board. When you're mitering, cut the miter on a piece a little bit longer than you'll need. Cut it to length by making a square cut.

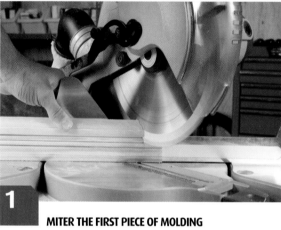

MITER THE FIRST PIECE OF MOLDING
Start with two pieces of molding, each a few inches longer than the section of wall they will cover. Set the saw blade 45 degrees to the right. Put the molding that goes on the left-hand side of the corner against the fence to the left of the blade. Cut the molding, leaving it long.

MITER THE SECOND PIECE
Turn the saw blade 45 degrees left. Put the second molding to the right of the blade and cut a miter in it that leaves the board longer than finished length.

LAY OUT THE LENGTH
The point of an outside miter sticks out beyond the corner by the thickness of a molding. To get the right length molding, measure the wall, add the thickness of the molding, and make a mark that distance from the point of the miter. It's sometimes easier if you do it in steps, as was done in the photo. The molding shown here runs along a short wall of an alcove, which measures 10⅜ inches. The molding is ½ inch thick. If you look closely, there's a light mark on the molding at 10⅜ inches; the second mark, which shows where to make the cut, was made by measuring over the thickness of the molding.

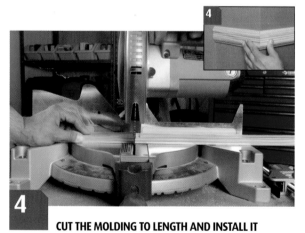

CUT THE MOLDING TO LENGTH AND INSTALL IT
Set the blade for a square cut (0 degrees) and lay the molding on its back on the saw table. Cut the molding at the line. Test fit the pieces. Nail one of the moldings on the wall, dab wood glue on the mitered surface, and rub it in with your fingers. Rub glue into the mitered surface of the second piece, and nail it in place too. Reinforce the joint by driving 1-inch brads through the faces of both moldings, through the miter joint, and into the other molding.

Mitering when the corner is out of square

WORK SMARTER

TAKE THE EASY WAY OUT
A molding that has a difficult miter on one end often has a simple butt joint on the other end. If so, cut the miter first (and keep cutting until you get it right). Once the miter is ready, make a square cut at the other end to cut the piece to length.

1 CHECK THE CORNER FOR SQUARE

Moldings that are mitered together at an out-of-square corner will have gaps between them unless you cut the miters at something other than 45 degrees. Check the corner with a framing square before you start. This corner is out of square by ¼ inch in a little more than a foot.

2 DRAW A LINE PARALLEL TO EACH WALL

The first step in finding the proper miter angle is to draw a line parallel to each wall. Trace along a piece of scrap to draw the line.

3 CONNECT THE CORNERS

Put the handle of a T-bevel against the wall. Set the arm so it runs from the corner of the wall to the corner created by the lines. This is the angle at which you want to miter the moldings.

4 SET THE SAW TO MATCH THE T-BEVEL

If the baseboard were narrower, you could just set the back against the fence to make the cut. The baseboard on this project is too tall for this saw to cut, however, unless you lay the baseboard flat on the bed. Clamp the saw to the fence, and temporarily hold the guard out of the way with a pencil while you set the saw to the proper angle.

5 MITER THE MOLDING

Put the molding in the box facedown, with the bottom edge against the fence, and make a cut. Miter the second molding facedown with the top edge against the fence. If you can make the cut with the molding standing up, make the first cut with the saw set to one side, then reset the saw to the other side to miter the second piece.

6 CHECK THE MITERS

When set in place against the wall, the moldings should form a tight corner with no gaps. If not, check your settings, and recut before nailing the molding in place.

3

FINISH CARPENTRY

Out-of-plumb corners

Even in the best-built houses, nothing is perfect. Sometimes you'll come to a corner where one or both of the walls are out of plumb. Unfortunately, placing a square-cut molding in an out-of-plumb corner leaves you with a gap, as shown here. Sometimes you can get away with leaving it alone. Sometimes there's a molding on the out-of-plumb wall that you can shim to close the gap. Usually, however, it's better just to fix the problem by cutting the end of the molding to match the slope of the wall. To do so, you'll use a tool called a sliding T-bevel to measure the angle at which the wall slopes. Once the T-bevel is set to the proper angle, you'll put it on the saw and turn the saw to the left or right to match the angle.

Cutting an out-of-plumb joint

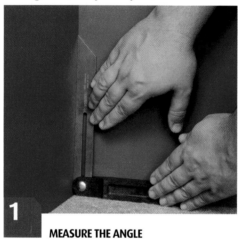

1

MEASURE THE ANGLE

Put a sliding T-bevel in the corner. Loosen the nut that holds the blade in place, set the bevel to match the angle of the wall, and then tighten the nut. If the nut is against the wall, as it is here, lift the bevel gently, and tighten it. Once you tighten the nut, double-check to make sure the T-bevel is still at the right angle.

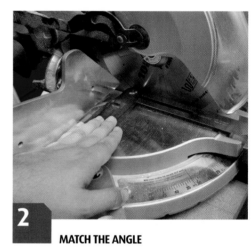

2

MATCH THE ANGLE

Lock the saw in the down position. Put the T-bevel on the saw, with its handle against the fence and its blade against the saw blade. Loosen the handle on the saw so that you can turn the saw from left to right, and turn the saw to match the angle on the T-bevel.

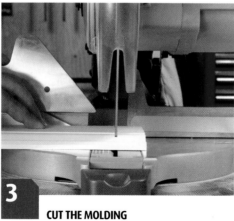

3

CUT THE MOLDING

Lock the saw in place at the proper angle, and double-check to make sure the T-bevel blade rests against the saw blade with no gaps. Make any necessary adjustments; then cut the end of the molding.

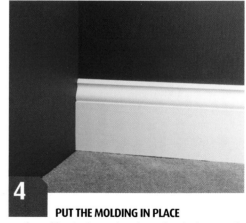

4

PUT THE MOLDING IN PLACE

Put the molding in place and see how it fits. The first cut isn't always perfect—sometimes the T-bevel gets knocked out of position, or an uneven floor throws off the angle. If the angle isn't right, move the blade a half a degree, cut a piece of scrap, and test fit it. Change the angle of the saw as necessary until you're satisfied with the fit.

Cutting mitered returns

A molding will sometimes end in the middle of a wall instead of running into another piece of molding. The apron below a windowsill is the most common example, but in the course of putting up molding you'll run into others.

When a molding ends trim carpenters don't just cut the piece to length, nail it up, and move on. The most common solution is just to cut a miter in the end of the piece, so that it slopes back into the wall.

A mitered return is another approach that gives you a more finished look. On a mitered return you put a small piece of trim on the end of the board so that the end appears to be molded to match the face. Cutting the joint is pretty easy on a miter saw; gluing a tiny piece onto another can be a bit tricky, but masking tape makes a great clamp.

1 **MARK WHERE THE MOLDING SHOULD END**
Sometimes, putting the molding where you want it means you run into an obstruction, such as an outlet. If so, put a "mitered return" on the end of the molding, as shown below and on the following page. Start by choosing a point near the obstruction at which on you want the molding to end. Mark it with a pencil, and measure the distance from there to the corner of the wall.

2 **MITER THE END THAT WILL HAVE RETURN**
Mitering leaves one side of the board longer than the other. Miter the end near the obstruction, creating a board on which the front is slightly longer than the back. Cut the other end square so the front will be the length you measured in step one. (If you're coping the end without the return, cut the cope first, then miter.)

Mark precise cut lines with a utility knife.

3 **MITER THE END OF A SECOND PIECE**
You won't need much molding for the second piece, but make sure you've got enough to keep your fingers away from the blade—cut a piece that's at least 18 inches long.

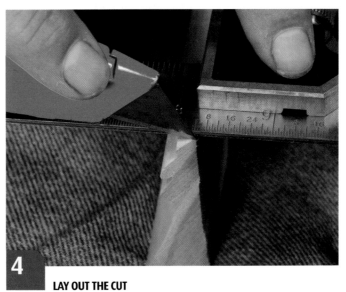

4 **LAY OUT THE CUT**
Draw a line with your square that begins at the back edge of the miter and comes to the front of the molding. Using a utility knife to mark the cut results in a very precise cut line and a more accurate cut.

Cutting mitered returns *(continued)*

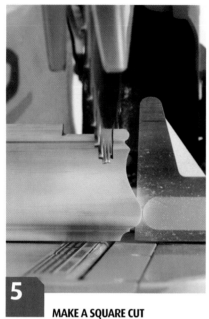

5 MAKE A SQUARE CUT

Make a cut along the line, positioning it so that you're cutting off the entire miter. To cut precisely, make a shallow cut starting well on the waste side of the line, and slide the board until the blade just touches the line. Cut at the line to cut off the miter. This will be the return you put on the other molding.

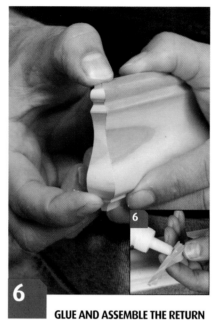

6 GLUE AND ASSEMBLE THE RETURN

Glue the return in place before you install it. Apply glue to both mitered surfaces, as shown in the inset, and wipe off the excess with your finger. Fit the pieces together.

7 CLAMP WITH MASKING TAPE

The return is far too small to clamp. Hold it in place instead with masking tape. Apply tape to the back, pull it tight over the return, and keep it taut as you attach the tape to the front.

8 DRILL PILOTS AND NAIL PIECES TOGETHER

On hefty moldings you can reinforce the joint with a finishing nail or wire brad. On smaller moldings driving a nail through the thin section will split it, so drive the nail only through a thick section, if at all. Drill a pilot hole for the nail, using the nail as a drill bit, and then nail the pieces together.

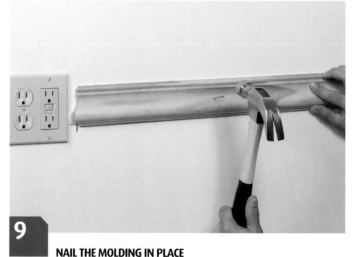

9 NAIL THE MOLDING IN PLACE

Put the molding on the wall, and nail it in place. If the return is more than a few inches from a stud you can nail into, apply construction adhesive to the back of the molding first.

Splicing molding

If you don't have a piece of molding long enough to span the wall you're working on, you can splice two pieces together. The joint, which is made by making opposing miter cuts on the pieces to be joined, is called a scarf joint. If you measure and cut precisely, the scarf joint will become almost invisible. That's because the miter cut emphasizes the profile of the molding, making it blend more effectively, especially if the joint is to be painted.

WORK SMARTER

STAY OUT OF THE LINE OF SIGHT
Position the splice so that it's not obvious from the main viewing areas of a room such as from a doorway or near a window.

1

LAY OUT THE SPLICE
The splice needs to be directly over a stud, so lay out both the bottom of the molding and the studs before you start.

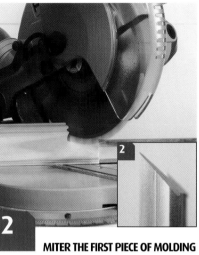

2

MITER THE FIRST PIECE OF MOLDING
Set the blade to 45 degrees, and position the molding to miter it so that the molded face will be the longer of the two sides, as shown in the inset. Put the molding tight against the fence. Cut the miter. Cut the other end square, cutting the molding to a length that puts the miter over the middle of a stud. (If the end opposite the splice will be coped, cut the cope first, then cut the splice.)

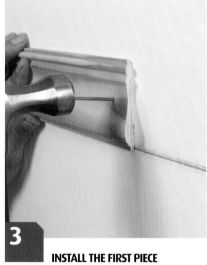

3

INSTALL THE FIRST PIECE
Nail the molding in place, driving the nails into the studs. When you nail the mitered end in place, drive the nails as shown, positioning them so that they don't come out through the miter.

4

MITER THE SECOND PIECE
Set the saw to 45 degrees again, angling it to the same side as it was when you cut the first miter. Put the molding on the other side of the fence, as shown. Miter, and then cut the other end square, cutting the molding to length in the process. (If the end opposite the splice will be coped, cut the cope first, then cut the splice.)

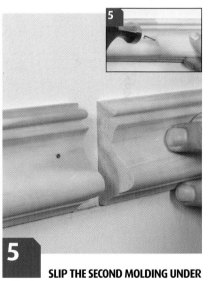

5

SLIP THE SECOND MOLDING UNDER THE FIRST
Put the molding on the wall, sliding it under the first piece of molding. Drive a nail through the center of the joint to hold both pieces in place.

3

FINISH CARPENTRY

3

Coping a baseboard or chair rail

A cope joint is a joint in which one piece of trim is cut to nest against the other without having to cut a miter. It's used for two reasons—one, because coping allows you to mate materials without knowing the exact angle of the miter and two, because miters can open up with changes in humidity or as the house settles. A coped joint can be easily adjusted to make up for imperfections. While the cope joint appears intricate, it's actually easier because you only cut one of the two pieces in any corner. The other piece gets a butt joint, which dead ends into the wall.

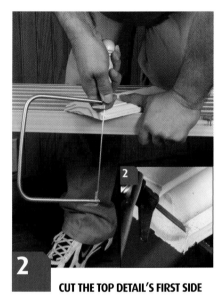

1 **MITER THE PIECE TO BE COPED**
Nail up the first piece of molding so it runs from wall to wall with a butt joint on each end. Miter a second molding on the end that meets the first molding. Angle the saw as shown, cutting a miter that leaves the back of the molding slightly longer than the front. For now, leave the molding longer than the final length required.

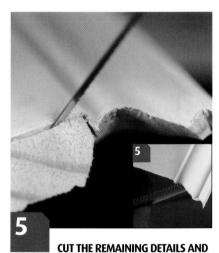

2 **CUT THE TOP DETAIL'S FIRST SIDE**
Start at top of the molding, or whichever edge is most fragile, and cut along the first shape, or detail, with a coping saw. When cutting, hold the blade at a steep angle, as shown, and follow the profile of molding, made easier to see here by the primer on the surface of the molding. Use a relatively quick stroke, but apply as little pressure as possible to keep the saw from binding.

3 **CUT THE TOP DETAIL'S OTHER SIDE**
Stop your first cut when the saw reaches the peak of the detail—the point nearest the face of the molding—and back the saw out of the cut. Start a cut from the back, as shown, and keep going until you've cut along the second side of the first detail and met your first cut.

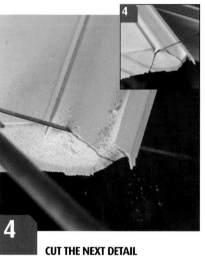

4 **CUT THE NEXT DETAIL**
Always start at the back, and cut toward the face of the molding in order to avoid having to make tight turns near the face of the molding. When the cut turns the corner and starts downhill, back the saw out. Start another cut from the back and cut uphill into the detail until the cut meets your first cut.

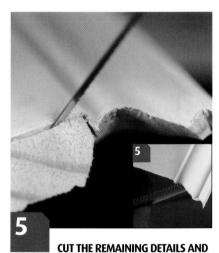

5 **CUT THE REMAINING DETAILS AND SMOOTH OUT THE PROFILE**
Continue cutting until you cut out the entire profile of the molding. If necessary, file the curves smooth with a rat-tail file. File the flats smooth with a flat file. Test the fit, and when you're satisfied with it, cut the molding to length by cutting a butt joint on the end opposite the cope joint.

Cutting a cope joint on crown molding

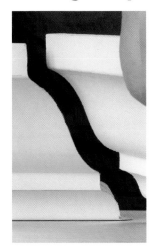

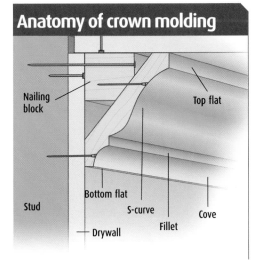

Anatomy of crown molding

Nailing block

Top flat

Stud

Bottom flat

S-curve

Cove

Fillet

Drywall

I n theory, at least, you could miter crown molding when two pieces meet in a corner. In fact, however, it would be a disaster. Crown only touches the wall at two points—the top and the bottom—so the vast majority of the joint is floating in midair, making it impossible to get a tight seam. Coping the corner pieces solves the problem. Here's how it works: One molding runs into the corner of room, where it meets the wall with a simple butt joint. It supports the second molding, the end of which is cut to fit against the first molding like a piece of a jigsaw puzzle.

Putting the first molding in place is a matter of cutting a butt joint and nailing the molding in place. Cutting the second molding to fit against it begins with a miter cut that makes it easy to see the shape you need to cut. You then cut along the shape with an inexpensive handsaw called a coping saw. Make sure you've got a fine blade in it (check it against a pack of replacement blades if you're not sure.) You'll also need a stable work surface one to three feet above the ground—a toolbox or sawhorses will do, but a platform like the one shown here supports more of the molding and is easier on your back.

Despite appearances, this is not a hard joint to learn, but practice helps. Buy an extra piece of molding before you start, and cut a few practice joints. It will give you confidence, and you'll get to throw out your mistakes instead of hanging them on the wall for the world to see. The next few pages show you how to cut the end of one molding to fit against the other. A look at the entire process follows; see Installing crown molding on pages 87–94.

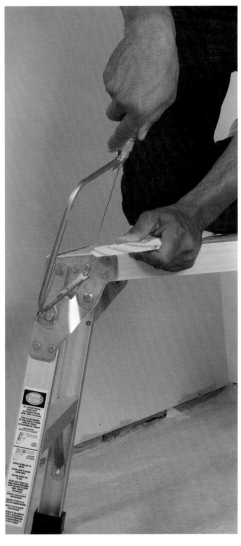

CLOSER LOOK

UNDERCUT THE JOINT

Don't hold the saw straight up and down when you cut a cope joint. Hold it at a 45-degree angle to the surface, so that when viewed from the side, the finished joint comes to a point. This creates a sharp edge that nests tightly against its neighbor.

Coping allows you to mate materials without having to know the exact angle of the miter. A coped joint can also be adjusted to account for imperfections or errors.

Cutting a cope joint on crown molding *(continued)*

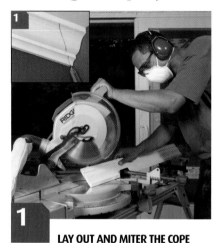

1

LAY OUT AND MITER THE COPE

Nail the first piece of molding in place. Hold the second piece temporarily in place, and lay out the direction of the miter by drawing a line that starts at the bottom of the molding and angles up and away from the corner. The line is only a guide, and doesn't need to be drawn at any particular angle. Put the molding on the miter saw, and set the saw to cut a 45-degree miter that angles in the general direction of the line you drew, and cut a miter.

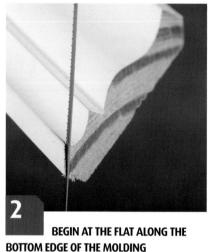

2

BEGIN AT THE FLAT ALONG THE BOTTOM EDGE OF THE MOLDING

Put the saw blade on the end grain just below the surface of the molding, as shown. (If the molding is primed, you'll lay the saw just a hair below the lower surface of the paint.) Make a few passes with the saw, making a shallow groove along the entire length of the flat.

3

CHANGE THE ANGLE OF THE SAW

Once you've made a shallow cut into the flat, lift the saw handle and begin cutting along the bottom corner of the molding. Cut from the corner to the point where the cove begins, following the groove you cut in step two.

4

CUT IN FROM THE BACK

Back the saw out of the cut you've made. Start a new cut from the back of the molding. Cut up towards the middle of the cove, and then follow the shape of the cove until you reach the cut you finished in step three. Remove the waste.

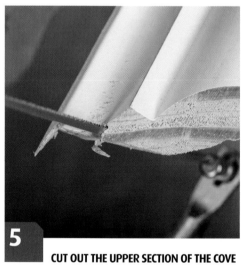

5

CUT OUT THE UPPER SECTION OF THE COVE

Turn the saw around, and cut along the profile of the upper section of the cove. Stop cutting when you reach the fillet.

💲 BUYER'S GUIDE

GET THE RIGHT BLADE
There are three grades of coping saw blades—fine, medium, and coarse. Use a fine blade to make cutting the joint easier.

📖 WORK SMARTER

USE THE CLAMP AS A STOP
Many saws come with a clamp to hold the stock in place while you cut. When you're mitering crown molding, use it as a stop instead of a clamp. Adjust the clamp so that when the molding rests against it, the back edges of the molding are resting on the saw table and saw fence. Rest the crown against the stop to keep it from moving up and down while you cut.

3

FINISH CARPENTRY

6

CUT OUT THE FILLET
Come in from the back of the molding, and cut along the fillet until you reach the cut you made at the top of the cove.

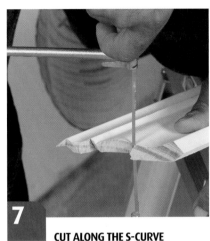

7

CUT ALONG THE S-CURVE
Start at the fillet and cut along the S-curve until you reach the flat at the top of the molding.

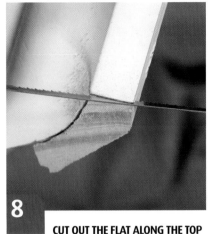

8

CUT OUT THE FLAT ALONG THE TOP OF THE MOLDING
Put the saw on the end grain just below the surface of the molding. Make a few shallow passes and then raise the handle so that the saw is cutting deepest at what will be the top edge of the molding. Continue cutting until the saw meets the cut along the S-curve and the waste falls away.

3

FINISH CARPENTRY

How to cut along a flat

The first and last cuts of a coped joint can be hard to start because they are along flats. The secret is to change the angle of the saw as the cut progresses. Set the teeth of the saw along the line you want to cut. Start the cut with a few gentle strokes in the **same direction** to cut a groove that will guide the rest of the cut and keep the wood from splintering. You can use either the downstroke or the upstroke. Once you have a groove raise the saw handle so that you're cutting along at the corner of the flat. Make a few more cuts with until the saw is about three-quarters of the way along the groove, as shown. Raise the handle, so the blade is straight up and down when viewed from the end of the molding, and finish the cut. When viewed from the edge of the molding, the saw should remain at a 45-degree angle throughout the entire cut.

If you're having trouble lining up the cut, use your thumb as a guide to support the blade and keep it on track until the cut is started.

Installing no miter/no cope molding

This type of installation is called no miter/no cope because all the joints are butt joints. Much Victorian door trim and baseboard are installed in this fashion. The trim is typically made of three parts—a plinth block at floor level, a rosette in the corners above the door, and molding in between. Because the eye is naturally drawn to the rosettes, common practice is to install the rosettes first, so that you can put them exactly where they should be. Install the corner of the rosette so that it aligns with the corner formed by the door jambs. The plinth should be the same width as the rosette, and installed so the inside edge is flush with the inside edge of the jamb. Center the moldings on the rosette and plinth. On windows there are no plinths—you install rosettes at each corner of the window, and run molding between all four.

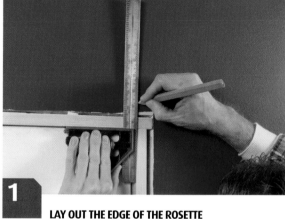

1

LAY OUT THE EDGE OF THE ROSETTE
Put a square against the top jamb of the door, and align the ruler with the inside edge of the side jamb. Draw a line marking the inside edge of the rosette.

2

PUT THE ROSETTE IN PLACE
Put glue or construction adhesive on the back of the rosette. Put a square on the side jamb, aligning the ruler with the inside edge of the top jamb. Rest the rosette on the ruler, align the rosette with the line you drew, and nail it in place.

3

INSTALL THE PLINTH BLOCKS
Plinth blocks, which sit on the floor, form a base for the door molding and are the surface against which the baseboard ends. Put a bead of glue or construction adhesive along the back of the block. Align the inside edges of the plinth with the inside edges of the jamb, and nail it in place.

4

CUT AND INSTALL THE SIDE MOLDING
Measure the distance between the rosette and the plinth. Cut the molding 1/16 inch longer than the measurement. Put the molding on the plinth block, flex it to fit between the plinth and rosette, and nail it in place.

5

CUT AND INSTALL THE TOP MOLDING
Measure the distance between the rosettes. Cut one end of the casing square; cut the other end to the exact length. Nail the molding in place. Cut and install the baseboard as you normally would.

3

FINISH CARPENTRY

 CLOSER LOOK

FIX THE FACTORY CUT FIRST
Factory cuts may look square, but there's no guarantee that they actually are. It's a good idea to square up the factory edge before you measure for the final cut on the other end.

WORK SMARTER

STAINING AND NAILING
If you're going to stain or varnish your trim, do so before you put it up. You're less likely to have problems with drips and sags if you do. In hardwoods, like the oak shown here, predrill holes for the nails so the nails don't split the wood.

Installing crown molding

3

FINISH CARPENTRY

PROJECT DETAILS

SKILLS: Measuring and layout; using power tools
PROJECT: Installing crown molding in an irregular room

TIME TO COMPLETE

EXPERIENCED: 6 hrs.
HANDY: 8 hrs.
NOVICE: 12 hrs.

STUFF YOU'LL NEED

TOOLS: Power miter saw and stand; hammer and nail set or nail gun and compressor; framing or combination square; ladder or folding platform; tarp; safety glasses; ear protection; stud sensor; latex gloves; caulk gun
MATERIALS: Crown molding; 16d finishing nails; 8d finishing nails; 3d finishing nails; primer and paint or stain and varnish; 2×4s for blocking; caulk; sandpaper

CLOSER LOOK

PREASSEMBLED CORNERS
Preassembled inside and outside corner pieces are available in some areas in a limited number of styles. These pieces attach to the corners and you simply butt the crown molding to them, eliminating the need to cope and miter joints. If they're carefully installed they look as good as the real thing but are much easier to put up on the wall. See page 99 for more information.

Crown molding adds depth and dimension to the junction where the walls and ceilings meet.

nstalling crown molding, like playing the piano, takes practice. Unlike playing the piano, however, most people can get the hang of it with only a little practice. Before you take the time to become a maestro, however, you may want to take a look at page 99, for more information on preassembled corner pieces that simplify the project tremendously.

The project on these pages shows you how to install crown molding using traditional finish carpenter's techniques. The heart of the process is the cope joint—a joint that looks like a miter, but which won't open up and leave gaps the way miters do. You'll see how to cope and how to approach the job the way a professional does. For a closer look at cutting the joint, see pages 83–85.

Plan ahead
The last piece of molding you put up is often the hardest, because it has to be coped to fit between the moldings on adjoining walls. Even the best carpenters plan ahead so that the last corner on the last wall is in a corner of the room that people seldom look at—a corner, for example, that's behind a door that opens into the room, or one that most of the furniture faces away from. On the other hand, if there's an outside corner somewhere in the room—as there is in this project—you don't have to cope both ends of the molding. Use that corner as your start and finish point.

Crown molding comes in lengths of 8, 10, 12, 14, and 16 feet. Any wall longer than that will require splicing two pieces together. The job is simple, but plan ahead: Choose a combination of lengths that requires the least amount of wood, and that keeps the splice away from the center of the room, where it would be most obvious. For a 17-foot wall, for example, buy a 12-foot length and an 8-foot length, instead of two 10 footers, or a 16 footer and an 8 footer.

Multiple choice
There are countless types of crown molding on the market—stainable pine, paintable pine, preprimed pine, hardwood, medium-density fiberboard (MDF), and polymer resin. You'll use the same tools and techniques no matter which molding you choose. Let your budget and the finish you're applying determine which material you buy. If you're staining, get a stain-grade molding, which is defect free and has no joints in it. If you're painting, you can save money by buying paintable molding, a preprimed molding in which each molding is made of smaller boards joined end to end. Medium-density fiberboard (MDF) molding is also preprimed, and the surface is probably the easiest to paint. Resin moldings come in every shape and form imaginable—plain, preprimed, stainable, and wrapped in a plain or finished hardwood. They're stable, cost less, and easy to work with.

WORK SMARTER

CHALK LINE BLUES

A lot of first-timers make a chalk line along the wall to show where the bottom of the molding should be. Not too many of them do it a second time. The chalk smears on the wall and the smudges remain visible after the molding is up. Repainting is about the only way to cover them up. Far better to make light marks in pencil, which you can erase.

3

FINISH CARPENTRY

Preparing the room

1

MARK THE TABLE TO SHOW THE SIZE OF THE MOLDING

Put the molding on the table with the top edge resting on the table and the bottom edge leaning against the fence, as shown. Mark the fence and table by drawing a pencil line along each edge of the molding. Use the lines to help you position the molding on the saw when you start cutting.

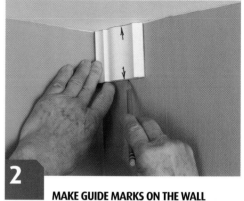

2

MAKE GUIDE MARKS ON THE WALL

Measure from the saw table up to the mark on the fence, and cut a piece of scrap to this length. Put the scrap against the ceiling, as shown, and draw a line along the bottom to mark where the bottom of the molding will meet the wall. Go around the room, making similar marks, sometimes called "witness marks," every few feet.

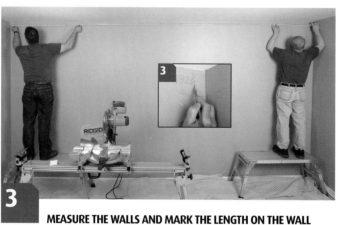

3

MEASURE THE WALLS AND MARK THE LENGTH ON THE WALL

Measure each wall from corner to corner. Measure carefully to the $\frac{1}{32}$ inch and mark the distance near the top of the wall, where it will be hidden by the molding. Mark the exact length of anything shorter than 10 feet. If the piece will be more than 10 feet long, add $\frac{1}{16}$ inch to the measurement for a snug fit, and write the total on the wall.

4

FIND THE STUDS AND MARK THEIR LOCATIONS

Find the studs in the wall with the help of a stud finder, which lights up when it's over a stud. Mark the center of each on the wall so it extends just below what will be the top of the molding.

5

MARK THE STUD LOCATIONS ON THE MOLDING

Measure the distance from the corner where you'll start to the first stud along the wall. Mark this distance from the same end of the molding. Then put the end of the tape on the mark, and make a mark every 16 inches on the molding to show where the studs will be when the molding is in place. (Adjust as necessary if the spacing is other than 16 inches from the center of one stud to the center of the next.)

Installing molding on the first wall

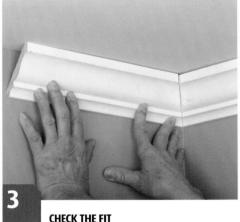

1 **CUT AND INSTALL THE MOLDING**

Cut the first piece of molding to the length you wrote on the wall. Have someone help you put it in place. If the fit is tight, flex the molding slightly to get it in place, then push it against the wall for a tight fit.

2 **NAIL THE MOLDING TO THE WALL**

To stay flat, crown molding must be nailed along both the top and bottom edges. Align the molding with the witness marks, and nail it in place. Start nailing about two feet from the end, at one of the lines you drew on the molding showing stud location. Drive an 8d nail into a stud at the bottom of the molding. Drive a 16d slightly above the middle of the molding into a joist, into a ceiling nailer, or into blocking. Leave about two feet of molding loose at each end for now. Set the nails, driving the heads slightly below the surface with a hammer and nail set.

3 **CHECK THE FIT**

Built-up plaster or drywall compound can twist the molding slightly out of place and cause gaps in a cope joint. To test the fit, cut a sample cope joint, as explained on pages 84–86. Fit it against each end of the installed molding before you nail it. If there's a gap between the two moldings in the top of the joint, tap on the installed molding with a hammer and piece of scrap to push the molding up and close the gap. If there's a gap in the bottom of the joint, tap on the sample to push the molding toward the wall and close the gap. Nail the ends of the molding to the wall once the fit is right.

Installing nailers

If you're lucky, the nails you drive through the top of the molding will always hit a piece of framing in the wall or ceiling. In older homes, however, at least two of the walls may give you problems: The walls parallel to the joists will not necessarily have framing directly above them, leaving you with nothing to nail to. If you find that nail after nail goes into the ceiling without resistance, there's no framing there, and your molding will eventually fall down. To solve the problem, put up nailers—triangles cut to match the slope of the molding. Set your miter saw to the slope of the molding— 38 degrees—and cut a triangle slightly smaller than the space behind the molding. On the next cut, set the saw for a square cut, and then alternate between the two settings until you have enough triangles to put one every 16 inches on center along the problem wall. Nail them into the top plate of the wall, and nail the molding to the triangle.

CLOSER LOOK

MAKE A CLEAN CUT
The end of a molding should be square when it comes from the factory. Often, however, it's either slightly out of square or damaged. When you cut a molding to length, cut one end square, measure from the cut, and then cut the molding to length. The ends will be cleaner, and your work will be better.

OLD vs. NEW

CUT IT ANY WAY YOU LIKE IT
Compound miter saws make it possible to cut a compound miter that replaces the cope joint. Before you abandon a time-honored joint, check the manual for the settings required on the saw. It will tell you that the bevel angle would be set at 33.85 degrees and the miter angle would be set at 31.62 degrees, *if the corner were perfectly square.* If the corner isn't square, and most aren't, you'll have to cut samples until you get the joint right.

3

FINISH CARPENTRY

Install molding along the second wall

WORK SMARTER

MITER THE CROWN UPSIDE DOWN
To make a proper miter cut the crown molding must be cut upside down on the miter saw. Think of the bed of the saw as the ceiling and the fence as the wall.

CLOSER LOOK

WHICH WAY IS UP?
You can install molding any way you want to, but traditionally, the small C-shaped cove goes at the bottom; the S-shaped curve goes at the top.

WORK SMARTER

FIXING A BAD JOINT
You can often fine-tune a joint with sandpaper or files. If you ruin a joint completely, cut off the mistake, and try again. Once you've succeeded, cut the other end and splice in a new piece as shown on page 81.

TOOL SAVVY

CAN'T COPE?
Coping saws often come with a coarse blade installed. For better results, get a fine blade. The coarser blade can be hard to guide through delicate cuts.

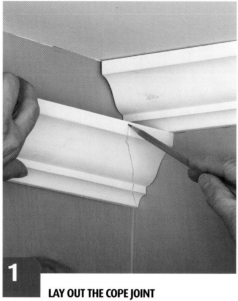

1 LAY OUT THE COPE JOINT
One end of this piece of molding will be coped—cut to nest into the piece that's already up. The joint starts with a miter cut. To make sure the miter angles in the right direction, hold the molding against the wall. Draw a pencil line that starts at the bottom of the molding and angles away from the wall.

2 CUT THE MITER
Label both the top of the molding and the saw table with pieces of tape. Put the molding in a power miter box so the top of the molding is on the saw table and the bottom leans against the fence. Set the saw at 45 degrees so that it follows the general direction of the line you drew on the molding.

3 CUT TO LENGTH
Cut the molding to length now, *before* you cut the cope joint. The edges of a coped joint are razor thin and it is hard to measure along them without either making a mistake, damaging the joint, or both.

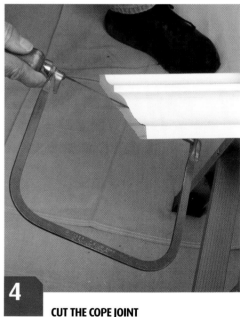

4 CUT THE COPE JOINT
The miter cut exposes the profile of the molding. Cut along the profile with a coping saw. Tilt the handle of the saw higher than the other end so that the cut removes more from the back of the molding than the front. Test-fit the joint against a piece of scrap. Nail the molding to the wall as before.

Installing molding on the third and fourth walls

1 FIND A JOINT THAT WILL SUPPORT A SPLICE
Crown molding comes in a maximum length of 16 feet. On longer walls you splice two pieces together to get the required length. Position any splices over a stud so that you can nail the boards to something solid. Find the stud with your stud finder.

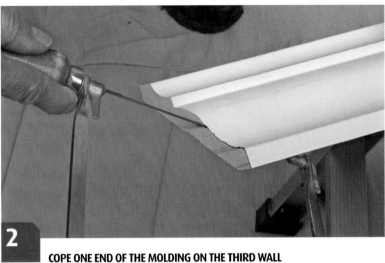

2 COPE ONE END OF THE MOLDING ON THE THIRD WALL
Begin with a piece that's a foot or so longer than the distance from the corner to the stud you'll use for the splice. Mark the top of the molding and the direction of the miter as before. Miter and cope the end that goes against the molding on the second wall.

3 LAYING OUT THE SPLICE
Put the molding temporarily against the wall, and sketch in a splice that begins about ¾ inch past the center of the stud you'll use.

4 CUT THE FIRST SIDE OF THE SPLICE
Put the molding on the saw table. Position it as usual—the top of the molding is flat on the saw table, and the molding slopes back so the bottom is flat on the saw fence. Turn the saw to a 45-degree angle that follows the general direction of the line you drew on the molding.

5 MEASURE THE LENGTH OF THE SECOND PIECE OF MOLDING

Nail the first piece of molding to the wall. Measure the distance from the corner of the room to the long tip of the splice. Add the width of the molding to the measurement to get the desired length of the molding that goes on the other side of the splice.

6 CUT THE SECOND PIECE TO LENGTH

The second side of the splice is cut with the saw at the same angle as the first, but with the molding coming in from the other side of the saw. Make a mark on the molding at the desired length, and cut the piece to length.

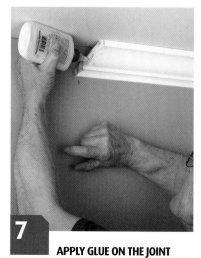

7 APPLY GLUE ON THE JOINT

The joint is held to the wall with nails, but glue helps keep the two pieces from separating. Squeeze some glue on both surfaces of the joint and brush off the excess with your finger.

8 NAIL THE SECOND PIECE OF MOLDING IN PLACE

Put the molding on the wall, and start nailing it in place, beginning at the splice. Work your way down to the end. Before you nail in the last couple of feet, use the sample joint to make sure the end is properly positioned.

 WORK SMARTER

COPING BOTH ENDS

Coping both ends of a molding on the fourth wall—which is sometimes necessary—is enough to make anybody nervous about a bad joint or cutting a molding that is too short. Relax. Cope each end, and if you don't like the one of the copes, cut it off. Cut a new joint on a separate piece of molding, and splice the two together, as explained on page 81.

9 PUT MOLDING ALONG THE FOURTH WALL

In a room with no outside corners, this is the most difficult wall, because the molding will have to be coped to fit against molding on both the first and third walls. If you're finishing against an outside corner, the job is simpler. Cope the end that goes against the third wall, and cut the other end square.

Installing outside corners

1

CHECK THE CORNER FOR SQUARE

Put a square against the wall to see if the corner is square. If it is, you'll be able to cut both moldings at 45 degrees. If the corner is out of square, you'll cut the moldings at an angle other than 45 degrees. Whichever the case, sample joints will help make sure you get the right setting.

2

MITER A SAMPLE PIECE FOR ONE SIDE OF THE CORNER

To cut the molding for right-hand side of the corner, put the molding in the saw in its usual position—top of the molding against the saw table, bottom leaning against the fence. Set the saw 45 degrees to the left as shown, adding or subtracting a degree to make up for an out-of-square corner. Make a cut on a piece of scrap.

 WORK SMARTER

ADJUSTING THE ANGLE OF THE CUT

If the corner you are putting molding over is out of square, a true 45-degree angle will leave you with a gap in the joint. Adjust the angle to close the gap. If the corner is out of square as shown in step one, set the saw to 44 degrees for your first samples. If the corner is out of alignment in the other direction, the ends of both arms of the square will touch the wall and the gap will widen as it gets closer to the corner. If this is the case, set the saw to 46 degrees when cutting your samples.

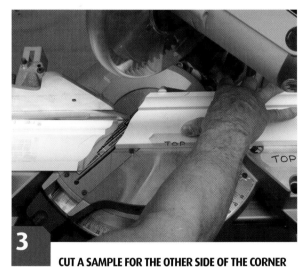

3

CUT A SAMPLE FOR THE OTHER SIDE OF THE CORNER

Turn the saw in the other direction, as shown, setting it to the same angle you used for the previous cut. Cut a sample for the second side of the corner.

4

TEST FIT THE SAMPLE

Put the sample on the wall, and see how it fits. If there are gaps in the seam, reset the saw and cut another sample corner until the fit is right.

 WORK SMARTER

TRY, TRY AGAIN

If there are gaps in your sample corner, set the sample aside, writing the saw setting on both pieces. Change the setting on the saw, and cut a new sample. If there's still a gap, write down the saw setting again. Compare how the first sample fit the wall with how the second sample fit. Compare the saw settings, and make an educated guess at what the right setting should be. It may take a few tries until you get a joint you're happy with.

3

FINISH CARPENTRY

5
COPE ONE END AND LAY OUT THE MITER ON THE OTHER

When you're happy with your sample joint, cope the end of a fresh piece of molding and put it on the wall. Make a mark where the bottom of the molding meets the corner of the wall. Repeat on the other side of the corner.

6
MITER THE CORNERS

Cutting this molding is just like cutting the samples. Put the molding for the first corner in the saw, as shown, and cut at the mark you made. For the other corner, put the board on the other side of the saw and turn the saw to cut the miter in the other direction.

Preassembled crown corners

Preassembled inside and outside corner pieces are available in some areas. They simplify the installation of crown molding because you only have to cut butt joints to mate the lengths of crown molding to the corners pieces. However, your choices in style and size are limited to what's available in your home center.

7
NAIL THE MOLDING IN PLACE

Nail the molding to the wall, starting at the coped end and working out to the miter. When you've nailed both pieces to the wall, lock the joint in place by driving a 3d nail in the corner so that it goes through one of the moldings and into the other.

8
PREP FOR PAINTING

Sand any splices smooth with 120-grit sandpaper. Run a bead of caulk along the top and bottom edges of the of the molding, and smooth it out with your finger. Fill the nail holes with window glazing, let it dry, and sand smooth.

Crown molding styles

Traditional crown moldings

Traditional crown was often built up from several pieces of molding and could get quite involved. The first example here is one such case, involving three separate pieces of molding to make the profile. The second example on page 96 may only be a single piece of molding, but architecturally, it's pretty complicated, too, starting at the top with a flat, followed by an S-curve, beading, and then a dentil molding. Both of these moldings reflect the nature of Traditional molding: Whether Colonial or Colonial Revival, it was urban, large in scale, and expensive. You might argue that it's more suburban than urban these days, but the cost is still high. Give traditional crowns a try before you commit. Buy a single piece or make a short section and temporarily tack it up on the ceiling. Live with it for a few days. Big molding is often designed to go on big walls—you may find that when put on a standard 8-foot ceiling, it looms a bit too closely overhead. If so, settle for a simple dentil molding, which can be bought separately, or turn the three-piece crown into two pieces, omitting the piece along the bottom.

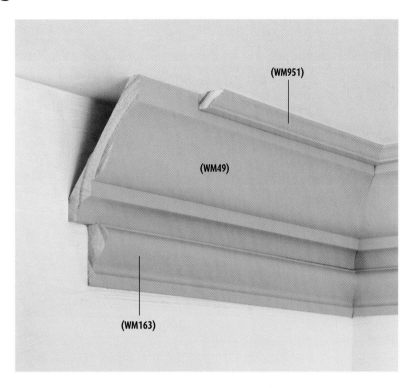

(WM951)

(WM49)

(WM163)

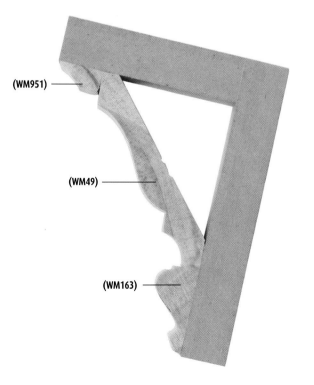

(WM951)

(WM49)

(WM163)

Three-piece crown

This traditional crown molding is made up of three commercial moldings—**(WM49)**, **(WM163)**, and **(WM951)**. Each piece is installed individually, which makes putting them up relatively easy.

■ Start with the center molding. This is ordinary crown molding **(WM49)**. Cut the pieces to fit and nail them in place. Miter any outside corners and cope any inside ones.

■ Next add the molding under the crown. This is actually base cap **(WM163)**, used upside down. Nail it in place right below the crown molding. Base cap is usually flexible enough to conform to any irregularities in the wall, so it will cover any gaps under the crown.

■ Finally, add the last molding to the ceiling. This is a profile called a stop molding **(WM951)**. It is thin and very flexible, so it will easily hide any gaps along the ceiling.

In some ceilings, you may have trouble finding anything to nail to. In this case, run a bead of construction adhesive along the surface of the molding and tack it to the ceiling with finish nails. They'll hold well enough until the adhesive dries.

Prefab traditional crown moldings

Wide and impressive-looking, this traditional molding might seem difficult to make, and it probably is. Don't worry about it. This is one of several elegant moldings you can buy off the shelf with the dentil work and carving already done for you. Simply buy what you need and nail it in place, mitering and coping the corner joints as necessary. Try to plan where the miters fall to make the spacing of the dentil "teeth" look nice. (Try not to break them off, either, or they'll need crowns.)

While these fancy moldings may be stock items, they are fairly expensive and may have been on the shelf for a while. Select carefully and avoid pieces that are excessively shopworn. In the event you end up with a bruised piece, a little sanding works wonders for renewing those crisp edges.

Country crown moldings

Country trim, in general, was simpler than its urban counterpart, and as a result there was not a lot of crown molding in country homes. It did exist, however, and moldings shown here are historic examples. They are in fact, variations on a theme. One has a quarter-round molding mounted against two flat pieces; the other has a cove molding mounted against the flat pieces.

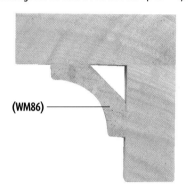

(WM86)

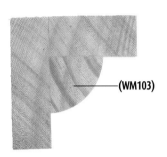

(WM103)

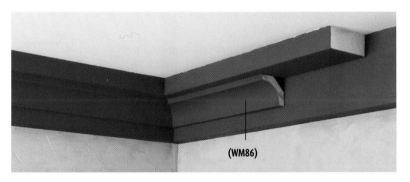

(WM86)

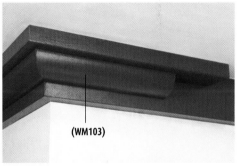

(WM103)

Making Country crown

Each of these crowns consists of three separate pieces: one length of 1× stock for the wall and one length of 2× stock for the ceiling with a piece of commercially made molding in between. The width of the stock depends on the scale of the crown molding and its relationship to the room. There's no general rule here, but the choice of this commercial molding determines the final "look" of the crown. In the right option above the molding is a quarter round (WM103). In the option on the left the molding is a cove listed as (WM86) by the Wood Moulding and Millwork Producers Association. If your wall surfaces are irregular, the cove molding is a lot more flexible than the quarter round and will install more easily.

You'll have the easiest time installing and painting (especially painting) the moldings if your stock has as few knots as possible. The easiest way to get knot-free wood is to buy select-grade wood. This, however, can get expensive, especially if you're making a lot of crown molding. This construction lets you save a few dollars by buying a lesser grade: Since only about ½ inch of the 1× pieces shows in the finished molding, all you need is one knot-free edge on each piece. With a little selective cutting, this shouldn't be very difficult to achieve in a cheaper-grade wood. No matter which wood you use, start by cutting the pieces to width—ripping the two pieces of 1× material. One should be 2½ inches wide and the other 1¾ inches.

This crown is installed as three separate pieces. On walls perpendicular to ceiling joists, nail the wider piece of 1× to the wall first, hitting the top plate or the studs. Then nail the narrower piece to the ceiling, hitting the ceiling joists. On walls that are parallel to the ceiling joists, there may not be anything to nail the second piece to. If not, screw the narrow piece to the wider one first with 1⅝-inch screws. Then simply nail the assembly to the wall without worrying about attaching it to the ceiling.

At outside corners, cut miter joints on the pieces of 1×. Butt the pieces together at inside corners.

Once the pieces of 1× are up, cut the cove or quarter-round molding to fit. Nail them in place with 3d or 4d finish nails. Miter any outside corners. You can either cope or miter the inside corners to fit.

Victorian crown moldings

Victorian-era carpenters may not have invented crown molding, but they certainly pushed it about as far as it can go. These are examples of Victorians at their oldest and newest. The built-up crown molding shown here is made of eight separate pieces, enough to keep a Victorian carpenter in clover for weeks. The second molding is what's called "egg and dart," a pattern that was already classic when it

became a Victorian favorite. Despite the elaborate carving—or what appears to be carving—this molding is made of polystyrene, making it reasonably priced. You can also buy prefab corner blocks that make installing it a matter of cutting a few butt joints. When painted, the molding is indistinguishable from its Victorian counterpart.

Built-up crown molding

This extravagant crown molding is an excellent example of the level of detail that is possible to achieve with off-the-shelf components. There are three commercial moldings featured here along with a number of pieces of 1× stock. They include crown molding **(WM53)** at the top, cove molding **(WM86)** in the middle, and base cap **(WM163)** near the bottom.

Start construction by building a C-shape assembly from 1× stock. Cut the top piece of the C to 4⅛ inches wide, the bottom piece to 2½ inches, and the connecting piece to 2⅛ inches. Before assembling the pieces, round over one edge of the top piece and two edges of the bottom piece

with a ⅜-inch roundover bit in a router table. Screw the top and bottom pieces to the connecting piece. Then add a 1⅛-inch-wide spacer piece on top of the bottom. Screw this assembly to the wall, mitering the corners as necessary.

Next rip pieces of 1×10 to 9 inches wide and fasten them to the wall under the C-shape assembly. You can butt any inside corners; however, you should miter any outside ones. Cut the various pieces of molding to fit and nail them in place. The top edge of the base cap molding should be 2⅞ inches above the bottom edge of the 1×10. Measure and mark this distance periodically as a guide. Cope or miter the ends of the moldings where they meet at the corners.

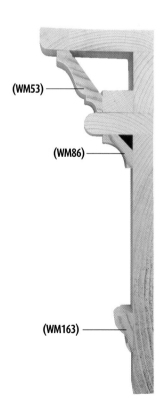

(WM53)

(WM86)

(WM163)

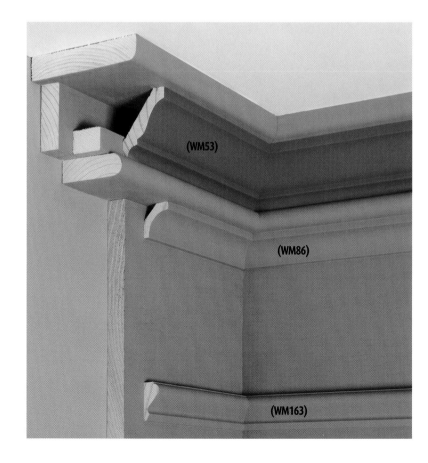

(WM53)

(WM86)

(WM163)

Miterless crown molding

While this ornate crown molding looks expensive, with its rich carved details and flowing curves, it is really fairly reasonably priced. This is because it is not made of wood. This molding (called an egg-and-dart profile) is one of many profiles available made out of rigid foam. Actually, the name rigid foam is somewhat misleading because the molding is really quite floppy until you have it installed. It comes primed and ready to paint and is suitable for both indoor and outdoor applications.

Along with the foam molding, this crown treatment also features a miterless plastic corner block. To install this molding, nail the corner blocks up first. Then simply cut the molding to length and butt it up against the blocks. Nail the molding in place as you would a piece of wooden crown. Be extra careful, however, not to whack the molding with your hammer so that you don't damage it.

Note how the shadows in the crown's egg-and-dart profile appear depending on which edge you designate as the top. The edge you choose as the top of the crown is up to you.

Arts and Crafts crown moldings

The Arts and Crafts style developed in reaction to the overly ornate Victorian styles popular in the mid to late 19th century. In comparison to Victorian, Arts and Crafts trim is very quiet and understated. Straight lines and simple profiles dominate with an emphasis on the material rather than the shape of the pieces. In keeping with this simple approach,

many Arts and Crafts homes didn't have crown molding. Many had an exposed beam—or what at least looked like a beam—instead. There are, however, a few examples available. This first profile is easily reproduced with a router table and a table saw. You make the second almost entirely on the router table.

Crown molding with rabbet

Start with 1× hardwood stock. Oak was commonly used, though cherry or maple would also be appropriate. Rip the pieces to 3 inches wide. Rout a 45-degree chamfer on the router table to create the edge that rests against the wall. Rout a second 45-degree chamfer to create the surface that rests against the ceiling. Put a dado blade in the saw, and set it at 45 degrees. Cut the notch at the bottom of the molding. When making cuts like these, it is a good idea to have a test piece or two the same size as your good pieces so you can make test cuts to check your setups.

Install the crown by nailing it in place. With hardwood, predrill the holes to make driving in the nails easier.

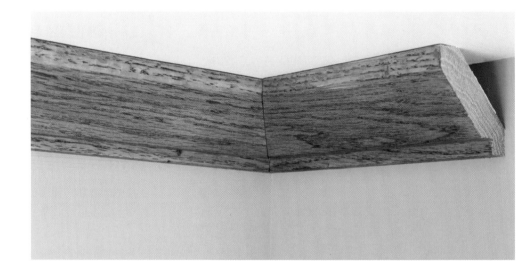

Stepped crown molding

Rather than running diagonally from wall to ceiling as many crowns do, this molding is positioned upright and nailed to the wall. The diagonal cut in the back corner is there to provide clearance should the corner formed by the walls and ceiling be less than perfect.

Start by ripping a piece of ¾-inch-thick stock to 1 inch wider than the final width. The extra width keeps the stock from rocking while routing.

You'll make three passes on the router. Start with a ¾-inch straight bit in your router table, set to make a cut ⅛ inch deep. Set the fence to cut a groove that begins 1¼ inches from the edge of the board. Rout all the stock, and reset the fence so that the resulting groove is at least 1 inch wide. Rout all the stock, and then raise the bit to make a cut just under ¼ inch deep. Reset the fence a third and final time. Set it so that it routs into the groove you just made, leaving it exactly 1 inch wide, and creating the bottom step in the process. Rout all the stock, and then cut it to final width.

Tilt the blade on the saw (the exact angle isn't important) and cut the upper inside corner off the molding to give yourself some wiggle room if the joint where the ceiling meets the wall is slightly irregular. Install the molding by nailing it in place along the walls. Miter or cope at the corners.

Arts and Crafts crown molding creates a minimal surface that provides subtle variations in light and shadow on the walls and ceiling.

Installing door trim

PROJECT DETAILS

SKILLS: Measuring and layout; using power tools
PROJECT: Installing door trim

TIME TO COMPLETE

EXPERIENCED: 1 hr.
HANDY: 2 hrs.
NOVICE: 4 hrs.

STUFF YOU'LL NEED

TOOLS: Miter saw; claw hammer; nail set; caulk gun; clamps; block plane; backsaw; safety glasses; hearing protection; dust mask
MATERIALS: Door trim; finish nails; caulk; 80-grit sandpaper; 120-grit sandpaper

CLOSER LOOK

DOOR TRIM FACTS

In practical terms, door trim serves to cover any gaps between the door jambs (the actual pieces that frame doorways to which the door hinges are screwed) and the wall surfaces surrounding the opening. Visually door trim (often called casing) helps to define the opening and helps dress up a room. In its simplest applications door trim consists of two side pieces, called legs, connected across the top of the door by a head casing. Note that any of the door casings would also work as window casings, and vice versa.

Door trim dresses up a doorway, giving it its character—Traditional, Victorian, Country, Arts and Crafts, or Modern. It covers up a multitude of shims, hiding the gaps between the framing and the jamb as well as the trouble you had to go through to get everything just right.

The trim itself consists of the head molding, which goes across the top of the doorway, and the legs, which run from the floor to the head molding. Standard practice these days is to miter the joints between the head and legs. The Victorians often used a piece of decorated wood, called a rosette, between the legs and head molding, allowing them both to dress up the trim and do the whole job with 90-degree angles. For directions on installing rosettes, see Installing no miter/no cope molding on page 86.

There are as many ways to install door trim as there are carpenters, and most ways work. This is one of the more commonly used methods, and removes much of the guesswork. The head molding goes in first so you can cut the legs to length without having to do a lot of fussy measuring. The mitered scraps that you clamp in place instead of the legs simplify laying out the two miters on the head molding.

No system is perfect. If you run into problems, see Solving door trim problems on page 105.

1 **LAY OUT THE REVEAL**
The trim sits back from the edge of the door jambs by a space that's called the reveal. Lay out the reveal, which is usually ³⁄₁₆ inch, with the help of a combination square. Set the square so the blade sticks out from the body of the square by ³⁄₁₆ inch. Put the body of the square against the jamb, and a pencil against the end of the blade. Slide the body along the jamb to draw a line the full length of all three jambs.

2 **PUT UP TEMPORARY SUPPORTS**
Miter two scraps of molding at a 45-degree angle. Tack or clamp them in place, positioning them as if they were the upper ends of the leg moldings. Align them carefully with the reveal lines, and make sure the inside corner of each miter is on the corner created by the lines.

3 MEASURE THE LENGTH OF THE HEAD MOLDING

Measure from point to point on the temporary supports to get the length of the head molding, sometimes called the top molding or head casing. Double-check by measuring between inside jambs at top of opening, and adding ⅜ inch—the combined distance of the reveals.

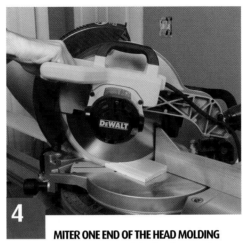

4 MITER ONE END OF THE HEAD MOLDING

Put the head molding in place, and sketch in the general direction of the miters—don't worry about the true length or the exact angle of the miter at this point. Set the miter saw to cut a 45-degree angle. Cut one 45-degree miter in one end of the molding, following the general direction of the line.

⊘ SAFETY ALERT

Unplug the saw when making adjustments.

📖 WORK SMARTER

LOOK FOR PROBLEMS

Look to see if the molding sits above the temporary supports, if the scraps sit above the molding, or if there is a gap between the wall and either the scraps or the molding. If any of these problems occur, see Solving door trim problems on page 105.

3

FINISH CARPENTRY

5 MITER THE HEAD MOLDING TO LENGTH

Measure along the edge of the molding from the point of the miter to the desired length of the head molding, and make a mark. Mark the face of the molding at the same point, and miter the molding to this length, following the general direction of the line you drew earlier.

6 NAIL THE HEAD MOLDING IN PLACE

Rest the head molding on the scraps, and adjust the scraps if necessary so the molding follows the reveal and is centered over the doorway. Nail the bottom of the molding to the jamb with 3d or 4d nails driven roughly every 12 inches. Drive 6d or 8d nails through the top of the molding into the framing. Keep the nails at least ¼ inch from the edge of the molding and 1 inch from the ends to prevent splitting. Remove the scraps and install the legs.

Installing the legs

⊘ SAFETY ALERT

Wear safety glasses, hearing protection, and a dust mask when cutting wood.

 GOOD IDEA

LEAVE THE NAIL HEADS EXPOSED

If you're worried about how the door frame is going together, don't drive the nails all the way home. Leave the nail head exposed instead, so you can remove it and reposition the trim if there's a problem.

 CLOSER LOOK

FINISHING UP

If you're painting the moldings, fill the holes with window glazing. Window glazing applies easily with no mess and dries quickly. Roll a ball in your hands, and push the glazing into the holes with your hands. Let the glazing dry, and then sand smooth with 120-grit paper if painting. Apply caulk along the seam between the door and wall. Run your finger along the seam to smooth out the caulk.

If you're staining there is no way to make the nails holes invisible. Your best bet is to use a stainable filler, made by the manufacturer that made the stain.

1 LAY OUT THE MITERS

Start with two pieces, each a few inches longer than the distance from the floor to the top of the header. Put one in place along the side of the door, and lay out the general angle of the miter. Repeat on the other side of the door.

2 MITER THE ENDS

Miter the end of each leg, following the angle of the lines you drew in step one. When you make the cut, position the boards so that the legs will be longer than finished length.

3 LAY OUT THE FINAL LENGTH

Put the left leg upside down against the right side of the header. Draw a line marking where the header meets the leg. Repeat with the right leg.

4 CUT THE LEGS TO LENGTH

Set the saw to make a square cut, and cut each leg so that the line you drew becomes the bottom of the leg. When you're ready to install the legs, apply glue to the mitered surfaces; wipe off the excess with your finger.

5 NAIL THE FIRST LEG IN PLACE

Put one of the legs in place. Hold the top end against the header, and drive a nail to hold it in place. Drive 3d or 4d nails every 2 inches along the inside edge, and 6d or 8d nails every 12 inches into the framing along the outside edge.

6 NAIL THE SECOND LEG IN PLACE

Repeat the process on the second leg. Reinforce the miter joint by driving a nail through the edge of each leg into the header. Wipe off any glue with a damp rag.

Solving door trim problems

In the best of all worlds, the back of the molding sits flat against the wall, and the front of the moldings meet each other on the same plane. All of this depends on a lot of little things coming together, and often the trim carpenter ends up in the worst of all worlds: Nothing meets the way it should. Here are some common problems and how to solve them.

Gaps between the casing and wall

Gaps between the wall and the molding occur when the jamb sticks out beyond the wall. A gap of up to a fat $\frac{1}{16}$ inch or even a full $\frac{1}{8}$ inch is no problem; it gets filled in by paintable caulk which will also help limit air flow around exterior windows and doors. If the gap is larger, use a block plane to shave down the door jamb. Remove the trim, rest the heel of the plane on the wall, and put the blade at an angle across the jamb. Plane the jamb flush with the wall.

When trim is uneven

Sometimes one molding sits slightly above the other at the miters, creating a small step between the two. The easiest solution is to push one of the moldings forward with a shim to bring it in line with the other molding. You can also take a more analytical approach: If the step is along the entire length of the miter, one of the jambs may be beyond the opening. If so, plane it back.

If the step is small, and only runs along part of the miter, something is pushing part of the molding out. Check for stray nails, blobs of drywall compound, and other obstructions. If removing them doesn't help, make a mark along the area of the miter where the problem is. Remove the molding, and sand the back of the molding along the marked area. Check constantly as you sand until the two sides of the miter meet as they should.

Sloppy joints

Often aligning a piece of molding with the reveal creates a gap in what was a tight miter. You may be working with a warped piece of molding—cut another piece and see how it fits. If the problem persists the sides of the doorway may be out of alignment. First check the door itself. If the gap around it is uneven, if the door's binding, if it's difficult to close, or if it won't stay open, you've got a bigger problem than the trim. Bring the door jambs into square, then take another look at your miter. If the miter is still open, you can sometimes put the pieces together to create a tight joint, and then flex the leg to follow the reveal, nailing it as you go. In the worst case install the molding temporarily. Put a backsaw along the joint, and cut through it to the wall. The cut averages out the differences, creating parallel edges in the joint. Remove the leg and reinstall it for a tight joint.

Door trim styles

 **CLOSER LOOK**

LOOKING CLOSELY AT DOOR TRIM

The pictures that follow show how door trim is reflected in our styles. They show the upper corner of doorway, because that is where most of the action takes place. With most doors the legs simply run straight down to the floor. Any moldings that adjoin the casing (chair rail, baseboard) simply butt into its side.

Traditional door trim

Traditional trim is perhaps at its best on windows and doors. Features like headers and "wings" are fun to mention, fun to look at, and (depending on your mindset and skill level) fun to make. The examples shown here are classic Traditional treatments. The first is easy to apply, but requires some work with the router to prepare. The second is the opposite—most of the stock is off the shelf, but you'll get to know your power miter saw really well in the course of applying the outer molding. Both are examples of common trim treatments in more expensive Colonial homes. You'll find few examples in modern interpretations of Colonial homes, but if you're willing to do the work, the results will be head and shoulders above the commercially made "Colonial" casing.

Door trim with header

The trim for this door is fairly simple, yet elegant. The actual casing is made from a piece of 1× stock, ripped to a width of 3½ inches. Rout a ⅜-inch bead along the inside edge of the pieces to dress them up a bit. Use a ⅜-inch corner-beading bit in a router table for best results. Nail these pieces around the door, mitering the corners.

To cap off the doorway, make a header for the top of the casing. This decorative touch is subdued, but still adds an ornate touch to an otherwise ordinary trim treatment. The header is made of a piece of 1× **(A)** sandwiched between two thinner pieces of stock. The top piece of stock **(B)** is

¼ inch thick by 1⅝ inches wide, and flat on all surfaces. The bottom piece **(C)** is 5/16 inch thick and 1 1/16 inches wide. Rout a bead on both ends and one side of the bottom piece of lath with a ⅛-inch edge-beading bit in a router table. The bead should be tangent to the top surface. Use a push block to guide the piece as you make the cuts across the ends.

Cut the 1× stock so it's 1½ inches wide. Rout a cove along one edge with a ⅝-inch cove bit in a router table. Nail and glue all three pieces together, then nail the assembly in place atop the doorway.

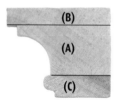

Winged casing

This Traditional trim treatment has a sophisticated look that belies how straightforward the molding is to make. Rather than being especially complicated, this molding just takes a little time and precision to carry out.

The basic casing is made from 1× stock that has been ripped to 3¼ inches wide. After you trim the pieces on the table saw, cut a rabbet on the good face of each piece with a dado blade. The rabbet should be 1⅛ inches wide and ³⁄₁₆ inch deep. As a final touch rout a profile on the inside (rabbeted) edges of the pieces with a ⁵⁄₃₂-inch beading bit in a router table. Cut the pieces to fit around the door opening, mitering the top corners.

To create the "wings" at the top of the legs, glue ¾-inch × ¾-inch by 8-inch-long pieces of scrap to the sides of the casing. Prepare these pieces carefully, cutting them square on both ends and making sure each is exactly 8 inches long. Glue the pieces to the sides of the casing, with the ends dead flush with the points on the miters. Nail the casing in place around the doorway.

The decorative trim around the casing is made from a commercial molding called brick mold. Rip the brick mold down in width so all that is left is decorative profile at the edge. Cut this to fit around the casing using a power miter saw. It's pretty standard work, except for the little pieces that wrap around the bottom of the wings. You may find it helpful to fasten the molding to a backer board with double-faced tape so the little pieces don't go flying when you cut them. Nail the modified brick mold to the sides of the casing.

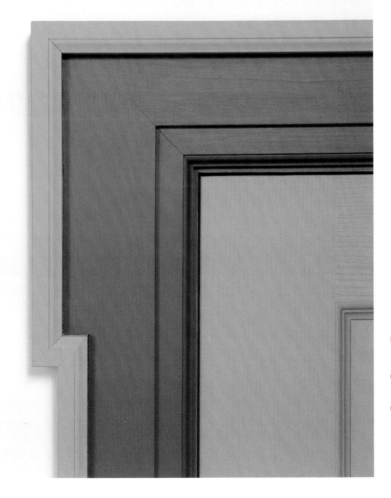

Combining stock and custom molding and trim can produce unique and personalized results.

Country door trim

Country door trim uses basic moldings such as coves and quarter rounds to create a touch of visual interest while remaining grounded in simplicity. Even well into the era of mass-produced trim and woodwork, rural carpenters relied on stock that they cut off their own land or on lumber that was plentiful in their particular region.

Most of the tools they used to create the trim that adorned their homes were basic—hand saws, chisels, hand planes, hammers, and mallets. But with these basic tools they were inspired to create simple but elegant combinations of trim that added dimension and simple elegance to their homes.

Beaded Country door casing

This door casing consists of a piece of 1× material with a thin piece of decorative commercial molding **(WM946)** applied on top of it. Start by ripping pieces of 1×4 so they're 3¼ inches wide. This will give you the chance to cut away any blemishes on the edge of the stock. Rout a bead on one edge of each piece with a ⅛-inch edge-beading bit—you'll get best results if you put the router in a router table.

Nail the routed stock around the door opening with the bead to the inside. Miter the corners where the legs meet the head casing. Nail the commercial molding along the outside of the 3¼-inch stock, mitering the corners where the pieces meet.

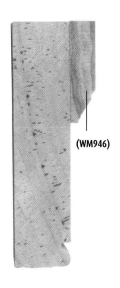

(WM946)

(WM946)

Wide Country door casing

This two-piece molding makes use of a decorative piece of commercial molding backed up by a 1½-inch-wide piece of 1× stock. The commercial molding **(WM163)** is sold as chair rail molding. To make it ready for use as door casing, you'll need to rip it to a width of 2⅜ inches. This cuts away a small cove on one side of the molding.

Cut the 1× stock to 1½ inches wide. (1×2s precut to this width are not the best quality. You'll be happier ripping down wider stock.) Round over one corner of the pieces with a ⅜-inch roundover bit in a router table.

Install the commercial molding around the doorway first, nailing it in place and mitering the corners. Then wrap the 1× around the outside of the commercial molding, also mitering the corners. You may find there isn't much to nail these second pieces of trim to. In this case apply construction adhesive to the back of the 1× molding, and nail it in place through the drywall. The nails will hold well enough until the adhesive sets.

(WM163)

(WM163)

Even built-up Country trimwork is simple and direct. Painting simple trim helps create depth and emphasizes subtle variations in the profiles.

Victorian door trim

Most people think of rosettes when they think Victorian, and with good reason: They were everywhere. But as classic as rosettes may be, Victorians reveled in detail, and there was a lot of detail to Victorian trim beyond rosettes. The S-curve and chamfer molding shown on the next page is copied from a Victorian mansion—the moldings downstairs were oak; the ones upstairs were painted.

Doors trimmed with rosettes and plinths

Rosettes are used for changing the direction of moldings that are the same size, such as the top of a door or window. Plinth blocks, shown below left, are used when joining two profiles of different widths as is the case when a wider baseboard molding joins a narrower door casing.

Dressing up a doorway with rosettes (also called corner blocks) and plinths is a classic Victorian design detail. It is also fairly easy—all cuts are at 90 degrees, and moldings and rosettes are widely available. Corner blocks are available in several sizes, and there are a number of Victorian casings that look good with them, including the **WM286** shown here.

Carpenters install the rosettes first, and then cut the moldings to fit. Make sure you get rosettes that are slightly wider than the molding, so that you can center the molding on them as shown here. For more on installing rosettes, see Installing no miter/no cope molding on page 86.

(WM286)

(WM286)

FINISH CARPENTRY

3

Door with S-curve and chamfer

This three-piece door casing has a lot in common with the built-up Victorian chair rail on page 142. It uses the same piece of commercial molding **(WM163)** and almost the same pieces of 1×. Start by ripping the 1× stock to width. The main casing should be 3¼ inches wide and the smaller piece that wraps around the outside should be 1⅜ inches wide. Cut a chamfer along one edge of each piece with a chamfering bit in a router table.

Nail the main casing in place around the doorway, mitering the corners. Add the narrower piece of 1× on edge around the outside of the main casing. Again miter the corners where the pieces meet. Finally nail the commercial molding in place into the corner formed by the two pieces of 1×, once again mitering the corner joints.

(WM163)

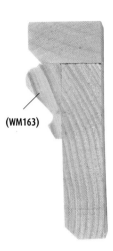

(WM163)

Victorian trimwork tended to be stained in public places such as a downstairs drawing room and painted in more private areas such as bedrooms.

Arts and Crafts door trim

The Arts and Crafts door, like the rest of the Arts and Crafts trim, wanted to be simple, but somehow it makes a statement that seems grand today. Instead of a mitered molding that simply wrapped around the door, Mission designers often settled on a wide three-piece molding, called a header, that sat on top or between two wide pieces of trim that ran up the sides of the door. Everything was nice and rectilinear, the way Arts and Crafts was supposed to be. Yet no matter how simple, the built-up header and hardwood construction point to a carpenter with skill, time, and good raw materials and to a homeowner who appreciated all three.

Work carefully when you build in the Arts and Crafts style. The absence of miters was supposed to make things simpler and more honest. Like any architectural theory, the proof is in the making: 4½-inch-wide butt joints can be just as demanding as miters.

Clean and simple

This doorway treatment is a textbook example of Arts and Crafts trim. No complicated molding profiles to worry about—just clean, simple lines and straightforward butt joints. Make the side casings first. Cut them to width (4½ inches) on the table saw, then rout the inside edge with a ⅜-inch roundover bit in a router table. Cut the casings carefully to length, then nail them in position on either side of the door.

The head casing is made of three separate pieces of wood. The main piece is a piece of 1× material that is 4½ inches wide. The bead underneath is cut on the edge of a piece that is ⅜ inch thick and 1 inch wide. Finally the top band is a piece of 1× stock that is 1⅝ inches wide. Rout the bead with a ⅛-inch beading bit on a router table. Rout a chamfer on the edge of the top band with a chamfering bit on the router table.

Glue and nail the three pieces together. Then nail the head assembly on top of the two casings. This headpiece would also work well over a window.

Basic profile

It doesn't get much simpler than this. None of the pieces in this door treatment have any profile—unless you count flat as a profile. Cut the two side casings and the head casing to width (4½ inches) on the table saw. Note how the side casings run past the head casing, trapping it in between. Install the side casings first, then cut the head casing to fit and nail it in place. Finally, add the top band—a piece of 1× cut to a width of 1½ inches. It should extend about 1¼ inches on either side of the side casings. When installing any hardwood trim, predrilling for the nails is a good idea. It's particularly important here, where nailing without predrilling could knock the head casing out of position.

Arts and Crafts trimwork is so basic that it almost seems unfinished, but closer inspection reveals very close attention to detail in matching grains and natural color in the wood.

Modern door trim

Like other Modern trim applications, creating a simple look around a door involves lots of work behind the scenes. Construction starts with the jamb, and then boards that function as baseboard and door trim are nailed in place and partially covered by drywall. It takes a good bit of experience and skill to keep everything plumb and level on the first try. Patience and the willingness to experiment until something is right are a good substitute for experience on this job, so work slowly, and keep at it until everything is properly aligned.

Baseboard and door trim

The door trim shown here is designed to work with the baseboard shown on page 146. Start by applying the doorjamb, which must be covered by both the door trim and baseboard. Apply baseboard next, ending it with a mitered return where it meets the doorjamb. Apply the trim around the door and caulk the seams. (Both the baseboard and door trim are cut away here so that you can see the doorjamb.)

Apply ¾-inch plywood to the studs so that the drywall can overlap the baseboard. Apply the drywall, and nail vinyl L-bead to the edges, mitering the corners where the bead along the door meets the one along the wall. Apply joint compound to edges, seams, and screws. When you're finished paint all the surfaces.

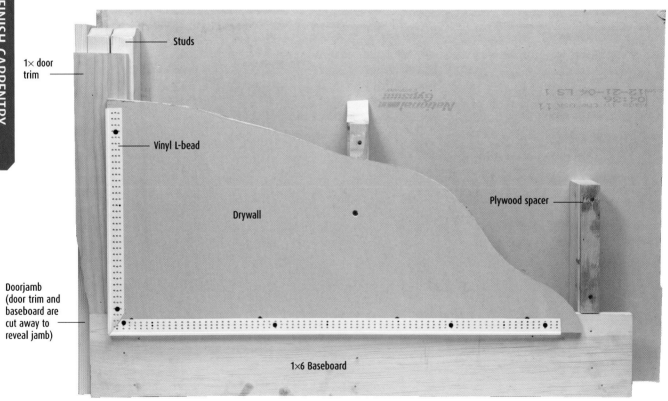

- Studs
- 1× door trim
- Vinyl L-bead
- Drywall
- Plywood spacer
- Doorjamb (door trim and baseboard are cut away to reveal jamb)
- 1×6 Baseboard

By eliminating intricate framing, Modern door trim focuses on the door as an object.

Passages from room to room that might be more ornately trimmed in another style are simple geometric planes.

Installing window trim

PROJECT DETAILS

SKILLS: Measuring and layout; using power miter and jigsaws
PROJECT: Installing window trim

TIME TO COMPLETE

EXPERIENCED: 2 hrs.
HANDY: 4 hrs.
NOVICE: 6 hrs.

STUFF YOU'LL NEED

TOOLS: Miter saw; hammer or nailer; tape measure; nail set; combination square; clamps; acid flux brush for applying glue; caulk gun
MATERIALS: Window trim; stools; jamb extension; shims; scribe; 4d, 6d, and 8d finish nails; caulk; 120-grit sandpaper

CLOSER LOOK

WINDOW TRIM FACTS
As with door casing, window casing serves to bridge the gap between the window jambs and the surrounding walls. It also serves as a decorative frame for the window and whatever view lies beyond. In addition to the side and head casings, window trim also includes a sill (sometimes called a stool) and an apron. The sill is a horizontal piece that typically juts out into the room somewhat, serving as a place to let pies cool or cats sleep. The apron is another horizontal piece, running under the sill. It serves as a transition between the underside of the sill and the wall surface.

You can apply window molding in one of two ways: The simplest to explain (but not necessarily the easiest to do) is called picture framing. The trim extends around all four sides of the window, and is mitered at each of the four corners, just like they would be if you hung a picture frame over the opening. The ease with which you picture frame a window depends on your ability to cut accurate miters and to create 90-degree corners once you've cut the miters.

The second, more common, approach involves putting in a windowsill. While the sill has to be cut to fit and has an additional piece of molding beneath it, the joinery is easier

and far less likely to result in gaps than on a picture-framed window. Because trimming a window with a sill is more traditional, and because it is more forgiving, it's explained first in this chapter. For information on picture framing, see Picture framing a window, on page 121.

Like most aspects of trim carpentry, applying molding has its own language. Applying the molding, or trim, is called trimming the window. The sill is referred to as the stool, and the trim beneath it is called an apron. The sides of the window framing are called jambs. A compass is called a scribe.

Cutting the stool

1 LAY OUT THE REVEAL
Trim molding usually sits back from the edge of the window by a small space, called a reveal. To lay out the reveal, set the blade of a combination square so it extends beyond the head of the square by ¼ inch. Put a pencil against the blade, and slide the head along the top and sides of the jamb to lay out the reveal.

2 LAY OUT THE LENGTH OF THE STOOL
Temporarily put a piece of scrap molding against the reveal and trace along it. Then flip the piece on edge, and draw a second line alongside the first, as shown in the inset. Repeat on the other side of the window. Measure the distance between the outside marks, and cut the stool to this length.

3 LAY OUT PART OF THE CUTOUT
The stool has to be cut out to fit around the wall, and you'll need to put the sill in place to lay out the cuts. Slip a couple of shims between the bottom of the window and the drywall, and rest the stool on it with the rounded edge against the wall. Align the ends with the lines you drew on the wall. Lay a combination square against the jamb, and draw a line along it. Repeat on the other side of the window.

Clean up the tool marks
Marks left by the saw will be visible through whatever finish you apply. Sand the ends of the stool with 120-grit sandpaper to remove the marks.

3

FINISH CARPENTRY

Undercut the sill

Adjust the sole of the jigsaw so that the saw cuts away more along the bottom of the sill than along the top. The angled cut will keep irregularities along the thickness of the sill from pushing it away from the wall—and you'll get a tighter seam along the top as a result.

4 LAY OUT THE REST OF THE CUTOUT
Turn the stool around so the rounded edge faces out. Measure in twice the thickness of the molding from the front of the stool, and make a mark. Set a compass (called a scribe by carpenters) to the distance between the wall and the mark. Slide the point of the scribe along each wall, and along the window frame, to lay out the wood that needs to be removed.

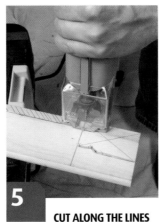

5 CUT ALONG THE LINES
If your saw has orbital adjustments, set it to make its smoothest cut, and set it so that it undercuts the lines slightly, as explained in Undercut the sill (right). Mark the waste side of the layout line to avoid confusion, and then cut along the layout lines with the jigsaw.

6 INSTALL THE SILL
Put the sill in place on the window, and nail it to the window with 8d nails.

Installing the top molding

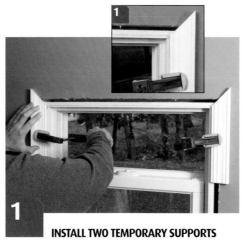

1 INSTALL TWO TEMPORARY SUPPORTS
It's easiest to cut and install the top piece of molding first if you have some supports to hold it. Miter two scraps of molding 8 to 12 inches long at 45 degrees. Slide down the window, and clamp the scraps in place. Align them carefully with the reveal lines, and make sure that the short corner of each miter is on the corner created by the reveal lines.

2 MEASURE THE LENGTH OF THE TOP MOLDING
Measure from point to point of the temporary supports to get the length of the top molding, sometimes called the head molding or head casing.

3 MITER THE TOP MOLDING
Set the miter saw to cut a 45-degree angle, and position the molding so that the short end of the miter will be on the inside edge of the molding. Cut the miter, and then set the saw to miter 45 degrees in the other direction. Measure from the point of the miter to the desired length of the molding, and make a mark. Miter the molding to this length.

4 INSTALL THE TOP MOLDING
Rest the head molding on the scraps, adjusting them if necessary so that the molding is on the reveal line and centered over the window. Nail the bottom of the molding to the jamb with 3d or 4d nails driven roughly every 12 inches. Drive 6d or 8d nails through the top of the molding into the framing. Keep the nails at least ¼ inch from the edge of the molding and 1 inch from the ends to prevent splitting.

Installing the side moldings

1 **MARK THE LENGTH**

Miter one end of each of the side moldings. Rest the molding upside down on the stool, aligning it with the reveal along the side of the window. Trace across the top molding to draw a line on the leg. Repeat on the other side.

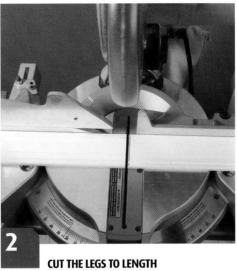

2 **CUT THE LEGS TO LENGTH**

Put the legs in the miter saw, one leg at a time, and make a cut at the mark.

3 **INSTALL THE LEGS**

Put the legs in place one at a time. Nail the inner edge to the jamb with 6d nails. Nail the body of the molding to the framing with 8d nails.

4 **NAIL THE MITERS**

Drill pilot holes to avoid splitting the molding and, if necessary, use small shims to make the joint fit tightly, then drive a 4d nail through the side of the molding, across the miter, and into the adjoining molding. This reinforces the joint and helps close any gaps. Remove the shims once the joint is nailed.

Cutting the miters

Cut the miters on the side moldings so that the short edge is the inside edge of the window trim. To do this keep the outside edge—the thick edge—against the fence for both cuts. Cut one miter to the left, and one miter to the right.

Gluing the miter

Some carpenters like to reinforce a miter joint by putting glue on the mating surfaces before they nail it in place. Others don't think it accomplishes much, and skip the step. It's up to you, but hey—what's wrong with a little extra insurance?

3

FINISH CARPENTRY

Installing the apron

Double rough sills

If you're framing the window that you're trimming, put in two rough sills, one below the other, to give you more surface to which you can nail the apron. If you're not doing the framing, you can nail the top of the apron into the rough sill, and the bottom of the sill into the studs.

1

MITER THE APRON

The apron is made from the same molding as the window trim. Each end is mitered, and then a small mitered piece is glued to the end to dress it off. Start by standing the molding up against the fence, and mitering one end. The left end of the molding is shown here.

2

MEASURE THE LENGTH

Rest the apron on the window stool so that one end is flush with the outside edge of the window trim. Trace along the outside edge of the other side, making a mark on the apron. Miter the apron along this line.

3

CUT THE RETURNS

Set the saw to cut a 45-degree miter to the right. Put a long piece of apron scrap against the fence with the top edge facing up, and cut a miter near the end of the scrap. Slide the stock so you can make a cut that cuts off the entire mitered section, but no more. Repeat, making the first cut with the saw turned 45 degrees to the left.

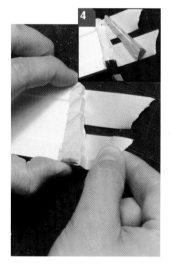

4

GLUE THE RETURNS TO THE APRON

Glue the returns to the apron before you put it in place. Start by putting masking tape along the front of the apron, as shown. Apply yellow glue to both surfaces of the return and brush it in with a plumbers acid flux brush. Put the return on the apron, mitered edge to mitered edge, and fold it in place. Pull the tape tightly around the return and onto the back of the molding. Repeat on the other end of the apron.

5

INSTALL THE APRON

Let the glue dry for at least a half hour, and then nail the apron to the sills with 6d nails.

A simpler return

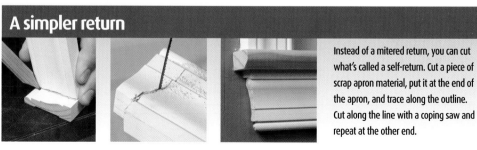

Instead of a mitered return, you can cut what's called a self-return. Cut a piece of scrap apron material, put it at the end of the apron, and trace along the outline. Cut along the line with a coping saw and repeat at the other end.

Picture framing a window

1

LAY OUT THE REVEALS

Picture frame trim wraps around all four sides of the window—like a picture frame. Start by laying out the reveal. Set your combination square so that the ruler sticks out ³⁄₁₆ inch beyond the body of the square. Put a pencil against the ruler and guide it all the way around the jamb.

2

LAY OUT THE DIRECTION OF THE MITERS

Put the trim in place and sketch out the direction of the miters. Cut one end of each piece, as follows: Right end of the top molding; left end of the bottom molding; top end of the left molding; and bottom end of the right molding. Cutting these ends will make sure that the long end of the miter fits against the stop when you set it up in step four.

3

LAY OUT THE LENGTH OF THE CUT

Put the bottom piece of trim in place. Align the miter with the reveal line on one end of the molding; mark where the other reveal line meets the other end of the molding. Repeat on the side pieces and the top piece. Lay out a 45 degree miter at each mark with the help of a combination square.

🔍 **CLOSER LOOK**

MAKE SURE THE WINDOW IS SQUARE

Measure the diagonals of the window before you start picture frame trim. If the diagonals differ by more than ³⁄₁₆ inch, the window is too far out of square—apply trim that includes a windowsill.

🔍 **CLOSER LOOK**

TAKE A DETOUR

Sometimes the best way to lay out a miter across the front of a piece of molding is to start by laying it out across the back. This is especially true on molding that has bumps or curves along the bottom edge. Once you've laid out a miter across the back, draw a square line across the top of the molding from where the miter meets the top. Use this line to lay out the miter across the front.

3

FINISH CARPENTRY

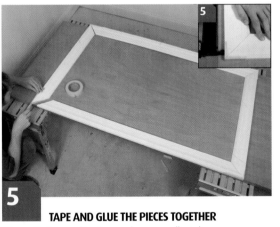

4

CUT TO LENGTH

Clamp a fence to the saw, and cut a miter on it. Align the miter you laid out with the miter on the fence. Clamp a stop block to the other end of the molding, and cut the piece to length. Put the matching piece of molding against the stop. Cut the piece for the opposite side to length. Reset the stop, and miter the other pieces of molding.

5

TAPE AND GLUE THE PIECES TOGETHER

When mitering, masking tape makes an excellent clamp. Line the four pieces end to end, and apply tape across the joints. Apply glue, and then fold the pieces together to form a frame. Measure the diagonals to check for square; if one diagonal is longer than the other, apply gentle pressure to bring the two to the same measurement. Reinforce the joints with brads, as shown in the inset.

6

HANG THE FRAME

Double check to make sure the frame is square. Let the glue dry 30 minutes, and then hang the frame, aligning it first with the reveal lines, and then nailing it in place. A pneumatic brad nailer makes short work of this installation. A hammer can force the pieces apart if you're not careful.

Window trim styles

Traditional window trim

🔍 CLOSER LOOK

LOOKING CLOSELY AT WINDOW TRIM

The pictures that follow in this chapter show the lower corner of a window where the casing joins with the sill. In most cases the casing is simply mitered at the top corners. Note that any of the door casings would also work as window casings. Also note that you don't have to include a sill with your windows. You can simply wrap the casing around the opening, much as you would a picture frame.

By and large, the profiles that you buy at the lumberyard or home center these days have been around since Colonial days. Two things make Modern molding different from Traditional molding—wood and time. Colonial carpenters worked with thick wood, and they had the time to combine moldings for a rich look. These two Traditional window trims recapture those aspects. The first uses a traditional casing known as "Colonial" but adds a custom-made skirt for richness. The second example also uses Colonial molding but is built in layers, providing a thick base that the Modern molding lacks.

Window with custom skirt

This window trim relies on commercial molding for the casing **(WM445)** and routed pieces of 1× stock for the sill and apron. Start by cutting the sill. The ears of the sill should be 1½ inches wide and 4 inches long. Rout an ogee across both ends of the sill and along its front. Use a ⁵⁄₃₂-inch ogee bit in a router table. Guide the sill with a push block as you make the cuts across the ends. Install the sill, then wrap the commercial casing around the window, mitering the top corners.

To make the apron, rip a piece of 1× to 3 inches wide. Cut a ⅛-inch-deep by 1-inch-wide rabbet along the bottom edge of the piece by running it over a dado blade on the table saw. Then rout an ogee along the bottom edge of the apron to match the one on the sill. Nail the apron in place under the sill.

(WM445)

(WM445)

Built-up window casing

At first glance, the casing on this window may appear to be a simple, off-the-rack piece of molding. With a second look, you'll probably realize the casing is considerably thicker than a typical piece of commercial molding. Both of these impressions are actually true. The main profile is a piece of commercial molding **(WM376)**, but it is backed up with a piece of 1× with a routed edge, thus giving the casing its rich, thick appearance. The sill is another piece of 1× stock, and the apron is similar to the casing—a piece of commercial molding **(WM210)** applied to yet another piece of 1×.

Start by cutting the sill. Shape the top edge of the sill with a ¼-inch roundover and the underside with a ½-inch cove. Both of these cuts should be made on a router table. Use a push block to help guide the piece as you rout across the ends. Install the sill.

Rip a 1× for the first layer of the casing so it's 2¾ inches wide. Rout the inside edge with a 5⁄32-inch ogee on a router table. Install the casing around the window, mitering the top corners. Add the commercial molding, cutting it to size, and fastening it so it is flush with the outside of the 1×.

For the apron, rip a piece of 1× to 3¼ inches wide. Rout a bead along the bottom edge with a ⅛-inch edge-beading bit. Nail this piece in place under the window. Cut the commercial molding to length and nail it to the 1×.

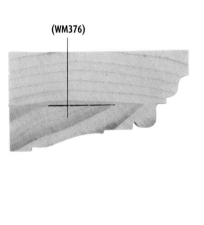

(WM376)

(WM376)

(WM210)

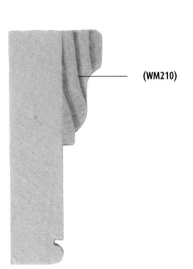

(WM210)

CLOSER LOOK

OGEE OR O.G.?

The word ogee is used by router bit manufacturers to describe a bit that cuts a specific ornamental profile. In finish carpentry the term is actually O.G.—an abbreviation for "ornamental gothic" and is used generically for any molding having the S-shaped profile such as the one routed into the window casing below. This shape is one of the most commonly used decorative profiles in molding today. It adds a subtle but dramatic finishing touch and is at home in many styles.

Country window trim

Of all five styles, Country is perhaps the most economical and efficient in that the materials used to create the trim are basic and easily accessible. Unlike the hardwoods used in the Arts and Crafts style, the pine, poplar, or engineered products such as MDF used for Country trim are easy to work with and finish nicely. These pluses add up to an advantage to beginning woodworkers who want a challenge but also want to grow their woodworking skills.

Just because Country trim is simple in look and feel doesn't mean it's not a challenge. Joints must meet squarely and fit tightly. Combinations of molding must exist together in harmony and all the aspects of the trim job from baseboard to crown must work together to create a unified design.

Country ogee casing

Rather than spend money on fancy commercial moldings, this treatment simply uses 1×4 stock routed with a couple of decorative profiles routed into the edges. The casings are stock 1×4s with a ⁵⁄₃₂-inch ogee profile routed on both edges. The sill is a plain piece of 1× material. It should extend 5⅛ inches beyond the inside of the jamb on either side and 1½ inches into the room. The apron is a piece of 1×4 with a bead routed along its lower edge. Make this cut with a ⅛-inch

edge-beading bit. All the router cuts are easier to make on a router table. Note: To cut the bead across the ends of the apron, use a push block to help guide the piece past the bit.

Start installation by cutting the sill piece to fit inside the jambs. Then wrap the casing around the window opening, mitering the two top corners and making butt joints where the casing sits on the sill. Nail the apron in place below the sill to complete the job.

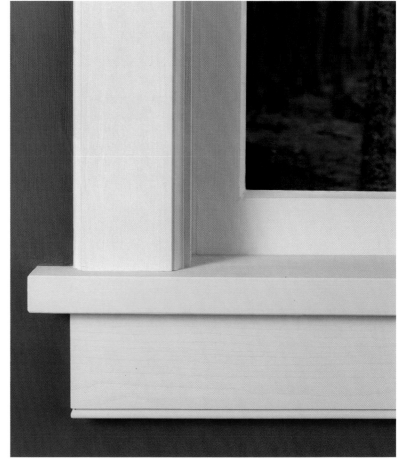

Backbanded Country casing

This option is even more straightforward than the first, because only the sill needs to be routed. The rest of the style comes from what's called back banding—pieces of square-edged 1× stock applied in a pleasing manner.

Make the sill first. Its ears should extend 4⅞ inches beyond the insides of the jamb and 1¾ inches past the surface of the wall. Round over the edges of the sill with a ⅜-inch roundover bit. These cuts are best done on a router table equipped with a fence. Use a push block to help guide the piece past the bit as you make the cuts across the ends of the ears.

Cut lengths of 1×4 for the casings. Wrap them around the window opening, mitering the top corners and butting the pieces into the sill. Rip a series of ½-inch pieces off a piece of 1× to create the decorative pieces that outline the casings. Nail these in place around the casing. Cut a 1¼-inch-wide piece of 1× to serve as the apron. Nail this in place under the sill with its ¾-inch dimension showing.

Country trimwork is solid and clean. At its best, Country's no-frills look and feel is comfortable and appealing to the eye.

Victorian window trim

These windows make use of fluted and reeded moldings, classical shapes that trace their origins back to the Greeks and Romans. Flutes are thumbnail-shaped grooves cut into the surface of a column or molding. Reeds are thumbnail-shaped bumps that run along the surface of a column or molding. In this case the reeding is narrow, and perhaps it's easier to think of them not as reeds, but as strips of spaghetti. Reeds and flutes flourished in Country, Traditional, and Victorian trim but lost their currency to the Arts and Crafts Movement's love of the rectilinear, and the Modernist's disdain of everything that had no function. To the Victorian eye, they were art for art's sake. The continued availability of reeded and fluted molding indicates the Victorians may have been right.

Reeded window trim

This trim is named for two pieces of molding along the outside edge, each of which has three small beads in it. As with most window trim, however, you'll start by making the sill piece. The width of this piece should equal the distance from the wall surface to the face of the window, plus 1½ inches. Cut the ears that extend past the jambs 1½ inches wide and 4⅜ inches long. Round over the top edge of the sill with a ⅜-inch roundover bit in a router table. Use a push block to help guide the piece past the bit as you rout the ends. Install the sill in the window opening.

The beaded strips are a commercially available molding called screen molding **(WM144)**. They're nailed to piece of 1×, and the whole thing is framed by a piece of ⅜-inch lattice around the outside. Start by ripping a 1× to 3½ inches wide. Cut the pieces to length and nail them in place around the window. Butt the casings on the sill, and miter the top corners.

Rip the **lattice** down to 1⅛ inches wide. Cut the pieces to length, miter the ends, and then nail them around the outside of the 1× casing. Finally cut the screen molding to length, and wrap two bands of it around the outside of the casing.

The apron is 1× that is 1½ inches wide with a commercial molding **(WM210)** nailed under it. Cut the 1× to length and nail it in place. Cut the molding to length, then cut the ends off at a 15-degree angle to dress them up a bit. Nail the molding in place under the 1×.

(WM144)

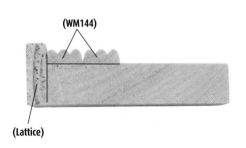

(Lattice)

(WM210)

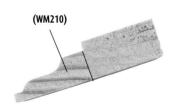

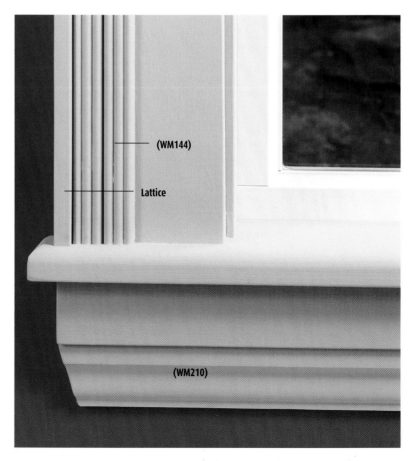

(WM144)

Lattice

(WM210)

3

FINISH CARPENTRY

Fluted window trim

The sill for this window trim is simply a squared-edged piece of 1×. The width of this piece should equal the distance from the wall surface to the face of the window, plus 1¼ inches. Cut the ears that extend past the jambs 1¼ inches wide and 4¾ inches long. Nail the sill in place.

The casings are made from a commercial molding **(A285)**. Cut the pieces to length and nail them in place. Miter the top corners, or use corner blocks as in the door with rosettes on page 110.

Make the apron from a piece of 1× that is cut to a width of 3¾ inches. Cut a 1⁹⁄₁₆-inch-wide by ³⁄₁₆-inch-deep rabbet in the face of the apron by making repeated passes with a dado blade in the table saw. Set the height of the blade to equal the height of the rabbet, and position the fence to control the rabbet's width. Cut the ends of the apron off at a 15-degree angle to dress them up a little.

(A285)

(A285)

Arts and Crafts window trim

Arts and Crafts windows were often treated like Arts and Crafts doors, with a three-piece header sitting on top of simple side moldings. In fact, the window shown here with the sill could be built with a header on it, but you often saw such windows with regular mitered corners. The second window shown here is the Arts and Crafts version of picture frame trim, shown on page 121.

Arts and Crafts window with sill

This window trim makes use of a ½-inch corner bead as its defining detail. Start by making the sill. The width of the sill should equal the distance from the wall surface to the face of the window plus 1½ inches. The ears on either side of the sill should be 1½ inches wide by ¾ inch long. Round over the corners of the sill with a ⅛-inch roundover bit in a router table.

Cut both the casing and the apron to width on the table saw. The casing is 4⅝ inches wide and the apron 4 inches. Rout corner beads on one edge of all the pieces with a ½-inch corner-beading bit in a router table. (A corner-beading bit looks like a roundover bit, except that the bearing is slightly smaller, so that it leaves a slight step before the roundover begins.) To achieve the look shown, cut the pieces by holding them on edge against the fence. Use a push block to help steady the apron as you make the cuts across its ends.

Nail the casing and apron in place. With the casing you can either miter the top corners and continue the same profile across the top of the window, or you can install a headpiece such as the ones shown with the Arts and Crafts door trim on pages 112–113.

3

FINISH CARPENTRY

Rabbeted window trim

Instead of a sill, this trim has molding on the top, bottom, and sides. It's called picture framing a window and works well with the casement windows poplar in Arts and Crafts architecture.

The casing molding is simply 1× oak with a ¼-inch-wide by ¼-inch-deep rabbet cut along one edge. Rout the rabbet with either a rabbeting bit or a ¾-inch-diameter straight bit in a router table. Use a fence to control the width of the rabbet and move the bit up and down to control the depth of the rabbet.

Cut the top and bottom pieces of trim to length and nail them in place above and below the window. Then nail the side casing in place on either side of the window. The side casings should extend past both the head casing and the apron by about 1 inch.

The simplicity of the Arts and Crafts style allows the natural beauty of the hardwood trim to take center stage.

CLOSER LOOK

DRYWALL RETURN BEAD
Some window manufacturers sell a drywall return bead which is essentially a molding profile used to cleanly join the the back of the window to the drywall. Check with the window manufacturer to see if they offer the return bead.

3

FINISH CARPENTRY

Modern window trim

Making window trim disappear involves slightly different drywall beading than that used in other Modern trim. The term for this technique is called a drywall return. You'll use corner bead to protect the corner formed by the wall and window. Protect the drywall edge that butts against the window with a piece of trim called L-bead. There are several types; the L-bead used here has a paper flange on each face. Trim one flange back so that one face of the bead is as wide as the drywall is thick. Plaster the other flange in place with drywall compound.

Trimming a modern window

If you're using a stock window in this application, it's designed so that the drywall will butt up against the jamb. In order to create a seamless look, the drywall has to overlap the jamb. Start the job by nailing plywood to the studs to create a surface flush with the edges of the jamb. In this case, and in most cases, you'll use ½-inch plywood, but measure to check, and be sure to take your baseboard and door treatment into account when planning the thickness of the plywood. Apply drywall, cutting out for the window before you put it in place, and placing the cut so the drywall covers the window jamb. Cut drywall to attach to the face of the window jamb, using drywall as thick as the window stop is wide. Cut the paper facing from one face of a piece of L-bead and put the metal face that remains between the stop and the drywall. Nail corner bead to the outside corner. When you apply joint compound, roll the L-bead back, and get plenty of compound between the paper flange and drywall. Flatten it into place with a drywall knife, and then cover the flange with more compound. Let it dry, and apply as many coats as needed to create a smooth surface. Apply compound to the corner bead the way you would to a regular corner. Paint all surfaces.

You can purchase corner bead with a tear-off strip that you can pull away after the compound dries to create a perfect finishing line.

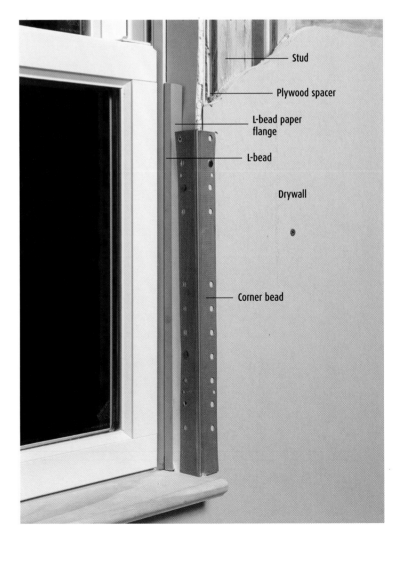

Stud

Plywood spacer

L-bead paper flange

L-bead

Drywall

Corner bead

Although there is no trim in the traditional sense, framing a window in the Modern style requires equally painstaking craftsmanship.

Installing baseboard and chair rail

PROJECT DETAILS

SKILLS: Measuring and layout; using power tools; coping joints
PROJECT: Installing baseboard or chair rail in an 8×10 room

TIME TO COMPLETE

EXPERIENCED: 8 hrs.
HANDY: 12 hrs.
NOVICE: 16 hrs.

STUFF YOU'LL NEED

TOOLS: Tape measure; chalk line with line level; stud finder; miter saw; hammer; nail set; 4- or 6-foot level; coping saw; glue; caulk gun
MATERIALS: Baseboard and/or chair rail; quarter round; 8d nails; paintable caulk; glazing compound

F or the most part, installing baseboard and chair rail is a matter of making a few cuts and driving a few nails. The hardest part may be getting it home. Both come in 16-foot lengths, which is more than you can fit in even the largest van or pickup. Most home centers have a hand miter box that you can use to cut the pieces to length, however. Cut pieces about a foot longer than you'll need. Buy an extra piece of the longest molding as insurance against mistakes.

Knowing where the studs are is one of the more critical things in installing baseboard and chair rail. Get a good stud finder, and mark the stud location on the wall, but don't stop there. Drive in a few nails at the mark, locating them along the path of the molding so that the molding will hide them. If you don't hit a stud, move over ¼ inch, and try again. Keep prospecting until you find the stud and repeat wherever the stud finder showed there was a stud.

Like most molding jobs, inside corners of baseboard and chair rail meet in a cope joint—a nesting joint described on page 82. It's easier than it looks, but almost no one gets it right on the first try. Practice on some scraps or an extra length of molding until you get the hang of it.

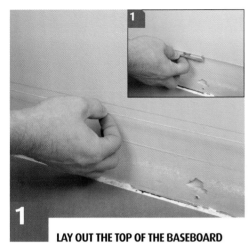

1
LAY OUT THE TOP OF THE BASEBOARD

Don't count on the floor being level. It may be, but if it's not, the molding can look out of kilter when you look at the chair rail or the windows immediately above it. Play it safe: Attach a line level to a chalk line, level the line, and then remove the level before snapping a level chalk line on each wall.

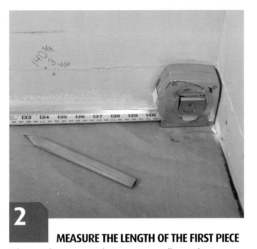

2
MEASURE THE LENGTH OF THE FIRST PIECE

When you're measuring between two walls, put the tape measure tight against each wall and read the measurement to the nearest sixteenth. Write the measurement on the wall and add in the length of the tape measure body—3 inches in this case. For a tight fit add another ¹⁄₁₆ inch to any measurement over 8 feet, and ⅛ inch to any piece over 12 feet.

3
MARK THE WALL TO SHOW WHERE THE STUDS ARE

Find the studs with a stud finder, and mark their location on the wall in an area that will be covered by the baseboard.

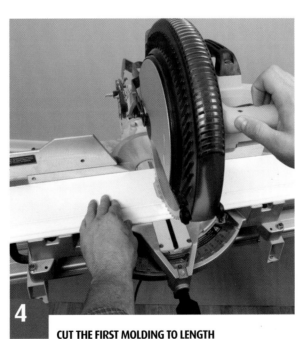

4
CUT THE FIRST MOLDING TO LENGTH

The first molding that you install is square on both ends. Check your measurement on the wall, and make sure you add in the extra required for long pieces. Cut a piece to this length, cutting it square on both ends.

WORK SMARTER

HELP ME, I CAN'T COPE

When you get to the end of this job, you'll discover that the baseboard along the fourth wall has to be coped to fit against the third wall and against the first wall. Plan ahead, so that the fourth wall is one with a door, an outside corner, or some other interruption. Cope the fourth wall's molding to meet the molding on the third wall, and then butt it into the interruption. Do the same against the first wall. You don't have to do it this way, but if the last wall you install is uninterrupted, you'll find you have to cope both ends of a single piece of molding. It's possible, but nerve-wracking.

GOOD IDEA

GET TIGHT-FITTING MOLDINGS

Carpenters add a little extra to any molding over 8 feet to ensure a tight fit:
- If the molding is over 8 feet, add ¹⁄₁₆ inch.
- If the molding is over 12 feet, add ⅛ inch.

If the molding is only a few inches long, subtract about ¹⁄₃₂ inch so that you don't have to force the molding in place.

3

FINISH CARPENTRY

3

FINISH CARPENTRY

TOOL SAVVY

HAMMERING AWAY

As you'll soon see there's a lot of nailing involved in installing baseboard. Carpenters use power nailers, and they do it for a couple of reasons. Not only does it save time, it's more accurate. With a nailer there's none of the vibration that makes things move every time you hit the nail. You hold the molding in place, pull the trigger, and the molding is fastened exactly where you held it. The price of nailers has dropped considerably, but they're still a lot of money if you only have one job in mind. Think about spending a few dollars at the rental counter instead. Renting a nailer can save you time and aggravation.

WORK SMARTER

GET A FINE BLADE

Make sure the coping saw you're using has a fine-toothed blade in it. Saws often come with coarser blades, which work fine for cutting out whirligigs, but not for cutting cope joints. To cut fine lines and make tight turns, you'll need a fine blade. And when you cut, let the saw do the work instead of pressing the blade forward and causing it to bind. If you have to invest a lot of energy in the cut, spend it moving the blade up and down. A quicker stroke makes a somewhat finer cut than a slow one.

5 **MARK THE BASEBOARD TO SHOW STUD LOCATIONS**

Lean the baseboard against the wall, and make a mark on it at each stud location. Marking the baseboard instead of the wall means you won't have marks on the wall that you'll have to paint over.

6 **SPRING THE FIRST MOLDING INTO PLACE**

Put the molding against the wall. If you've added either ⅛ inch or 1/16 inch for a tight fight, put an end in its corner and flex the molding until it fits against the other corner. Once both ends are in place, push the center of the molding against the wall.

7 **NAIL THE BASEBOARD TO THE WALL**

Drive two 8d nails at each stud. The first should be ¾ to 1 inch off the floor, so that it will hit the framing that runs along the floor. Drive the second nail closer to the top of the molding and into the stud.

Installing baseboard along the second and third walls

1

MITER THE BASEBOARD
Begin with a full length of molding, and miter the end. This is the first step in cutting the nesting corner joint, called a cope joint. Cut the miter so that the point of the molding is along the back of the baseboard. For now, don't worry about the overall length of the piece.

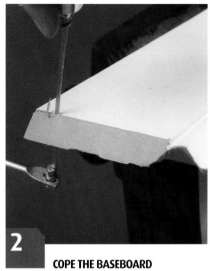

2

COPE THE BASEBOARD
Cut along the profile of the molding that was exposed by the miter cut. Make the cut with a coping saw, and let the saw do the work without applying pressure. For more on coping baseboard, see Coping a baseboard or chair rail on page 82.

3

NAIL THE MOLDING IN PLACE
Measure along the second wall from corner to corner; if the wall has a door in it, like this one does, measure from the corner to the trim. Cut the molding to the measured length, adding a bit extra to long pieces as described on page 133. Transfer the stud marks from the wall to the molding, as before. Put the molding in place, and nail it to the wall with two nails at every stud.

Little pieces

A short section of trim, like this one between the door and corner, requires a short piece of molding. Cut both ends square—and cut the piece about ¹⁄₃₂ inch short so that irregularities won't keep it from sitting flat. Nail the piece in place and cope the piece on the adjoining wall.

1

MITER AND COPE
Cut a miter in the end that will go against the second wall. Cope it to fit.

2

MEASURE, CUT, AND INSTALL
Measure the length of the wall, adding an extra ¹⁄₁₆ inch to any piece over 8 feet, and an extra ⅛ inch to any piece of 12 feet. Lay out the length on the baseboard, and cut it to length with a square cut at the end opposite the cope. Nail the molding to the wall.

Installing along the fourth wall

1

COPE THE MOLDING AND MEASURE
Cope a piece of molding to fit against the molding on the third wall. If you planned ahead, you saved a wall with some sort of interruption in it to be the fourth wall. If it's an outside corner, like this one, cut the piece somewhat longer, and then put the molding temporarily in place once you've coped it. Mark where the top of the molding meets the corner of the wall, and then trace along the wall to mark the required length on the molding. If the obstruction is an inside corner or piece of molding, measure from the obstruction to the third wall, and add the necessary fraction of an inch if the molding is over 8 feet long.

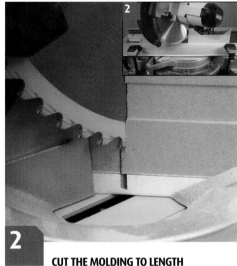

2

CUT THE MOLDING TO LENGTH
If the end of the molding is supposed to be square, cut it to length on the miter saw. If the end is supposed to be mitered, cut a piece of scrap as a guide. Clamp the scrap to the table, as shown in the inset, and cut partway through it. Line up the cut with the layout line on the back of the molding—as seen here from the back of the saw, the scrap is white and the layout line is along the back of the upright brownish molding. Make the cut and install both pieces of molding.

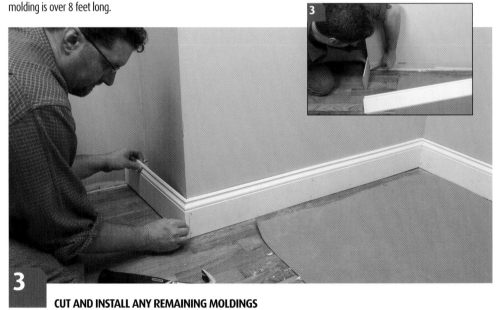

3

CUT AND INSTALL ANY REMAINING MOLDINGS
To cut the second half of an outside corner, miter it, and then put the molding in place against the wall. Trace along it, and cut to length as before. Nail the pieces you've cut to the wall. If you're painting, fill all the nail holes with glazing putty, and caulk any open seams. If you're staining, fill the holes either with a wood putty that matches the stain or a putty that absorbs stain.

Chair rail

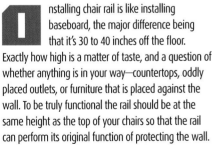

WORK SMARTER

CUTTING RETURNS

If the baseboard comes to an end at an opening that doesn't have any trim around it, end the baseboard with a mitered return, shown here. To cut a return, miter the baseboard wherever you want it to end. Miter a long piece of baseboard, and then cut off the mitered point. Glue the point to the baseboard, and then nail both in place. For more on mitered returns, see pages 79–80.

BUYER'S GUIDE

GETTING THE RIGHT STUFF

Wondering what kind of molding to buy? Pine is the traditional choice—if you want to stain it, get stain grade, which is clearer and more expensive than paint grade. If you're going to paint, get a preprimed molding, which already has the first coat of (white) paint on it.

The baseboards in this project are going to be painted, and the owner opted to save money by using medium density fiberboard (MDF) instead of pine. Its smooth surface is perfect for painting. It cuts with regular woodworking tools, but has no grain, so coping it is almost like cutting through butter.

If you're using oak, expect to bend some nails and damage the wood in the process. To solve the problem, predrill holes for the nails using a nail as a drill bit. Just put the nail in the chuck as if it were a bit, then drill, and drive the nail through the resulting hole.

I nstalling chair rail is like installing baseboard, the major difference being that it's 30 to 40 inches off the floor. Exactly how high is a matter of taste, and a question of whether anything is in your way—countertops, oddly placed outlets, or furniture that is placed against the wall. To be truly functional the rail should be at the same height as the top of your chairs so that the rail can perform its original function of protecting the wall.

Begin installing chair rail the same way you begin with baseboard: Snap a level line around the room, marking the bottom of the rail. Mark the location of the studs—there's no floor plate to nail into when you're this high off the ground, so it's important to know where every stud is and to be able to nail into it.

Before you start nailing, look around the room to find a wall where a door or window will interrupt the molding. Plan your work so that this will be the last wall you install. (If the last wall is uninterrupted, plan on coping both ends of the chair rail.)

Cut the molding along the first wall so that it runs from corner to corner and both ends are square. Cope a piece of molding to fit against the molding on the first wall, and cut the other end square so that it reaches into the corner. Repeat on the third wall. On the fourth wall, cope a piece of molding to fit against the third wall, and cut the other end so it meets the door or window in a butt joint. Repeat, coping a piece to fit against the first wall, and butt it into the other side of the door or window.

3

FINISH CARPENTRY

Baseboard and chair rail styles

Traditional baseboard and chair rail

Traditional trim was made of moldings pieced together to make an impressive whole. Originally each piece was hand cut with special planes, the sole and blade of which were shaped to mate with the shape they were cutting. In the Colonial Revival houses of the early 20th century, the molding was usually cut with a shaper, rather than by hand. The moldings shown here let you enjoy the joy (or tedium) of piecing molding together. Depending on which molding you're making, the pieces may either be entirely store-bought or entirely shop-made. Colonial molding was almost all painted, so don't be too hard on yourself at the sight of the occasional gap. Fill the gap with caulk, and then wipe it smooth with your finger. A latex glove will make cleanup a bit easier.

Two-piece chair rail

This two-piece chair rail gives you the look of a substantial, thick molding without the expense of buying a substantial, thick piece of wood. Start by ripping a piece of 1× stock to 2½ inches wide. Rout a bead along either edge with a ⅛-inch edge-beading bit on a router table.

Snap a level line on your wall to indicate the bottom edge of the chair rail. Align the bottom of the 1× molding with the line, and fasten the molding to the wall. While you can use nails, you can also drive screws down the center of this molding as the screw heads will be covered by the second piece of molding. Screws have the advantage of drawing the molding tight against any irregularities in the wall.

The second piece of molding **(WM984)** is a commercial molding called mullion. It is a thin decorative strip with a profile cut on either side. Nail this in place down the center of the 1× molding. While you can measure and mark the 1× molding to help you keep the mullion centered, most professionals will simply eyeball it.

Three-piece chair rail

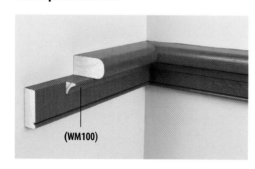
(WM100)

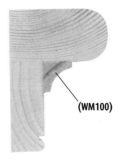
(WM100)

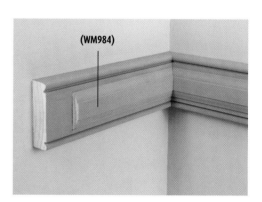
(WM984)

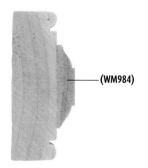
(WM984)

This Traditional chair rail is similar to the Country chair rail; however, the Traditional version is somewhat heavier and includes a third piece of molding. Rip pieces of 1× material to 2 inches wide to make pieces that go flat against the wall. Rout a bead along one edge with a ⅛-inch edge-beading bit in the router table. Make the cap pieces from ⁵⁄₄-inch stock that has been ripped to 2¼ inches wide. Round over the front edges of these pieces with a ½-inch roundover bit in the router table to create a bullnose profile.

Start installation by snapping a level line around your walls 1 inch below where you want the top of the rail. (This line will eventually be hidden by the molding.) Attach the beaded molding to the wall with its top edge aligned with your layout line. Nail the bullnose molding to the top of the beaded molding. Predrill the holes to avoid having to pound too much on the beaded molding. To finish the chair rail, attach a piece of ¾-inch cove molding **(WM100)** in the corner between the bullnose molding and the beaded molding.

Baseboard with molding

This four-piece molding mimics one of the Traditional profiles that appears in many historic American buildings. It makes use of three commercial moldings along with 1×6 stock. Start by nailing the 1×6 to the wall. You'll need to miter any outside corners, but you can simply butt any inside ones. The cap molding will cover the joint.

Next add the first commercial molding (**WM123**), ⅝-inch half round. Cut a scrap of 1× to a width of 4⅜ inches to serve as a guide so you can keep the molding parallel to the floor. (Be careful using this trick if the floor dips and rises significantly.) Rest the molding on the scrap, and nail the molding to the 1×6.

Nail the base cap (**WM166**) to the wall with the molding sitting on top of the 1×6. This flexible molding will help disguise any gaps between the baseboard and the wall. Finally nail the shoe molding (**WM126**) to the 1×6 at floor level. This helps disguise any gaps between the baseboard and the floor. It also provides a nice transition between the trim and the flooring.

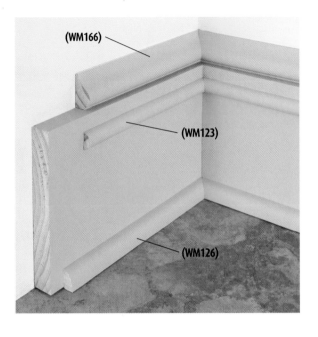
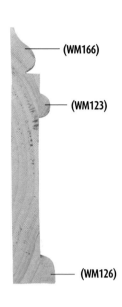

Baseboard from 1× stock

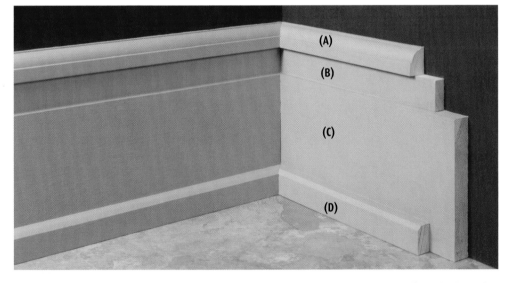
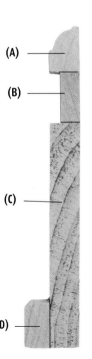

Unlike today's mostly skimpy baseboards, Traditional baseboard often featured wide, expansive boards cut with rich, detailed profiles. While it carries on this heritage, this example won't break the bank as it is made entirely of 1× material rather than expensive commercial molding.

The baseboard (**C**) is a piece of 1×6. Start installation by nailing it to the wall. Rip more 1× to a width of 1¼ inches, then turn the pieces on edge and cut them to ½ inch in thickness. Nail these thin pieces (**B**) to the wall on top of the 1×6s. Cap off this assembly with another piece of 1×. This

piece (**A**) is 1⅛ inches wide and has a ½-inch bead routed on one corner. This cut is best accomplished with a ½-inch corner-beading bit in a router table.

Install a shoe molding (**D**) at the bottom, where the baseboard meets the floor. Rather than using commercial shoe molding, use another piece of 1×. This piece should be cut to 1⅛ inches wide and ⅝ inches thick. Rout a chamfer along one edge of the shoe molding with a chamfering bit in a router table.

Country baseboard and chair rail

In addition to its decorative duties, chair rail stands guard, protecting fragile drywall and plaster surfaces from the dings and bruises that chairs and other furniture can mete out.

Typically applied about 36 inches above the floor, chair rail can stand alone, or as the top edge of a series of wainscot panels.

Bullnose Country chair rail

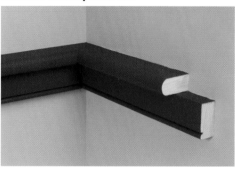

This two-piece molding is made from lengths of 1× stock that have been cut to shape on a router table. Start by ripping the pieces to width. Each piece is 1⅝ inches wide, which means you can get two pieces from a length of 1×4. You'll have the easiest time painting if you choose the clearest (knot-free) pieces you can find. This is a Country molding, however, so a few knots would not be out of character.

The front edge of the top piece is a profile known as a bullnose. While a commercial shop would cut this profile in a single pass with a specialized cutter, you can reproduce it with a simple ⅜-inch roundover bit in a router. You'll find it easier to cut the pieces if you put your router in a router table. Set up a fence on the router table with its face flush with the ball bearing on the bit. (With the fence set up this way, the majority of the bit will be behind the face of the

fence.) Make the bullnose by running the piece past the bit twice, routing first the top edge and then the bottom edge. Cut the bead on the lower piece of the rail with a ⅛-inch edge-beading bit. Again you'll find it easier to cut if you use a router table.

Once you have the pieces cut and routed, sand them to remove any mill marks and fuzz. To install the chair rail, draw a level line on the walls where the molding is to go. The line should be ¾ inch lower than you want the top of the chair rail to be. Nail the beaded piece to the wall, aligning the top edge with the line. Then nail the bullnosed piece in place on top. Predrill these holes so that you won't have to hit the nails so hard that the beaded piece gets knocked out of position. Miter the pieces at any corners. At outside corners apply glue to the ends of the bullnosed pieces where they meet.

Beaded chair rail

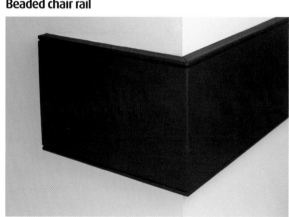

Making this chair rail is quite simple. Start with 1×8 stock and rip it to 7 inches wide, cutting away any damage on the edges of the boards. Rout a bead on either edge with a ⅛-inch edge-beading bit. You'll find this cut is easier to make if you use a router table. Draw a level line on the wall to indicate the lower edge of the chair rail. Nail the boards in place, aligning them with the layout line. Miter the pieces where the chair rail goes around corners.

In many old Country houses, chair rails like this were often installed before the walls were plastered. Plasterers used the rail as a gauge to make sure the wall was flat.

Baseboard

The humble baseboard sits at the bottom of a wall, helping to protect the wall surfaces from errant vacuum cleaners and careless soccer cleats. In addition to its guard duties, baseboard also serves as a visual anchor for the wall, and helps to cover any gaps where the floor and wall meet. Most builders today use a single-piece molding here, but traditionally, builders used to use two or even three separate pieces of molding to make up a baseboard.

Using multiple pieces of molding for baseboard has some distinct advantages, especially if your walls and/or floors aren't especially straight and flat. The actual baseboard is typically a wider piece of 1× stock. On top of this piece goes a piece of molding called base cap. This piece is usually smaller than the baseboard and is usually cut with a decorative profile. Because it is smaller than baseboard, it is more flexible and can be bent to conform to any irregularities in the wall. Some baseboards employ a third piece of molding at the floor. This is called base shoe (or simply shoe) molding. Like base cap, shoe molding is flexible and can be bent to conform to irregularities in the floor.

Country baseboard

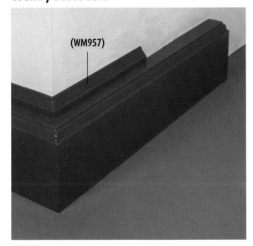

(WM957)

(WM957)

This option offers a somewhat fancier look, while still remaining Country at heart. The baseboard itself is a robust piece of ⁵⁄₄×4 material. To dress it up a bit, rout the corner with a ⁵⁄₃₂-inch ogee profile. As with most molding profiles, this operation is easiest on a router table. Nail the baseboard in place, mitering the corners as you go.

The base cap is a very small piece of commercial molding **(WM957)**. It is very flexible and will help hide any gaps between the chunky baseboard and the wall surface. If the molding tends to split, you may find it helpful to predrill the holes for the nails before driving them.

Baseboard with quarter round

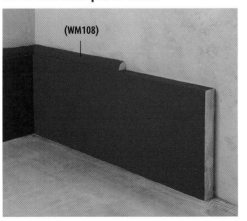

(WM108)

(WM108)

Like most of the other Country moldings, this baseboard is simple and straightforward. Start with pieces of 1×6. You can simply butt the pieces at inside corners, though you'll want to miter them for outside corners. Once you have the 1×6s installed, cap them off with lengths of quarter-round molding **(WM108)**. You can miter or cope the inside corners and miter the outside ones.

Victorian baseboard and chair rail

Victorian molding was perhaps more varied than any other style. One Victorian stylebook, printed in 1888, shows 24 molding combinations for doors, windows, and wainscoting, 18 styles for exterior cornices, and 38 styles of balusters and posts. This page is a small sampling of the richness of Victorian molding—there's a built-up chair rail; a chair rail embossed to look like it's carved; a baseboard with corner block; and a wide baseboard made out of a single piece. The last two, by the way, are made from a material that is far from Victorian—a pressed fiberboard called MDF. If you're painting your trim—and Victorians did—it's an economical way to get nice, wide pieces to work with. Don't turn up your nose: The Victorians were on the leading edge of the Industrial Revolution and didn't hesitate to use engineered materials that looked like more expensive natural materials—embossed Lincrusta, a linseed oil-based material that looked like elaborate paneling, and wood painted to look like marble are two examples.

Built-up chair rail

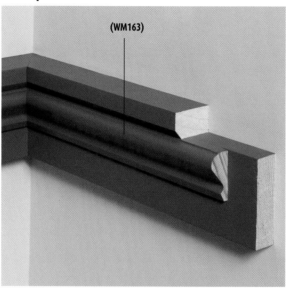

(WM163)

(WM163)

This three-piece chair rail makes use of one commercial molding **(WM163)** combined with two pieces of 1× stock. Start by ripping the 1× to width—the vertical piece is 2⅜ inches wide and the horizontal piece is 1⅜ inches wide. Rout a chamfer on the edge of the horizontal piece with a chamfering bit in a router table.

To begin installing the chair rail, draw a level line around the room ¾ inch below where you want the top of the rail. Align the top edge of the vertical pieces with this layout line, and fasten the pieces to the walls, mitering or butting the corners. Keep the nails slightly above the center line so the applied molding will cover them.

Nail the horizontal piece in position atop the vertical piece, mitering the corners. Predrill the holes to avoid having to pound on it too hard. Finally nail the commercial molding into the corner formed by the horizontal and vertical pieces.

Embossed chair rail

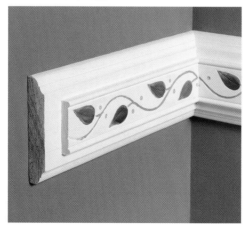

This chair rail makes use of embossed wood molding, a commercial wood product with a design pressed into the surface. The overall effect is one of hand-carved elegance. Back it up with a piece of 1× molding that has been cut to 3½ inches wide. Before installing the 1×, rout a profile along each edge with a ¼-inch cove-and-bead bit in a router table. To install the molding, draw a level line around the room for the bottom edge of the rail. Align the 1× on this line and fasten it to the wall. Keep the fasteners in the center where they will be covered by the applied molding. Miter the corners as necessary. Cut the embossed molding to fit, coping the ends where they meet at the corners. Nail the embossed molding to the 1×, centering it between the routed profiles. While you can measure and mark the 1× to help position the applied molding, most finish carpenters would just eyeball it.

Baseboard with corner block

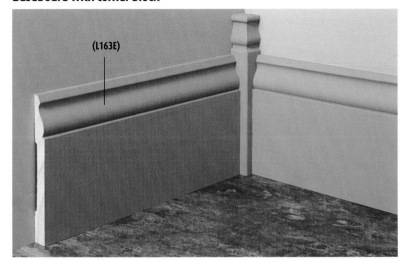

(L163E)

While it may appear to be made of more than one piece, this Traditional baseboard is a single-piece commercial molding **(L163E)**. It is fairly thin, so it will conform well to wavy walls. Nail it in place as you would any baseboard. The corner block makes installing baseboard much easier, because it does away with mitered or coped joints at inside corners. Simply nail the corner block in place, and then cut the baseboard so it butts up tightly to the corner block. Corner blocks are also available for outside corners.

WORK SMARTER

NAILING OUTSIDE CORNER BLOCKS IN PLACE
Outside corner blocks, which are resting on the metal corner bead, are easier to set accurately if you first drill a pilot hole from the inside or back of the block to the face. Then set the corner block in place and drill back into the wall through the metal corner bead and into the stud.

Baseboard with coped joints

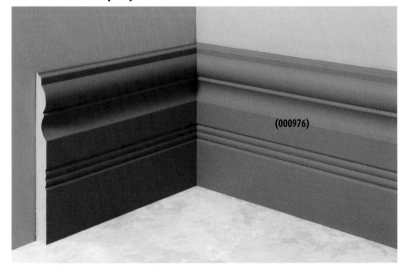

(000976)

(000976)

This reasonably priced baseboard is a great reproduction of a classic Victorian profile made out of MDF. Other standard wood profiles are also available in MDF. The profile is number **(000976)**. MDF cuts well with sharp tools and paints beautifully. It generates a lot of dust when being cut, so wear a high-quality dust mask. Nail the baseboard in place as you would with wood molding. You'll find that MDF moldings are very flexible and conform well to irregularities in the wall. Cope the inside corner joints; miter the outside ones. You can add a shoe molding at floor level to finish off the job.

3

FINISH CARPENTRY

Arts and Crafts baseboard

Arts and Crafts baseboard was simple—sometimes nothing more than a 6-inch-wide board nailed to the wall. The top of some baseboard was chamfered; rarely, you'd see a baseboard with an S-curve cut into the top. Gustav Stickley, who published *The Craftsman,* an Arts and Crafts magazine that included floor plans for homes, was fond of wide, simple baseboard. His plans included one baseboard that was 10 inches wide. The molding was flat on top and had a ⅜-inch-thick shoe base with a rounded edge. He also used a baseboard that was 12 inches wide, with a 1½-inch-high shoe base that was chamfered on the top. A 10-inch-wide baseboard Stickley designed had a chamfered shoe base that was 4 inches wide. It was beefy: The baseboard was nearly an inch thick, and the shoe base was another ¾ inch thick. Because of the difficulty in getting thick, wide stock, the baseboard shown here is a more modest 3½ inches wide.

Chamfered baseboard

In keeping with the rest of Arts and Crafts trim, this baseboard is made of oak. It is a two-piece molding—a piece of 1× with two decorative cuts, accompanied by a separate base shoe that also has a decorative cut. Start by ripping the pieces to width. The baseboard itself is 3½ inches wide and the base shoe is ½ inch wide. Rout a chamfer on the top edge of the pieces with a chamfering bit in a router table. Note that the chamfer on the shoe molding is narrower than the one on the baseboard. Complete the decoration by cutting a shallow groove the width of a saw blade along the length of the baseboard. The kerf should be positioned about ½ inch from the edge of the chamfer.

Because the baseboard is made of oak, it may not conform to bumps and dips in the wall surface. If you have gaps, fill them with a brown or tan caulk.

Rabbeted Arts and Crafts baseboard

Baseboard profile   Chair rail profile

Along with the window trim on page 129, this baseboard profile makes use of a simple rabbet as its one source of decoration. Cut the pieces to width (3½ inches) on the table saw. Cut ¼-inch by ¼-inch rabbets on one edge using a rabbeting bit or a ¾-inch-diameter straight bit in a router table. No matter which bit you use, position the fence to control the width of the rabbet and adjust the height of the bit to control its depth. Nail the baseboard to the wall, keeping in mind that you may need to use caulk to fill in any gaps. Hardwood tends to be stiff and doesn't conform well to any irregularities in the wall. Miter the pieces where they join at any corners. Rabbeting both edges of a piece of 1× will create a simple chair rail as seen in the profile to the near left.

Because the joinery is so simple, it requires precise measurements and cutting to create a pleasing look and feel.

Modern baseboard

In Modern architecture the joint between the wall and floor appears to happen without the help of the baseboard. In fact, a clear 1×6 functions as a baseboard and is so integral to construction that you actually install it first, before you put on the drywall. Make sure you use a clear 1×6; knots and other defects are hard to hide with paint. Creating a wall with recess in it requires building up entire sections to create the higher of the two surfaces. In this case strips of plywood were nailed to the studs to create the effect.

Recessed baseboard

Start with a wall that has exposed studs. Nail a clear 1×6 baseboard to the studs with 8d finishing nails. Cut and apply strips of ¾-inch plywood to each of the studs, nailing them in place. Install the drywall as you ordinarily would, allowing it to overlap the baseboard by about an inch. Overlapping the baseboard not only makes for a stronger edge, it creates a cleaner seam than it would if the drywall sat on the top edge of the 1×6. Nail the trim in place, and apply three coats of joint compound to cover it and create a smooth transition with the wall. This trim is L-shaped and applies easily over installed drywall. If you use metal J-bead, install it before you put the up drywall, and make sure you buy bead with a dimpled surface. Joint compound won't stick to smooth metal surfaces.

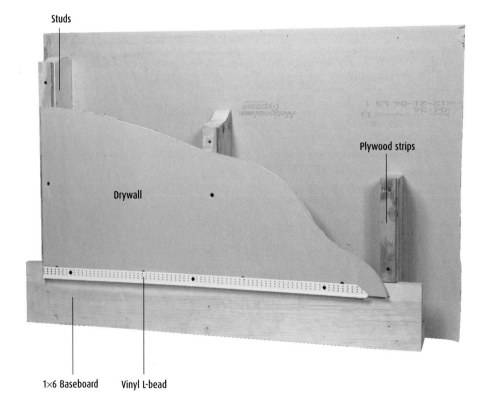

Studs

Plywood strips

Drywall

1×6 Baseboard   Vinyl L-bead

Modern trim requires a combination of finish carpentry and general construction techniques, including working with drywall, to achieve a seamless look.

Baseboard with reveal

On this baseboard, the drywall and the baseboard are on the same plane. A few inches from the ground, however, they step back into the wall, to reveal a recessed piece of drywall. Start by cutting a ¼-inch-deep rabbet (groove) about ¾ inch wide in the top of the baseboard. Nail the baseboard in place, taking care to keep the top of the board level. Once the baseboard is in place, slip a narrow strip of ¼-inch drywall into the groove, and screw the drywall in place. Apply strips of ¼-inch plywood to the studs, bringing the surface out to the same plane as the ¼-inch drywall. Cover the strips, and part of ¼-inch drywall with ½-inch drywall, to create the reveal. Cover the edge with vinyl L-bead, and cover with three coats of joint compound.

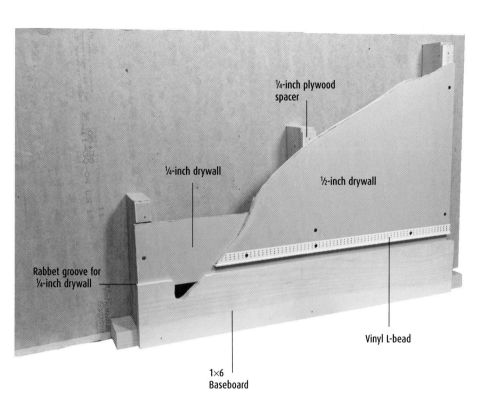

¼-inch plywood spacer

¼-inch drywall

½-inch drywall

Rabbet groove for ¼-inch drywall

Vinyl L-bead

1×6 Baseboard

A reveal on Modern baseboard can be as narrow as ¼ inch or as wide as 4 inches depending on the desired effect.

Trimwork projects

Once you've learned the basic trim techniques—mitering, coping, installing baseboard, and so on—you can apply them to some more advanced projects.

Try something new

In this chapter you'll see how some larger projects go together. In some cases, like installing beaded-board wainscoting, installation is a matter of doing what you already know how to do, only on a larger scale.

Installing gingerbread trim on a porch is pretty straightforward, too, as long as you measure correctly.

Advanced finish work

Frame and panel wainscoting, however, can involve extensive work in the shop before it gets near the wall it's intended for. And the window seat in this section involves cabinetmaking skills—you'll see how to cope with corners that aren't square, and wavy walls that are seldom parallel.

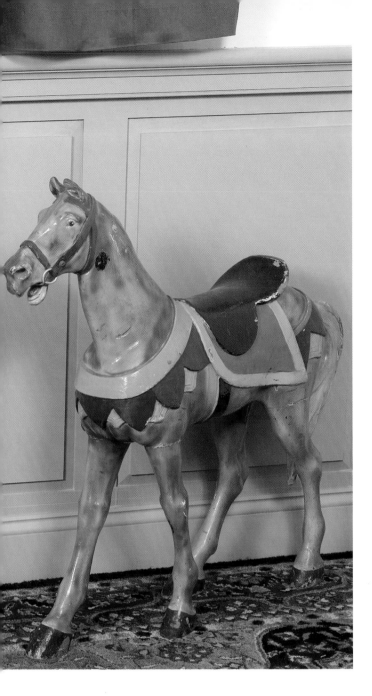

Chapter 4 highlights

INSTALLING WAINSCOTING
Beaded-board wainscoting is a fixture of Country style.

150

MAKING FRAME-AND-PANEL WAINSCOTING
Frame-and panel is a standard element of Traditional style.

155

INSTALLING FAUX PANELING
Faux paneling is easy to install and adds an instant touch of elegance.

160

MAKING A WINDOW SEAT
A paneled window seat is a cozy connection to the outdoors.

162

INSTALLING GINGERBREAD TRIM ON A PORCH
Gingerbread is a hallmark of Victorian style.

169

MAKING COLUMNS
Traditional fluted columns made with stock molding dress up the plainest door.

174

Learn the basics, then grow your skills

You may want to wait until you've mastered some basic woodworking techniques and are comfortable with using power tools before you attempt some of the projects in this chapter, but the more you know about trim carpentry, the sooner you'll be ready to tackle a window seat or a wainscoting project with confidence.

Installing wainscoting

 PROJECT DETAILS

SKILLS: Measuring and layout; using power tools; scribing
PROJECT: Installing wainscoting in an 8×10 room

 TIME TO COMPLETE

EXPERIENCED: 10 hrs.
HANDY: 15 hrs.
NOVICE: 20 hrs.

 STUFF YOU'LL NEED

TOOLS: Tape measure; power miter saw; clamps; sawhorses or other work surface; compass; jigsaw; level; hammer; nail set; drill and drill bits; table saw; caulk gun
MATERIALS: Wainscoting; 1×6; base cap; quarter round; 4d finishing nails; 8d finishing nails; sandpaper

 **WORK SMARTER**

ACCLIMATE THE WAINSCOTING
Your wainscoting will be less affected by changes in humidity and seasonal changes if you allow it to acclimate to the room before you install it. General guidelines for acclimation are 24 hours per ¼ inch of thickness of the stock.

Wainscoting is a general term that applies to any sort of wood applied to the lower section of a wall. The origin of the word is Dutch and the term probably referred to the paneling on the sides of a wagon or coach. Today the most common wainscoting is made of tongue-and-groove boards with a bead routed along the length to dress up the surface. One of the beads usually runs down the middle of the board, so that a single board ends up looking like two boards.

There is no great trick to installing wainscoting—adhesive is applied to the back of the board and it's nailed to the wall with 4d nails. Nothing will go wrong as long as you check your work with a level periodically to make sure the edges are plumb. The top edge of the wainscoting is covered with a molding, and the bottom is covered with baseboard. For best results you should cope the joints of both moldings.

Paneling is a great shortcut if you're looking to put up wainscoting quickly and cheaply. While this project concentrates on doing the job with solid wood, pages 160–161 shows you how to do the job with molding.

Space the boards to suit the season

Wainscoting will expand and contract with changes in humidity. Boards installed in the winter will grow wider in summer humidity. Use the head of a 4d finishing nail as a spacer to leave a small space between the visible edges of adjoining boards. If you're putting wainscoting up in the summer, snug each board against its neighbor. Adjust the position of the boards by tapping against a piece of scrap wainscot with a hammer.

Installing wainscoting

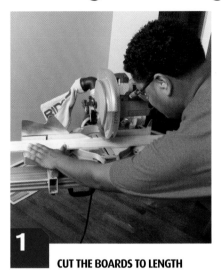

1

CUT THE BOARDS TO LENGTH

Wainscoting typically sits ¼ inch off the floor, so that bumps in the floor won't push the top edge of some boards higher than they should be. Later you'll apply baseboard that covers the gap. Cut all the wainscot boards to length—miter saw stands like this one have a built-in adjustable stop that controls the length. Put the boards in the room they'll be in for a least a day to adjust to the room's humidity before work begins.

2

LAY OUT THE PANELING

Snap a chalk line on the wall to show where the top of the paneling should go. Draw a second line to show where the top of the chair rail will be. Find the studs with the help of a stud finder, and draw lines on the wall marking the center of the studs. Draw level lines marking the top and bottom of outlets, and plumb lines marking the sides. Mark where the plumb lines meet the floor.

3

SCREW IN A LEDGER

Screw a board along the line marking the top of the paneling so that you can line the top of the wainscoting against it as you work. The board should be absolutely straight and level. Use the table saw to cut a long strip from a piece of plywood for best results, or have the store cut a piece for you. Drive the screws into studs along a section of wall that will be covered by the chair rail.

4

TEMPORARILY INSTALL THE FIRST PIECE

Each piece of wainscot looks like two boards from the front. Put the first piece of wainscot in a corner, grooved edge first. Put a level against the tongue, and adjust the board so it's straight up and down. Tack the piece temporarily in place.

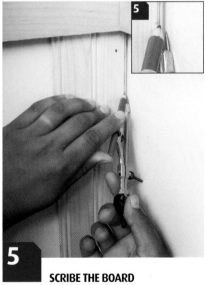

5

SCRIBE THE BOARD

Set a compass as shown in the inset so that the point and pencil are a bit farther apart than the depth of the groove in the edge of the wainscoting. Guide the compass—carpenters call them scribes—along the wall, drawing a line on the wainscot that is parallel with the wall and any irregularities in it.

6

CUT ALONG THE SCRIBE LINE

Remove the board from the wall, and cut along the scribed line with a jigsaw. This cut lets you plumb the board—put it straight up and down—while still fitting it tightly in the corner. Sand the edge smooth with 120-grit paper.

☾ OLD vs. NEW

DON'T FORGET ADHESIVE

You may be tempted to put up beaded board without using adhesive. Don't give in to temptation. A 4d nail driven into drywall or lath doesn't have enough bite to anchor the board in place. And you can't count on the studs to provide any extra nailing surface. Because of the nailing pattern you use with beaded board, chances are good that you'll miss every stud in the wall. Always apply construction adhesive, and nail the board in place to hold it while the adhesive dries.

⊙ TOOL SAVVY

CRACKED TONGUES

In some woods—oak in particular—blind nailing can cause the tongue to crack. Predrill nail holes if cracking is a problem. Put a finishing nail in your drill as if it were a bit, and use it to drill holes in the tongue wherever you want to drive a nail.

7   NAIL UP THE FIRST BOARD

Put the board back on the wall, plumb it, and nail it in to the corner with 4d (1½-inch) finishing nails. Start by driving a nail through the bottom of the board into the framing that runs along the floor behind the wall. Space the other nails every 16 inches above it. Apply adhesive to the second board as shown in the inset.

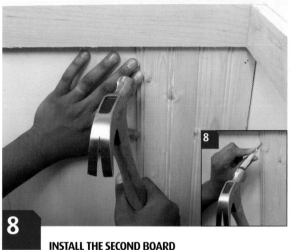

8   INSTALL THE SECOND BOARD

This board and its neighbors will be blind nailed—you'll drive a nail through the tongue of the board into the wall. Put the second board next to the first, spacing it as required by the season—tight spacing in the summer, looser in the winter. Apply adhesive and place a 4d nail in the corner formed by the tongue and the edge of the board, and drive the nail at an angle into the wall. Blind nail roughly every 16 inches along the tongue; set the nails with a nail set so the heads are flush with the tongue.

9   WORK YOUR WAY DOWN THE WALL

Install the next board and work your way down the wall. Check every couple of boards to make sure the edge of the board is plumb; if not, tilt each of the next few boards slightly until you've corrected the error. Slip a pry bar under the wainscoting as shown. The weight pushes the wainscoting tightly against the ledger.

Cutting holes for outlets

If a board covers an outlet or switch plate, install boards right up to the edge of the opening. Put in the next board, covering the opening. Use your level to transfer the marks you made earlier onto the board. Cut along the lines to create an opening for the outlet. Nail the board in place, and keep working your way down the wall.

Installing the last board

ENDING AT AN OUTSIDE CORNER

If the last board comes to an opening in which there is no trim, put the board in place, trace along the edge of the opening to mark the back of the board, and cut along the line. Cut along the waste side of the line with the jigsaw, just to make sure you don't take away too much wood. Sand the cut surface smooth.

GOING AROUND AN OUTSIDE CORNER

If you want to continue the wainscot around the corner, cut the first board to remove the groove. Position it against the last board on the adjoining wall, and plumb it, making sure it covers the adjoining board completely. Nail the board in place.

GOING AROUND AN INSIDE CORNER

If the adjoining wall forms an inside corner, start the second wall the same way you started the first. Plumb a board and nail it in place. Scribe, trim, and then install the board.

WORKING TOWARD A SECOND CORNER

If the wainscoting ends against some trim, like this wainscoting does, or if it ends in a corner, start as you normally would, then install boards until you come to the second-to-last board. Temporarily fit the last board in place. Set a scribe to the width of a board, minus the tongue. Guide the scribe against the trim to mark the board. Remove the board, cut along the line with a jigsaw, and set the board aside. Install a full board in the opening, and nail it in place. Put the scribed board in place, and face-nail it to the framing.

Installing chair rail and baseboard

GOOD IDEA

DEALING WITH BASEBOARD HEATERS

A baseboard heater shouldn't keep you from installing wainscoting, but if you want it to work, the heater has to remain exposed. A three-piece painted baseboard helps camouflage the heater. Install the baseboard on adjoining walls as you normally would. When you reach the heater, install base cap across the top. Paint the baseboard heater to match the baseboard.

Alternate chair rail

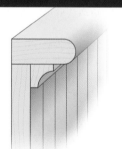

There are nearly as many ways to trim wainscoting as there are styles of molding. Base cap is a traditional approach; the trim shown in this drawing is another favorite. Make the nosing on the router table and install it first. Install the cove molding next, to dress up the job and cover any gaps between the nosing and the wainscoting.

1

INSTALL THE BASEBOARD

On this installation the baseboard is a three-piece installation—a 1×6, topped with base cap, and protected across the bottom by quarter-round molding. Start by nailing the 1×6 to the studs and the framing, butting the pieces in the corners.

2

INSTALL THE BASE CAP

Nail the base cap to the 1×6 and to the studs in the wall. Butt the first piece into the corners, and cope the neighboring pieces to fit. Work your way around the room, coping as you go. For more on cope joints, see page 84.

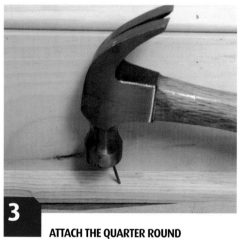

3

ATTACH THE QUARTER ROUND

Drive finishing nails into the molding at a 45-degree angle so that it catches the framing behind the wall and will stay anchored regardless of expansion and contraction in the floor or baseboard. Cope the molding the same way you coped the base cap.

4

INSTALL THE CHAIR RAIL

Wainscoting is traditionally topped off with a molding. On this installation the molding across the top is also base cap that matches the one on the baseboard. Butt the first piece into the wall at the corner, and cope adjoining pieces to fit against it.

4

TRIMWORK PROJECTS

Making frame-and-panel wainscoting

PROJECT DETAILS

SKILLS: Measuring and layout; using power tools; cutting mortise and tenon joints
PROJECT: Building a 12-foot section of frame-and-panel wainscoting

TIME TO COMPLETE

EXPERIENCED: 2 days
HANDY: 3 days
NOVICE: 4 days
Panel installation should take an additional 4 hours.

✓ STUFF YOU'LL NEED

TOOLS: Table saw with combination blade and dado blade; 2- to 3-hp router with electronic speed control and soft start; panel-raising bit; wing cutter; router table; tape measure; framing square; combination square; pipe clamps; hammer, nail set; safety glasses; dust mask; hearing protection
MATERIALS: 1× pine; 5/4 pine; medium-density fiberboard; cove molding; wood glue; finishing nails; baseboard

BUYER'S GUIDE

PREASSEMBLED FRAME-AND-PANEL WAINSCOTING
In some areas you may be able to find finished MDF panels in 36- and 48-inch widths. When assembled they provide the look of a hand-crafted panel.

Frame-and-panel wainscoting was the province of the rich in Colonial times. It used as much wood as a good piece of furniture and was labor-intensive, especially when hand planing the molding profiles. Modern machinery has made the job simpler, but you will need some special tools: a wing-cutter router bit for cutting grooves, a panel-raising router bit, a router big enough to do the job, and a good router table.

Wainscoting is generally made and assembled offsite. Grooves are cut in the horizontal rails and vertical stiles. The raised panels slide into the grooves, which hold them in place and allow for expansion in humid weather. A tenon on the end of the stile also fits in the groove in the rails, giving the frame structure.

The tools you'll need for this project are available at home centers. The router table is usually a stock item, and the bits can be special ordered at the contractor's desk. As for the router, the size of the panel-raising bit means you'll want a router with soft start and electronic speed control. The big bit starts up with an unsettling jerk when the outer edge of the bit spins too fast. Adjust the speed as low as it will go.

This set of frame-and-paneling was made with clear pine and medium-density fiberboard (MDF). It gives you a wonderfully smooth surface for painting and looks great.

Because it comes in 4×8 sheets (actually 4 feet 1 inch × 8 feet 1 inch) you can get wide panels without having to glue together narrower pieces of wood. If you want to make the paneling out of a solid wood, you can follow the same steps shown here. The widest stock boards you'll be able to get are 11¼ inches wide. Glue together boards for wider panels, leaving the pieces a little long and cutting them to size after you glue them up.

This stretch of paneling is 142½ inches long—just under 12 feet, the longest 1× that stores commonly carry. It's 35 inches tall—36 inches once you put the chair rail on top. The top rail is 3¾ inches wide; the lower rail is 3¼ inches wide. Panel openings are 19⅞ inches wide and 28 inches tall. The panels, which fit in ½-inch-deep grooves cut into the frame, measure 20⅝ inches × 28¾ inches, which leaves room for the panels to expand.

Since wainscoting differs from room to room, you'll have to design your wainscoting to match your needs. Draw it out on graph paper until you get proportions that please you.

Once you've designed your wainscoting, plan your cuts so you use the wood most efficiently. Nothing can be as frustrating as needing a 4-foot piece, only to find that all you have is two 3-foot pieces because you didn't plan ahead. Figure out what will give you the most efficient use of your wood, and lay it out roughly in chalk before you start cutting. When you're ready to cut, measure carefully, and mark your cuts with a sharp pencil.

Making the frame

4

TRIMWORK PROJECTS

Centering the groove

The best way to rout a groove down the center of the rails and stiles is to rout it twice. Rout it once with one face on the table, and then rout it again with the other face on the table. Draw an X on one side of each piece before you start so you can tell the sides apart.

Dust

Routing panels raises huge amounts of dust. Attach a vacuum to the router fence. If fine MDF dust clogs the filter, run the vacuum without it.

1

RIP THE RAILS AND STILES

Cut all the pieces of a given width at the same time, then move the fence and cut the next batch of pieces.

2

CUT THE PARTS TO LENGTH

Put a piece of wood in a crosscut jig (see page 50), cut one end square, and then draw a line to mark the actual length of one of the pieces. Cut at the line, and without moving the stock in the crosscut jig, clamp a stop against the end farthest from the blade. Cut all similar parts by resting a square edge against the stop block, and then move the block and cut the next batch of pieces. Continue working in batches until you have cut all the pieces to length.

3

ROUT GROOVES FOR THE PANELS

Cut the grooves with a router bit called a wing cutter. Put the bit in the router, and set it so that the wing will cut a groove down the middle of the board. Move the fence so that only about ⅛ inch of bit is exposed when the wing is perpendicular to the fence. Test the setup by routing a groove in a long piece of scrap left over from cutting the pieces. Make any needed adjustments, and rout a groove on the two long edges of the stiles and on one long edge of each rail. Reset the fence and cut a groove about ⁵⁄₁₆ inch deep.

Adjusting panel size

To make assembly easier, subtract ¹⁄₁₆ inch from both the length and width of the panel size you calculated, and cut the panels to this size. If you are using wood panels, make them ¹⁄₁₆ inch shorter and ⅛ inch narrower than calculated to allow for expansion in humid weather.

4

CUT THE TENONS

Tenons are the tongues that fit in the grooves. You'll cut one on each end of the stiles, which are the vertical pieces. Put a dado cutter on your table saw, and set up to cut a ¼-inch × ¼-inch groove on the end of the board as described on page 49. Use the miter gauge to guide a sample across the blade, and then flip the sample over and cut again to create the tenon.

5

TEST THE FIT

Put the tenon you cut into one of the grooves. A tenon that fits perfectly will slip into the groove with almost no friction. If the tenon is too thick, raise the blade and recut it. If it's too thin, lower the blade and make the cuts on another sample. Check, too, to make sure that there's a little bit of space at the bottom of the groove to collect excess glue during glue-up. Cut tenons on all the stiles.

6

MEASURE TO GET THE PANEL SIZE

Put all the stiles in a groove and slide them together at one end of a rail. Measure from the other end of the rail to where the stiles begin. Divide the measurement by the number of panels to get the size of each opening. Add in twice the depth of the groove to both length and width to get the maximum size of the panel.

Making the panels

Solid wood

If you want to make the panels out of solid wood, count on three things. You'll have to glue up the panels to get pieces wide enough. You have to make the pieces ⅛ inch narrower than the distance from the bottom of one groove to the bottom of the next groove to allow for expansion during humid weather. And be very careful during glue-up so that you don't glue the panel in the groove. If you do, it will crack as it tries to expand with changes in humidity.

WORK SMARTER

END GRAIN FIRST
If you're using solid wood, rout the end grains first, so that the splintering you get when routing it will be routed away when you do the sides.

1   CUT THE PANELS
Once you've calculated the size of the panel, cut it to size on the table saw. If you're using MDF, you can guide the cuts for both length and width against the rip fence. For safety, cut the widest dimension first, so that you can guide it against the fence for the second cut. If you're using solid wood, cut the panels to width against the rip fence, and then cut them to length in a crosscut jig.

2   SET UP THE ROUTER FENCE
A panel-raising bit has a bearing on top that needs to be flush with the fence. This means that at any given time, half the bit is outside the fence routing the panel, and the other half is away from the panel and somewhere behind the fence. Commercial router fences have an adjustable opening to keep the outside edge of bits from routing through the fence. Adjust the opening as needed.

3   ADJUST THE POSITION OF THE FENCE
Move the fence so it's flush with the bearing. Use a ruler as a guide. If the fence is difficult to set, it's better to have the bearing a tad behind the plane of the fence rather than in front of it.

4   ADJUST THE BIT
A panel-raising bit is one of the largest bits made. Don't try to rout the panel in one pass—the strain would be too great on your router. Lower the router so that the bit is just peeking up above the table. Lock the router in place so that it won't drop out while you're routing.

5   ROUT A SAMPLE
Set up a featherboard to help hold the panels in place while you work. Rout the edge of a long piece of scrap left over from cutting the panels. (Don't rout end grain if using a solid wood sample.) Raise the bit ⅛ inch, and rout again. Test-fit the scrap in one of the grooves in the frame. Keep raising the bit in small increments until the sample just slides into the groove.

6   RAISE THE PANELS
Move the fence forward, so that only about one-fourth of the bit is exposed. Rout all four edges of each panel. Turn off the router, and move the fence so that about one-half of the bit is exposed. Rout all edges of all the panels. Repeat, until the bearing is flush with the fence, and you've routed all the edges of all the panels.

4

TRIMWORK PROJECTS

Assembling the frame

1

TEST-FIT THE FRAME

Put the frame together, including rails, stiles, and panels. Make sure everything goes together smoothly—this is a trial run for the glue-up. Make any necessary corrections.

2

GLUE PART OF THE ASSEMBLY TOGETHER

Disassemble the frame. This is a big glue-up. To avoid problems, glue up part of it and let the glue dry before you glue up the rest. Start by brushing glue on both sides of a tenon and putting the tenon in the groove of the rail. Slip in a panel, and check to make sure the stile is square with the rail. When the stile is square with the rail, clamp it in place, protecting each end from the clamps with small blocks of wood. Work your way down the rail, gluing and clamping one stile at a time.

3

GLUE THE REST OF THE ASSEMBLY TOGETHER

Remove the clamps and brush glue on both faces of the remaining tenons. Put the rail in place, and clamp it to the rest of the paneling.

4

INSTALL THE ASSEMBLY

Take the frame-and-panel assembly to wherever you're installing it. The frame is somewhat fragile at this point—there's not a lot of tenon compared to the amount of paneling. Turn the piece on edge when you transport it. This assembly was designed to sit 3½ inches off the ground, with baseboard covering the gap. Rest the assembly on a support, and nail it to the studs.

5

INSTALL BASEBOARD

Put a scrap in the opening to support the bottom of the baseboard and nail the scrap in place. Nail baseboard across the opening, and nail quarter round across the bottom of the baseboard.

4

TRIMWORK PROJECTS

Making the chair rail

1   ROUT THE EDGE OF THE CHAIR RAIL

Make the rail from ⁵⁄₄ (five-quarter) stock, which is 1 inch thick. Put a ½-inch-radius roundover bit in your router table. Rout one edge on a piece of scrap, flip the piece over, and rout the other edge. Adjust until you're satisfied with the profile. Put featherboards on the table to hold the wood in place, and rout each face of the wood to create an edge called a bullnose.

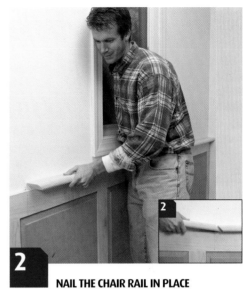

2   NAIL THE CHAIR RAIL IN PLACE

Apply glue to the top of the face board and frame, and nail the chair rail to it. If the frame-and-panel section is longer than the stock you have for the chair rail, splice the chair rail together as shown on page 81.

3   ROUT A FACE BOARD

The face board nails to the paneling just below the chair rail. It has a decorative bead along the edge. Set up featherboards and rout the bead on a piece of scrap. Make any necessary changes, and then rout the face board.

4   NAIL THE FACE BOARD IN PLACE

Nail the face board to the face of the frame so that the top edge is flush with the top edge of the frame. Splice as needed.

5   NAIL A COVE MOLDING IN PLACE

Nail a cove molding to the paneling so it bridges the space between the face board and chair rail. Set all the nails with a nail set.

4

TRIMWORK PROJECTS

Installing faux paneling

PROJECT DETAILS

SKILLS: Measuring and layout; using power tools; mitering corners
PROJECT: Installing 12 feet of faux paneling in an 8×12 room

TIME TO COMPLETE

EXPERIENCED: 4 hrs.
HANDY: 6 hrs.
NOVICE: 8 hrs.

STUFF YOU'LL NEED

TOOLS: Miter saw; brad gun and compressor; tape measure; chalk line; level; stud finder
MATERIALS: Molding; chair rail; baseboard; 1¼-inch brads

Nailing jig

A jig can be as simple or as complex as you want it. Generally speaking, simpler is better. This jig is designed to hold two pieces of the frame at right angles while you nail them together. The smaller piece of plywood keeps the frame pieces at 90 degrees when you nail them together; the larger one provides a flat work surface. The mitered molding keeps the shorter piece from moving when you drive a nail into it through the longer piece. The small flat piece helps hold the molding in place, freeing up a hand to use the nailer. It won't take 5 minutes to make and helps guarantee tight joints.

F aux paneling creates the effect of frame-and-panel wainscoting by nailing frames made of molding to the walls. For a fraction of the cost and effort of real frame-and-panel, you can dress up your walls dramatically.

Sketch out your plans on a piece of graph paper, using a simple straight line to represent whatever molding you choose. The key to good design is proportion: Make the long side of the square about 1.5 times as long as the short side. It's a formula based on Greek and Roman architecture, and the relationships between the sides of a right triangle and its hypotenuse. It's overly technical, but it works, so forget the theory and remember the results: If the short side of the frame is 20 inches, the long side should be 30 inches.

Almost any molding works in this application. The one shown here is called a shingle panel **(WM210)**, but baseboard, base cap, or even door and window casing will work on the right wall.

When you're nailing together lots of frames like these, it's worth using a pneumatic brad nailer to do the work. Unless you've got a lot of experience, driving brads by hand tends to force the pieces apart. Get a brad gun rather than a finish nailer. A finish nailer has a wider tip, the center of which can easily miss the molding entirely, causing the nail to fly across the shop instead of into the wood.

1 LAY OUT THE HORIZONTALS

Faux framing is a combination of the baseboard, chair rail, and the frames. Before you start installing, lay out the top of the chair rail and baseboard by drawing a pencil line or snapping a level chalk line on the walls. Then snap a line to lay out the top edge of the frame. Repeat to lay out the bottom edge. For more on using a line level see page 35.

2 LAY OUT THE EDGES OF THE PANELS

Measure and lay out the outside edges of the panels with the help of a level. Stand back to make sure you like the layout and make any changes you'd like.

3 CUT THE MOLDING

This wall has four frames, each of which is 20 inches high and 30 inches long, for a total of eight 20-inch pieces and eight 30-inch pieces. Cut them in batches: Cut a right-hand miter on all of the 20-inch pieces, leaving each one long by twice the thickness of the molding. Repeat on the 30-inch pieces, but cut a few extra pieces, just in case. Reset the saw, and cut all the 20-inch pieces to length, using the stop on the saw stand as a guide. When you're finished with the 20-inch pieces, reset the stop and cut the 30-inch pieces.

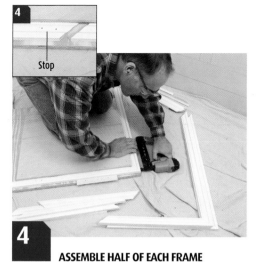

Stop

4 ASSEMBLE HALF OF EACH FRAME

Put adjacent sides of the frame in a nailing jig like the one shown here, and nail through one side and into the other. On large frames (over 20 × 30 inches), you may want to nail through both sides of the corner. Make sure your jig has a stop like the one in the inset to hold the piece you're nailing into. If not, it will be very hard to get a tight joint.

5 ASSEMBLE THE FRAMES

Put two half frames together around a piece of plywood with 90-degree corners, and nail the frames together. You may want to have a stop to nail against. It can be a simple block of wood that holds the end opposite the nail against the plywood. On a smaller frame, like this one, you may be able to hold the frame in place with your knee as shown here or use a clamp with plastic protectors.

6 NAIL THE FRAMES TO THE WALL

Hold a stud finder on the wall along one of the horizontal lines you drew, and mark the location of the studs on the line. Hold the frames on the lines, and nail into the studs.

7 INSTALL CHAIR RAIL

Cut and install chair rail along the lines you drew for it. For more on installing chair rails, see Installing baseboard and chair rail on pages 132–137.

8 INSTALL THE BASEBOARD

Put the baseboard on the floor, and align it with the line you drew marking the top. Nail into the studs to attach it.

Making a window seat

PROJECT DETAILS

SKILLS: Measuring and layout; using power tools; making butt joints with a plate joiner
PROJECT: Building and installing a window seat with concealed storage compartment

TIME TO COMPLETE

EXPERIENCED: 2 days
HANDY: 3 days
NOVICE: 4 days

STUFF YOU'LL NEED

TOOLS: Table saw; router; rabbeting bit; plate joiner; drill with drill bits and screwdriver bits; hammer; nail set; tape measure; combination square; straightedge; chisel; clamps; rubber mallet; hearing protection; safety glasses; dust mask; cotton swab

MATERIALS: ¾-inch plywood; 1×6 pine; 2-inch and 1¼-inch drywall screws; ¾-inch brads; 6d nails; glue; ½-inch plywood; wood joiner biscuits; piano hinge; baseboard

A window seat adds both grace and storage to a room. It's not something that works everywhere, nor is it something that you can go out and buy at the store. Each room is different, and if you want a window seat, you'll have to make one yourself, or have it made.

There are three distinct stages to building this window seat—building the box, building the frame-and-panel facade that goes over it, and installation. Building the box is relatively easy, as it simply screws together. Given that the home center or hardware store will cut the pieces for you, and given than they'll do a better job than even the most skilled craftsman can do on a table saw, there's not a lot that can go wrong.

Building the facade is slightly more complicated, but the use of simple plate joinery keeps it from getting out of control. If you can make square cuts and handle large but flat glue-ups, you'll do fine. The plate joiner handles what would otherwise be difficult joinery. It cuts a groove in each of the pieces to be joined; a football-shaped spline goes halfway into one groove. The groove in the other piece goes over the other half of the football. Assemble it with some glue, and you have a tight joint.

When you look at the steps involved in installation, it may seem complicated. In fact, there are just a lot of little steps, most of which involve covering up plywood with solid wood or screwing a support to the underside of another piece of wood.

Designing your window seat

You'll have to design the seat to fit the nook beneath your window, so there's no comprehensive parts list here. Use the following information to sketch out your own seat and to make your own parts list.

A window seat is typically about 20 inches tall; the box inside is about 2¼ inches shorter—pieces added during assembly bring it up to its final height. From side to side the box is 1 inch narrower than the opening it fits into, so that it will slip in the opening with no problem. Measured from front to back the box is an inch or two longer than the opening you're putting it in—both for looks, and so that you won't have to align it with walls that may not be in line with each other.

The overall length of this seat is 69 inches; the bottom rail is 5½ inches wide; the top rail is 3 inches wide; and the stiles that run between them are 2¾ inches wide.

Making the box

1

ASSEMBLE THE SIDES
The heart of the window seat is a box made of ¾-inch birch plywood. Have the pieces cut to size when you buy your plywood. Start construction by screwing the front, back, and sides together with 2-inch drywall screws.

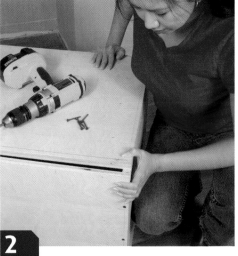

2

ATTACH THE BOTTOM
Draw a line ⅜ inch in from the edge all the way around the bottom. Put the bottom over the sides. Drive screws through the line into two corners along one of the ends. Go to the other end, and slide the plywood over so it closes any gaps and squares up the assembly. Screw through the lines at the corners. Drive screws every 8 to 12 inches along the lines on all four sides.

Cut the plywood at the home center
Wrestling big pieces of plywood across the table saw can be tricky, hard, and even dangerous. Lumberyards and home centers have special saws that simplify making accurate cuts. Draw up your plans, figure out how big the pieces need to be, and then have the store cut the parts to size for you. The pieces will be more accurate than any you could cut at home.

3

ATTACH THE FEET
Screw three or four strips of plywood to the bottom, spacing them equally along the length. This lifts the bottom off any irregularities in the floor, helping to keep the box from rocking.

4

PUT THE BOX IN PLACE
Slide the box into the opening by the window, pushing it against the back wall, and centering it between the two side walls of the opening. Screw it to studs in the back wall with 2-inch drywall screws.

Making the facade

Use a crosscut jig

Whenever you have a job that requires cutting pieces so that they are perfectly square and all the exact same length, consider using a crosscut jig with a stop block. Cut one end of each piece first so that it's square, and then clamp a stop block to the fence. Position the stop block so that pieces butted against it will be cut to the desired length, and then tighten the clamp. Put the square end of the piece against the block, slide the jig forward to cut it, and then repeat. For more on crosscut jigs, see page 50.

1 CUT THE PIECES TO SIZE

The facade is made of a frame that looks a bit like a ladder, with plywood panels that fit between the rungs. The rungs of the ladder, called stiles, are 2¾ inches wide. The sides of the ladder, or rails, are two different widths. The top rail is 3 inches wide; the bottom is 5½ inches wide. Rip the pieces to width, and then cut them to length.

The plate joiner

The joints in this facade are made with a plate joiner. A plate joiner cuts a groove in each of the pieces of wood to be joined together. When it comes time to assemble the joint, you put a football-shaped piece of compressed wood into one groove and fit the mating groove over it. The glue makes the compressed piece of wood, called a biscuit, expand for a nice, tight joint.

2 FIND THE CENTER OF THE STILES

Because the biscuit joint must be centered on the stiles, you need to find the center of each stile, and mark it on each end of the stile. Set a combination square to the proper distance, hold it against the stile, and make a mark. Mark both sides of all pieces.

3 DRY FIT THE FRAME

Put the frame together without using glue. Equally spaced stiles make assembly easier down the road, so cut a spacer to position the stiles in the frame. Assemble the frame, clamping the stiles in place as you go. If necessary, trim the spacer or cut a new one, and reposition and reclamp the stiles.

4

TRIMWORK PROJECTS

4
TRANSFER THE LAYOUT LINES
Use a straightedge to transfer the lines from the stiles to the rails. These lines mark the center of where each joint occurs on the rail.

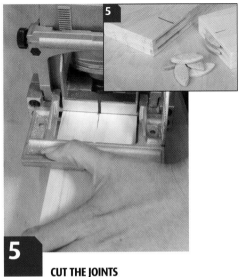

5
CUT THE JOINTS
Set the plate joiner to cut a groove about ⅛ inch from the top of a stile. Align the line on the joiner with the line marking the center of the joint. Push the joiner forward to cut the groove. Turn the stile over and cut a second groove on the same piece, so that you get pieces that look like those in the inset. See The plate joiner on page 164.

GOOD IDEA
NO STICK SOLUTION
The last thing you want is to glue the frame to the work surface. Cover the surface with wax paper before you start to keep the two from bonding together.

4

TRIMWORK PROJECTS

6
TEST ASSEMBLE THE FRAME
Put biscuits in each joint and put the frame together. Clamp the pieces in place, check for square, and fix any problems that occur.

7
GLUE THE FRAME TOGETHER
Squeeze glue into the grooves on one rail, and put biscuits into the grooves. Apply glue to the grooves in each stile, and slip them over the biscuits in the rail. The stiles can move back and forth on the rail, so align the pencil marks on the rail with those on the stiles in order to get the proper spacing. Repeat on the upper rail, and then clamp the assembly together. Check to make sure the rails and stiles are square with each other, and make any necessary adjustments.

WORK SMARTER

CLAMP CATASTROPHES

You have to have clamps to hold the pieces together while the glue sets, but clamps can cause as many problems as they solve. To keep clamps from causing problems like knocking things out of square, twisting the joints, or warping the frame, apply the least amount of pressure possible. Always center the clamp in the joint. Center it in the wood too. Having the clamp too high on an edge will close the side of the joint you can see while forcing the underside open.

8 **ROUT THE BACK OF THE FRAME**

The panels sit in a recess, called a rabbet, in the back of the frame. Let the glue dry, and then rout the recess with a ½-inch rabbeting bit, routing all four sides of each opening. Make the groove so the panels are flush with or slightly above the back of the frame. When you attach the frame, the box will keep the panels firmly in place.

9 **SQUARE THE CORNERS**

The router leaves rounded corners instead of square ones. Use a ruler to draw in a square corner, and chisel away slivers of wood working toward the lines until you've created a square corner.

10 **CUT THE PANELS TO SIZE**

Measure the size of the openings. For an easy fit, cut panels that are smaller than the opening by ⅛ inch in each direction. The panels are made of ½-inch plywood, which is easier to handle than the plywood for the box. When you buy the plywood, have the home center cut the sheet into 24-inch strips, so it's easier for you to rip and crosscut at home.

WORK SMARTER

CUTTING WIDE PIECES

Depending on the width of your saw table and the size of the plywood, it may be easier to run the cutoff against the fence, where it is supported by the saw table. The narrower piece—the one you want to keep—will run on the narrower stretch of table to the left of the saw blade. Set the fence so you cut the keeper piece a bit wider than needed. Once you've cut it, reset the fence, and cut it to final width to remove any ragged edges.

11 **APPLY GLUE**

Apply glue to the edges of the recess with a cotton swab. Put on plenty of glue, but don't leave puddles that will squeeze out and cause a mess when you put the panels in place.

12 **PUT IN THE PANELS**

Put the panels in their openings. Tack the corners in place, and drive tacks every 10 or 12 inches along the sides of the panel to hold the panel while the glue dries.

4

TRIMWORK PROJECTS

Installing the window seat

Scribing the wings

Unless you are lucky, at least one of the sidewalls surrounding the seat is out of square. If so, you may have to scribe the side wings to fit. For more on scribing see page 151.

1

ATTACH THE FRAME
Center the frame on the front of the box, and clamp it. Screw it in place with 1¼-inch drywall screws.

SAFETY ALERT

SUPPORT THE LID
The lid for a window seat is large and heavy enough to hurt someone if it accidentally slams shut. Protect yourself—and others—from possible injury by installing a lid support. The support shown here automatically locks and holds the lid in place when you open it, and is easy to install. There are several other supports in the hardware aisle of your home center. Pick one that works best for the window seat you build.

2

ATTACH FILLERS
The assembled seat has lots of exposed plywood edges that you want to cover. Cut pieces to fit across the back, front, and sides of the plywood box. Glue and nail them in place.

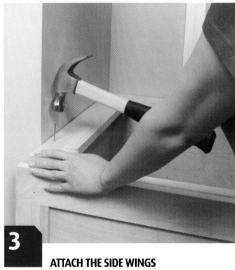

3

ATTACH THE SIDE WINGS
You will need to attach three more pieces of to create an opening for the lid. The first are two pieces about 3 inches wide that go against the side walls. They will keep the lid, which fits between them, from getting close to the wall and scratching it. Cut the wings so they reach from the back wall to the frame.

4

ATTACH THE REAR SUPPORT
The lid needs a lip to rest on in the back. Cut a piece of 1× stock about 2 inches wide, and screw it in place so that about 1 inch extends into the opening.

4

TRIMWORK PROJECTS

Installing the window seat *(continued)*

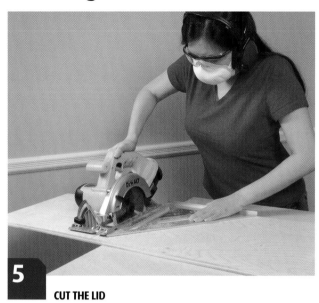

5 CUT THE LID
The lid comes from the same piece of plywood as the panels. Lay out the lid so that there's a gap of about ⅛ inch between it and each of the side wings. Rip it to a width that leaves the top edge of the front frame exposed, and then crosscut it to length.

6 ATTACH THE HINGES
Screw a piano hinge to the lid. Put the lid in place, and screw the hinge to the window seat.

7 APPLY BASEBOARD
Apply baseboard across the front of the seat, mitering the ends. A short section of plywood is visible when the box is viewed from the side. Cover it with wood, and nail baseboard to the side. Nail quarter round to the baseboard.

8 APPLY MOLDING TO THE LID
Nail a piece of molding to the edge of the lid and to the side wings. Choose a molding that is wider than ¾ inch, so that it can hold the cushions in place. Paint the seat, and cover the lid with cushions.

4

TRIMWORK PROJECTS

Installing gingerbread trim on a porch

PROJECT DETAILS

SKILLS: Measuring and layout; using power tools including paint sprayer; working at heights
PROJECT: Installing 40 feet of gingerbread trim

TIME TO COMPLETE

EXPERIENCED: 3 hrs.
HANDY: 4 hrs.
NOVICE: 5 hrs.
Time will vary depending on the size of the porch and complexity of the trim you choose.

STUFF YOU'LL NEED

TOOLS: Ladder; combination square; tape measure; drill and bits; screwdriver; spray painter
MATERIALS: Gingerbread trim, including rails, spandrels, and brackets

The Victorians loved to dress up everything with frills. In part they did it because they could—for the first time mass production made fancy trim available to the middle class. But even if they overdid it, they often did it right, too, and nowhere is it more obvious than the gingerbread trim that adorns the Victorian porch. Much of the same trim is available today, whether you're replacing trim removed by an overzealous (or lazy) painter, or want to add charm to a tract house. Most of the trim falls into one of four categories. Headers are scrollwork designs that mount over the window. Rails hang between porch posts and are made of turned spindles running between two strips of wood. Brackets either support rails or stand on their own on porch posts. Spandrels are a combination of rails, brackets, and other fancy details and also mount between porch posts.

Since no two porches are exactly the same, spandrels and rails are tailor-made to fit the porch they're intended for. As a result they're special-order items, which can't be returned. Measure carefully—and then measure again—before you place your order.

4

TRIMWORK PROJECTS

Using a paint sprayer

1

POUR IN THE PAINT

You'll need a good exterior latex paint—a gallon is more than enough for most gingerbread jobs. Pour the paint into a five-gallon bucket attached to the sprayer.

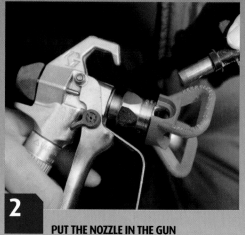

2

PUT THE NOZZLE IN THE GUN

The size of the hole in the nozzle depends on the material you're spraying. Tell the people at the rental counter what kind of paint you're spraying and have them select the proper size. Slip the nozzle in its hole, and tighten the nut against it.

3

PRIME THE MACHINE

The compressor in the machine is filled with air at first. Set the control knob to "prime" and flip the switch to turn it on. The compressor will blow the air into the paint bucket, causing the paint to bubble. When the bubbling stops, turn the control knob to "spray."

4

SPRAY PAINT INTO THE BUCKET

The hose is still filled with air, which will cause the spray gun to sputter. Spray paint into the bucket until the sputtering stops.

Nozzle set to spray up and down

Nozzle set to spray side to side

5

SET THE NOZZLE

A spray gun shoots paint in a flat, fan-shaped pattern. You can turn the nozzle to control whether the fan is upright or horizontal. For spraying in a motion that travels from side to side, turn the nozzle so the fan is upright. For spraying in a motion that goes up and down, set the nozzle for a horizontal pattern.

Preparing to install

1 TEST FIT THE PIECES

Gingerbread is usually a special-order item and is tailor-made to your measurements. Test-fit each piece to make sure it will fit. Open-ended pieces, like this rail, can usually be cut to fit. Spandrels, which have an end piece that screws to the post, can be cut a fraction of an inch shorter, but will fall apart if they are too small. Check with the supplier if you have any questions about the fit of your gingerbread.

2 SAND THE SURFACE

Even though the surface may appear to be smooth, sand the surface with 180- or 220-grit sandpaper to remove any fuzziness on the surface. Exterior surfaces take an extraordinary amount of abuse from the elements. Your new trim will survive longer if you take a little extra time with the prep before installing.

3 SPRAY PRIMER AND FINISH COATS

Like any paint job this one requires a primer to seal the wood. Turn the nozzle so the fan-shape spray pattern is upright. Hold the gun about 12 inches from what you're going to spray and off to the side. Pull the trigger and move the gun along a path parallel to the surface you're spraying. On short pieces you can make the motions with your arm, but don't swing your arm in an arc. On longer pieces hold the gun steady and walk to move the gun along the surface. To minimize drips stop spraying when you reach the end of the piece. Go back to the beginning and start spraying again.

Installing the rails

1 FIND THE CENTER OF THE POST

Measure to find the center of the post, and make a mark. Make a mark on the center of the rail too.

2 DRILL HOLES FOR THE SCREWS

Screwing the trim in place makes it easy to take it down when you need to paint it. Drill clearance holes for screws the same diameter as the screw shank in the rails. Spacing for the holes depends on the weight of the rails. The holes in this rail were spaced about every 2 feet.

Some assembly required

Longer pieces may be too big to make all at once or too long to ship. If so, they'll arrive as two pieces, with dowels in the end of one piece and holes for the dowels in the other piece. Put glue on the dowels and in the holes, and slide the pieces together. Tie the pieces together and set them aside for at least 30 minutes to let the glue set. When you hang the trim, screw both halves in place so that you don't have to count on the glue alone.

Installing the rails *(continued)*

3

CLAMP SUPPORTS TO THE POSTS

Even if you have someone helping you, positioning the rails can be tricky. Clamp a 2×4 to each post so that you can rest the rails on it as you work.

What if the rails are too long?

If the rails are too long, you can cut them to fit. To lay out the cut, put the rail flat on the 2×4s you clamped to the post. Center the rail so that the overhang is equal on each side, and then trace along the 2×4 with a knife to make a mark on the rail. Cut along the line on a power miter box or table saw. If you use the table saw, use the jig described in Making a crosscut jig on page 50 and have someone help support the piece as you cut.

Drilling for screws

Clearance hole

Pilot hole

When you screw two pieces of wood together you should drill holes in each piece for the screw. Drill a clearance hole the size of the screw shank in the first piece; drill a slightly smaller hole in the piece you're screwing into. The best way to get the right size hole is to trust your eyes. Hold a drill bit in front of the screw as shown. If the bit just barely blocks out sight of the screw, as shown in the top photograph, it's the right size for a clearance hole. If the full width of the threads is visible behind the bit, as in the bottom photograph, it's the right size for a pilot hole.

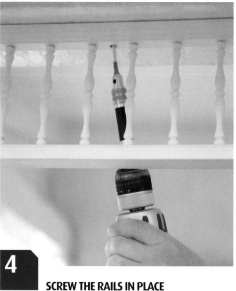

4

SCREW THE RAILS IN PLACE

Put the rails in place, aligning the center marks on the rails with the center marks on the posts. Use the clearance holes as a guide to drill pilot holes in the porch that are slightly smaller than the screw. Screw the rails in place with steel screws to cut threads in the wood; remove them once they're in and replace with brass screws, which won't rust. Brass is soft and the heads may strip if you don't drive steel screws first.

5

SCREW THE BRACKETS IN PLACE

Predrill clearance holes in the bracket. Hold it against the bottom of the rail, and drill pilot holes in the post. Screw it in place with brass screws.

4

TRIMWORK PROJECTS

Installing spandrels

A spandrel is fancier than a simple rail and is made up of several architectural elements. Because it's made to fit in a given space, it should fit snugly when you slide it into place. Drill holes for the screws with a combination bit that drills both clearance and pilot holes. Screw it in place by first using a steel screw to cut threads. Remove the steel screw and replace with a brass screw.

Installing headers

1 MARK THE CENTER OF THE WINDOW

A header is a piece of trim that mounts over a window. Mark the center of the window and of the header, and align the two when you install the header.

2 INSTALL THE HEADER

If you're installing the header in wood trim or siding, you can nail or screw it in place. If you're installing a header over stucco, use construction adhesive.

Making columns

 PROJECT DETAILS

SKILLS: Measuring and layout; using power tools; using power nailer
PROJECT: Building a pair of 8-foot columns

 TIME TO COMPLETE

EXPERIENCED: 4 hrs.
HANDY: 6 hrs.
NOVICE: 8 hrs.

STUFF YOU'LL NEED

TOOLS: Tape measure; work bench, work platforms, or saw horses; router and fence; ¾-inch cove bit; finish nailer; combination square; compound miter saw; utility knife; level; pneumatic nailer
MATERIALS: 1× pine; baseboard (WM618); base cap (WM163); 1- and 2- inch finish nails to fit finish nailer; construction adhesive

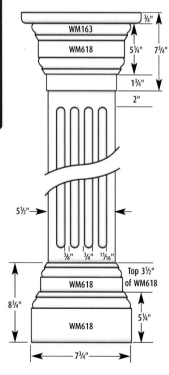

Columns dress up a doorway or a bookcase and can even stand on their own as a decorative element on a wall. But they're actually not columns at all. The vertical elements are called pilasters and the horizontal element is called a pediment. Together the pilasters and pediment are referred to as a surround.

Because this project relies on commercially available moldings, you can easily build a pair in a day. Be prepared to master the miter in the process—each column has 10 miter joints in it, and many of the pieces are small. Two vitally important tools for this project are a power miter saw and a pneumatic nailing gun.

The power miter saw assures true 45-degree angles. You'll want a compound miter saw: It handles the wide pieces shown here and simplifies layout by letting you lay out cuts on the back of the stock as well as on the front.

A nail gun lets you nail the small pieces in place quickly and easily. Of course, you can use a hammer and nails but if you do, prepare for pieces sliding out of position or splitting as you nail them. A nail gun will make the job easier, especially if you're doing several doors.

What's the proper proportion?

The column for this project is illustrated at left but there are no firm rules for determining the proper proportions for a door surround. There are, however, some basic guidelines.

The top should align width some horizontal line in the room—this surround was designed so the capital could be carried across the top of the door. If you wanted to incorporate a column into the faux framing that appears in some of the column pictures, you might consider a smaller column width for a more delicate look.

For a longer column, stick with a 1×6; anything wider will overpower the room; anything narrower will look skinny. Once you pick the width of the column, in this case a 1×6, the length of each piece of molding you apply is predetermined. Use the same molding on the top that you use on the bottom; if you're going to introduce a second type of molding, have it repeat a detail in the first type.

The base of the column should be taller than the capital or top to keep the column from looking top-heavy. Our base is one inch higher than the capital.

The stock molding chosen for the surround is very common and seen all around the country in Traditional homes. But you can also experiment with different looks. Get ideas from architectural magazines and period homes. Buy several samples and try them out. Lay the boards on

a workbench, cut a few pieces of molding and slide them around until you find a combination and sense of proportion you like, then tack them in place and see how everything looks. When you're satisfied use the assembly as a pattern to build the real thing.

Experiment with different molding combinations until you find a look for the columns you like.

Making the fluted pilaster

1   ROUT THE OUTER FLUTES

This column begins with a pilaster, a 1×6 into which you rout grooves called flutes with a ¾-inch cove bit. Draw pencil lines on the wood to show where the flutes should start and stop (2 inches from the base and top). Clamp stop blocks at each end so you won't go over the line. Check your layout and set the router fence to rout one of the outer flutes. Guide the router first along one side of the pilaster, and then along the other, to rout the two outer flutes.

2   ROUT THE INNER FLUTES

Check your layout again and reset the fence to rout one of the two inner flutes. Guide the router fence along one side, and then the other side, of the pilaster to rout the inner flutes

Routing flutes

You rout flutes with a cove bit in a handheld router, using a fence to guide the router along the edge of the pilaster. Fence attachments are usually sold separately and one size doesn't fit all. If you can't find a fence made for your router, contact the manufacturer.

The fence usually slides back and forth on rods that fit in the router base. Slide the fence and lock it in place, positioning it to rout a flute on your column. Test the setup on a scrap—you can even use the back of the pilaster if the flutes aren't too deep.

Start the flute by tilting the router up while keeping the fence against the edge of the wood, as shown. Don't try to hit the line that marks the point where the flutes start. Bring the bit down an inch or so in front of the line, and then back up until the cut just bumps into the line. Change direction again, and rout the length of the flute. Stop when the cut hits the line at the other end of the column; back up, turn off the router, and wait until the bit stops spinning before you lift it out of the groove.

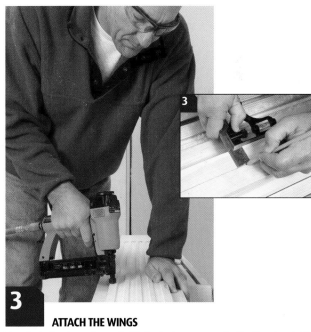

3   ATTACH THE WINGS

The pilaster has two wings nailed to the back—one on each side. The wings build up the thickness of the column and move it away from the door, so that the moldings that wrap around the pilaster won't interfere with the door. Draw a line on the back of each wing to help position it, and then nail the wings in place. The wings measure 2¾ inches with 1½ inches of the stock visible.

Installing the baseboard moldings

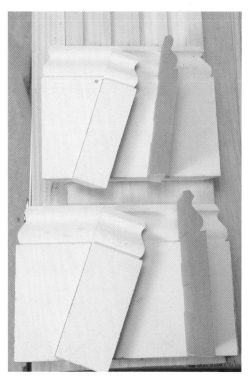

There are two tiers of baseboard attached to the bottom of the pilaster. The upper tier is applied directly to the pilaster; the lower tier overlaps the upper, and is nailed to it. The parts of each tier are mitered so that the baseboard can wrap around the pilaster. You'll be cutting each of these parts, so it helps to get an idea of what each is. Pictured above are the six pieces used to make the bottom of the pilaster. The total height of the column base including both tiers is 8¾ inches.

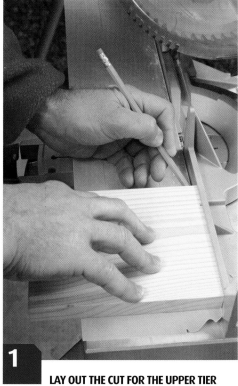

1 **LAY OUT THE CUT FOR THE UPPER TIER FRONT PIECE**

Start the upper tier with the front piece of baseboard. The inside face of the piece is the same width as the pilaster. To lay out the width cut a miter on one end of the baseboard. Align a cutoff from the pilaster with the miter, and trace along the other edge. The line marks the location of the miter.

2 **CUT AND NAIL THE UPPER TIER FRONT PIECE**

Put the piece you're cutting on a compound miter saw, and turn the saw to cut at a 45-degree angle. Cut along the pencil line and nail the piece in place. Note that since the baseboard is only 5¼ inches tall, the top tier will not run all the way to the bottom of the base.

4

TRIMWORK PROJECTS

3
MEASURE AND LAY OUT THE SIDE PIECES

Put a combination square on the front piece, and set it so the ruler rests on the wing. Miter two pieces of baseboard, one along the left edge and one along the right edge. Trace along the miters with the square, as shown in the inset, to lay out the length of each piece.

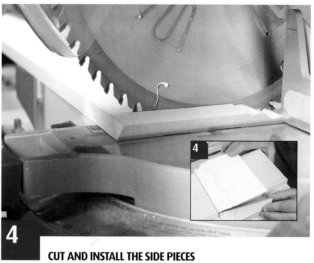

4
CUT AND INSTALL THE SIDE PIECES

Make a square cut along the line you drew, and nail the pieces in place.

5
LAY OUT THE LOWER TIER BASEBOARD

Miter one end of a piece of baseboard, and lay it on top of the upper tier, as shown. Put a utility knife in place along the side of the upper tier, and use it to make a mark on the back of the lower tier baseboard. Miter the baseboard at the mark. Lay out and cut the side pieces as before.

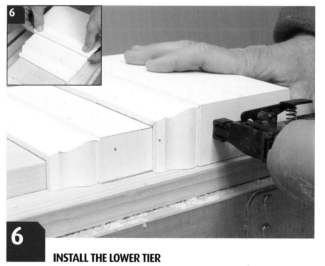

6
INSTALL THE LOWER TIER

Nail the front piece to the upper tier, and nail the side pieces in place. If you're using a hammer it is a good idea to pre-drill before you nail. The piece being nailed in place in the photo above is $1\frac{7}{8}$ inches, but lay it out as in step three.

To keep small pieces from flying away while cutting, put a strip of double-stick tape on the saw table.

Installing the capital moldings

Getting to know capital moldings

There are three tiers to the capital at the top of this column. All three sit on a blank filler piece that helps make the assembly thicker and more dramatic. Pictured (from the lower left) are the preprimed left and right sides of the lower tier, both of which rest on the front of the lower tier. The unprimed left and right sides of the second tier sit just below the front of the second tier. The front of the third tier is immediately above, and the sides of the third tier are above it. Note that the left side of the second and third tier have parallel miters that fit into neighboring moldings.

1 **PUT IN THE FILLER**

Cut a filler piece of 1×6 to size, and nail it in place so the top and sides are flush with the top and sides of the pilaster.

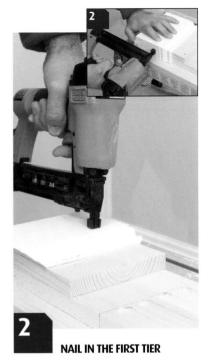

2 **NAIL IN THE FIRST TIER**

Lay out the first tier the same way you laid out the upper tier of the base, and nail the parts in place.

3 **ATTACH THE FRONT OF THE SECOND TIER**

Lay out the front molding of the second tier the same way you laid out the lower tier of the base. Miter one end, put it in place, and mark the back with a knife. Miter along the line, and nail it in place.

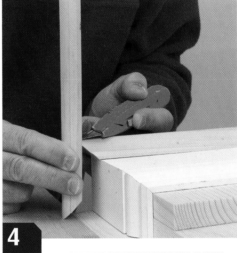

4 **LAY OUT THE OUTSIDE MOLDING OF THE SECOND TIER**

The two sides of the second tier are different from each other. The side that faces the door is mitered so that the molding can continue across the door. The other side molding butts into the wing. Lay out the piece that butts into the wing first. Start by mitering one end. Then put the miter point down on the wing. (If the wing is too narrow, as it is here, place a piece the same thickness next to it, and rest the point on it.) Trace along the installed piece to make a mark on the back of the side piece, and make a square cut on the line to cut the piece to length.

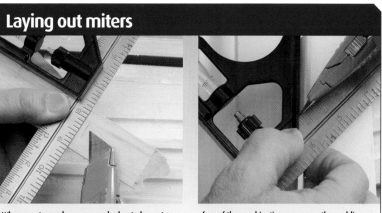

When you trace along a curved edge to lay out a cut, you'll get a curved line. Slide a combination square along the piece until it touches the surface of the curve that will give you the longest piece, and then make a straight knife mark along the square. Roll the piece on edge, put the 45-degree face of the combination square on the molding, and align the ruler with the mark on the back. Trace along the ruler to make a mark on the edge you're cutting, no matter how narrow the edge of the molding may be.

5 LAY OUT THE MOLDING THAT FACES THE DOOR

Lay out this molding in much the same way you laid out the other side. Miter one end and put the tip on the wing, or on a temporary piece the same thickness as the wing. Make a mark on the front of the piece to mark how long the front of the molding will be. Miter the piece, cutting a miter parallel to the existing miter.

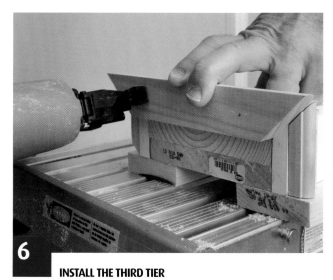

6 INSTALL THE THIRD TIER

Make the molding for the third tier by routing a ⅜-inch roundover on the edge with the router table. Layout and installation are exactly the same as in the second tier. Cut the pieces to length, and nail them to the top of the column.

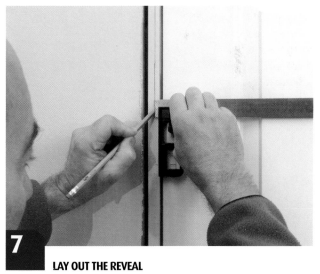

7 LAY OUT THE REVEAL

When all is said in done, columns like these are just fancy door trim. Like other door trim there is a slight space, called a reveal, between the edge of the door jamb and the edge of the column. Set your combination square so that ¼ inch of the blade extends beyond the head, and trace along the jamb to lay out the reveal.

Installing the capital moldings *(continued)*

8

INSTALL THE COLUMNS

Hold a column against the reveal, and make sure it's plumb with a level—it's better to have the reveal a bit wider at one end than it is to have the column out of plumb. Apply construction adhesive to the back, and nail the wings to the jamb and wall.

9

INSTALL THE HEADER FOR THE PEDIMENT

Cut a piece of 1× to fit between the two columns, and nail it in place over the door. In this case the header is the width of the fluted piece plus the wings, making it 8⅝ inches.

10

PUT A PIECE OF MOLDING ALONG THE TOP

Place a third-tier molding along the top of the header, resting on a spacer, as shown. Trace along the miters in the third tier of the column to lay out miters on the molding. Cut the miters, and nail the molding to the top of the header.

4

TRIMWORK PROJECTS

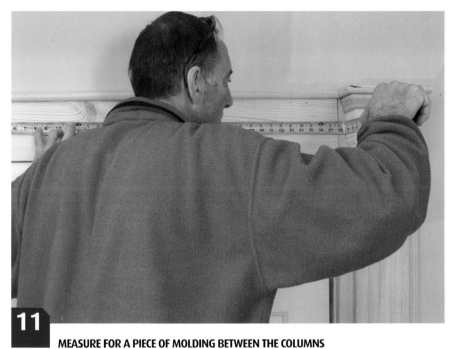

11

MEASURE FOR A PIECE OF MOLDING BETWEEN THE COLUMNS
Measure the distance between the first-tier moldings. Miter a piece of second-tier molding to this length.

12

TEST FIT THE MOLDING AND NAIL IT INTO PLACE
Slip it into place and nail it to the header molding. Fill nail holes with wood putty; then sand and clean up the molding edges. Seal the wood with a wood sealer; then prime and paint.

▶ Most of the trimwork techniques discussed in this book, including use of power tools and combining custom moldings with commercial varieties, come together to create this Traditional pilaster.

General carpentry

General carpentry is the nuts and bolts of building a home. General carpentry is studs, joists, rafters, roof, and subfloor. If you're really ambitious, it's also the nuts and bolts of remodeling—cutting through a wall and framing an opening for a new door; installing a window; putting up drywall to finish the job.

Some of the work is common sense; some of it is even commonplace. But don't doubt for a moment that working with 2×4s can be rewarding—especially if you've got the skills to finish the job. Building a header and framing a window may seem mundane, but structure emerges quickly out of that pile of lumber delivered from the home center and it's satisfying to walk through a series of stud walls, imagining your new room.

Beyond basic framing

But even if you know your way around construction, a great deal of general carpentry isn't commonplace. Installing the details that make your home special require some careful planning. In this section you'll see how to install a bay window, build an archway, cut pockets for hinges, hang a slab door, and install a pocket door for a closet.

Chapter 5 highlights

Meeting the carpenter's challenge

The finish carpenter's work is always there for the world to see—and a badly mitered joint can haunt you forever. General carpentry demands its own set of skills, not the least of which is the courage it takes to cut a hole in the walls of your home, and the assurance it takes to rebuild them.

Remember, when you alter or add to the structure of your home you will need to make sure you're complying with local building codes. They exist to guard your safety by making sure approved materials are used and installed properly. Check with your local building inspector and if you need a permit, get one. Better to be safe than sorry.

Framing a door

Y ou'll need two things if you're planning on putting in a new doorway: You'll need the guts it takes to cut a hole in your wall, and you'll need the patience it requires to put in a new door.

Putting the door in the opening is covered in Installing a prehung interior door, pages 194–197. A door that isn't prehung is called a slab door; hanging a slab door is covered in Hanging a slab door, pages 204–207. This project tells you how to get ready for the door by cutting a hole in the wall and by framing the new opening. In simplest terms you'll cut away all the drywall or plaster up to the first stud on either side of the opening. Once that's done you'll remove the studs you exposed, and then frame the new opening. The framing consists of two "king" studs that run from the soleplate to the top plate; two slightly shorter "jack" studs are nailed to the king studs and support the "header" above the door.

The size and shape of the header depends on the wall the door will be in. Load-bearing walls require a header that is essentially a built-up beam. Non-load-bearing walls have a much lighter-duty header. All exterior walls are load bearing, as are many interior walls. For tips on telling them apart, see Supporting load-bearing walls, page 185.

The wall shown here is a non-load-bearing interior wall. Information on framing load-bearing walls and on cutting through the siding on exterior walls is located in special boxes throughout the directions.

Working with headers

The header sizes given on page 187 reflect common building practice, but don't apply in all situations. They assume, for example, that the house was properly built in the first place, and that no modifications have been made since the house was built. The addition of a slate roof, a hot tub, or any significant amount of weight can turn a non-load-bearing wall into a load-bearing one, or require an oversize header in a load-bearing wall. Poorly done alterations made before you begin the job could have robbed a load-bearing wall of its load-bearing capacity, or put an improper amount of weight on a wall not built to support it. Any of these situations could result in the collapse of the wall you're working on. When you're removing studs in a wall it isn't safe to assume anything. Have a structural engineer look at the house, and advise you about installing proper support during construction and about proper header construction.

Cutting the opening

1 **REMOVE THE BASEBOARD**
Score along the top of the baseboard with a utility knife to break any paint binding the wall and baseboard together. Pry off the baseboard with a pry bar, protecting the wall with a scrap of wood.

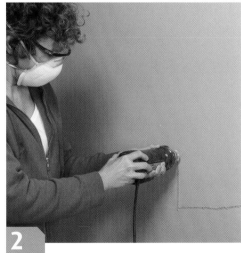

2 **LAY OUT THE DOOR AND FIND THE STUDS**
Pick the spot on the wall where you'll put the door, and draw it in with the help of a level. Framing requires that you remove drywall to the first stud beyond the door. Find the stud by driving the bit of a drywall router into the line you drew, and then moving it away from the door until you hit something solid. Rout along the entire length of the stud. Repeat on the other side of the door.

3 **REMOVE THE DRYWALL**

Use a flat pry bar to pry away a corner of the cutout drywall, then pull away large chunks with your hands. Once all the drywall has been removed, pry out any nails. Remove and carefully roll up any insulation.

Cutting and removing plaster

If you have an older home with plaster walls, cutting the opening is more involved than cutting through drywall. Start by drilling holes to find the studs that are on the outside edge of the opening, and use a level to mark the edge on the wall. Cut along the line with a circular saw that has a masonry blade in it. This creates a tremendous amount of dust, but cuts through the plaster without breaking it. Cut along the edges of studs you'll remove with a reciprocating saw, which raises less dust. Pry some of the lath loose with a pry bar and remove the rest of it by hand.

4 **REMOVE THE STUDS**

Remove all the studs you exposed when removing the drywall. (Leave any studs covered by drywall in place.) If you're working on an interior wall, use a reciprocating saw to cut through the nails that go into the top and bottom of the studs, and then pull the stud loose. If you're working on an exterior wall, especially one with plywood sheathing, it may be easier to make a diagonal cut in the middle of the stud, and then knock the stud loose, as explained in Framing a window, pages 218–224.

Supporting load-bearing walls

If the wall you're putting the door in is a load-bearing wall, you'll need to support it while you work. You can't tell a load-bearing wall by looking at it from the outside, but it's fairly easy to tell once you know what you're looking for. All exterior walls are load-bearing. Any wall with a double top plate—two 2×4s across the top—is load-bearing. A wall with another wall above or below it on another floor is load-bearing. And if there's a wooden beam or I-beam directly below the wall on the floor below it, the wall is load-bearing.

The quickest and most reliable way to provide support is with a floor jack and some 2×s, as explained in Framing a window, pages 218–224.

 SAFETY ALERT

Wear a dust mask and safety glasses when removing drywall or plaster.

Seal the room

Cutting a hole in a wall creates dust, dust, and more dust. Tape plastic sheeting over doorways to keep dust out of the rest of the house.

 TOOL SAVVY

FINDING STUDS

A drywall router makes quick work of finding studs and cutting through the drywall, but you can do the job without one. Use an electronic stud finder, or drive nails or drill holes until you hit a stud. Push the sharp end of a drywall saw into the wall on the edge of the stud nearest the door. Guide the saw along the stud until you've cut along its entire length.

5

GENERAL CARPENTRY

Making a non-load-bearing header

WORK SMARTER

1 LAY OUT THE STUDS ON THE SOLEPLATE
Measure and mark the edges of the opening on the soleplate. Draw a second line 1½ inches farther away from the center of the opening than the first line. Moving in the same direction, draw a third line 1½ inches away from the second. The jack stud, which supports the framing that goes across the top of the door, will go between the first two lines. The king stud, which supports the jack stud, will go between the second and third lines.

2 PUT IN THE KING STUDS
Put a stud on one of the marks you made for the king stud, and plumb it with a 6-foot level. Toenail the stud in place. Repeat on the other side of the opening.

3 ATTACH THE JACK STUDS
Measure from the finished floor and mark the top of the rough opening (it will be ½ inch above the top of the door jamb) on the king studs. Measure from the soleplate to the marks, and cut a jack stud to each of the measured lengths. Nail the studs in place by driving a pair of 16d nails through the jack stud every 16 inches or so.

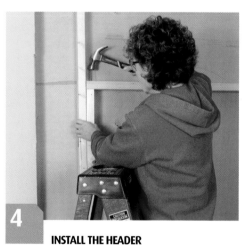

4 INSTALL THE HEADER
On non-load-bearing walls, the header is a 2×4 laid flat on the jack studs. Cut the 2×4 to length, put it in place, and nail it to the jack studs with 16d nails.

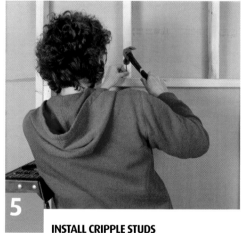

5 INSTALL CRIPPLE STUDS
Cut short studs, called cripple studs, to fit between the header and the top plate, and space them 16 inches on center. Toenail or nail up through the header to attach the bottom, and toenail the upper ends into the top plate.

Installing a load-bearing header

If you're putting an opening in a load-bearing wall, you'll need to build a load-bearing header. The header is a layer of ½-inch plywood sandwiched between two 2×s. The exact size of the header depends on the size of the opening.

Conform to local codes

The chart below gives you standard header sizes, but codes vary, so check with your local building authority and bring in a structural engineer to inspect the structure and provide you with specifications for the header that will guarantee a safe installation that meets building codes. See the introduction to this project on page 184 for more information on dealing with load-bearing walls.

1 BUILD THE HEADER

Cut the 2×s to the length given in the chart. Cut the plywood to width and length, and nail all the pieces together.

2 INSTALL THE HEADER

Rest the header on the jack studs, and toenail a 16d nail through the header and into the king studs to fasten it. The number of nails depends on the size of the header: Divide it into imaginary 2×3s and drive a single nail into each. A header made of two 2×6s requires four nails at each end.

Header size

HEADER MATERIAL	MAXIMUM OPENING	
	HEADER SUPPORTS ONE FLOOR, CEILING, AND ROOF	HEADER SUPPORTS CEILING AND ROOF ONLY
2×4 and ½" plywood	3'	3'6"
2×6 and ½" plywood	5'	6"
2×8 and ½" plywood	7'	8'
2×10 and ½" plywood	8'	10'
2×12 and ½" plywood	9'	12'

3 INSTALL CRIPPLE STUDS

Cut short studs, called cripples, to fill the opening between the header and top plate. Put one on each side of the opening, and space them 16 inches on center throughout the opening.

Finishing the opening

1

CUT AND REMOVE THE SOLEPLATE
Use a reciprocating saw to cut through the soleplate at either end. Pry away the soleplate, and remove any nails.

2

PUT IN A DRYWALL NAILER
Screw or nail a 2×4 to the studs that are on the outside edges of the opening. These studs provide support and a nailing surface for the edge of the new drywall. Attach the drywall to the nailers and the studs with #8 1¼-inch drywall screws.

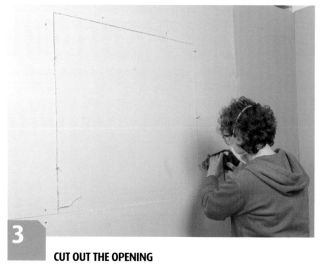

3

CUT OUT THE OPENING
Rout or cut around the inside of the opening. A drywall router makes short work of trimming out the opening. Wear ear protection and a dust mask when using a drywall router.

4

REMOVE THE SCRAP AND TAPE THE NEW JOINTS
After cutting out the opening remove the scrap and finish the new drywall by taping the seams and applying joint compound, as explained in Installing drywall, beginning on page 236.

Building an archway

PROJECT DETAILS

SKILLS: Measuring and layout; using power tools

PROJECT: Building an arch in an existing wall

TIME TO COMPLETE

EXPERIENCED: 6 hrs.
HANDY: 8 hrs.
NOVICE: 10 hrs.

STUFF YOU'LL NEED

TOOLS: Chalk line and marker; pry bar; drywall router or drywall saw; reciprocating saw; combination square; hammer; 6-foot level; clamps; ladder; paint roller and pan; drill and screwdriver bit; drywall knives; surform plane

MATERIALS: ½-inch drywall; ¼-inch drywall; flexible corner bead; metal corner bead; mesh drywall tape; setting-type drywall compound mixed from powder; drywall screws

Building an arch is probably the first job you'll do that makes drywalling fun. (There are those who say it's the only job that makes drywalling fun.) You'll have to do all the regular stuff—screwing, taping, and sanding—but you'll also get to bend drywall.

There are three ways to bend drywall: You can simply push ¼-inch drywall into place and screw it to the framing; for a sharper diameter (up to 36 inches), wet the drywall first; and for very small diameters, score the back surface perpendicular to the bend at 1-inch intervals to ease stress on the face of the drywall.

Of course an archway requires framing that's slightly different from the norm—you can't put a curved piece against a square header and expect it to work. To make the header, you'll cut two pieces of ¾-inch plywood to the radius of the arch, and then screw them to the framing on either side of the door. Once you've prepared the drywall and the opening, installing the bent drywall is pretty much like installing any other drywall. But the vinyl corner bead is a happy surprise—it bends like a slinky until you staple it in place.

This project shows you how to cut an opening and build a 40-inch diameter arch in an existing wall. If you're building the wall from scratch, however, the technique is pretty much the same. Frame as you normally would, and then start with Making an arched header, on page 191.

Preparing the wall

1
LAY OUT THE ARCH
Find an arch size and opening that works for you by using a chalk line, a screw, and a pencil to lay out the arch on the wall. Drive the screw in the wall at a point that you think will be both the bottom of the arch and center of the doorway. Experiment with different-size arcs; try the screw at different heights and choose an arc that gives you enough headroom to walk through the arch comfortably. Write down the measurements when you find the right combination.

2
REMOVE THE BASEBOARD
Once you've settled on the right size and location for the archway, you need to remove part of the existing wall. Start with the baseboard, running a knife along the top to cut through any caulk or paint that's holding the baseboard to the wall. Pry off the board with a pry bar, protecting the wall from damage with a piece of wood.

3
CUT THROUGH THE DRYWALL
Cut through the drywall with a drywall saw or drywall router. You'll need to remove drywall to the first stud on either side of the opening. Start at the line you drew marking the outline of the archway, and cut away from the arch until you hit a stud. Cut along the stud from ceiling to floor.

5

GENERAL CARPENTRY

Preparing the wall *(continued)*

4

REMOVE THE DRYWALL
Pry the drywall loose with a pry bar, and then remove the rest of it by hand.

5

CUT THROUGH THE STUDS
Cut through the nails that hold the studs in place at the top and bottom of the wall. Make the cut with a reciprocating saw that has a demolition blade, which is designed for cutting through both wood and nails.

6

REMOVE THE STUDS
Pull the studs out of the openings. If the wall is drywall, the stud will still be screwed to the other side of the wall, but it will still pull loose easily. If the wall is plaster and lath, cut through the plaster on the other side first so that you don't crack plaster beyond the area you're going to remove.

Framing the new opening

1

LAY OUT THE NEW FRAMING
Draw lines on the soleplate marking the outside of the opening. Draw a second line, ½ inch farther from the center of the opening, marking the inside face of the drywall. Draw a third line 1½ inches farther yet from the center and make an "x" marking where you'll put jack stud that supports the framing for the arch. Draw a fourth line another 1½ inches from the center and make a second "x" marking where the king stud that supports the jack stud will be.

2

INSTALL THE KING STUDS
Put in the king studs first. Cut a 2×4 to fit between the top plate and the soleplate. Put it in place over the "x" you made for it, and plumb it with a 6-foot level. Toenail the stud to each plate.

3

INSTALL THE JACK STUDS
Look at the measurements you made earlier, and make a mark on the king stud showing where the bottom of the arch will be. Measure and cut two 2×4s to this length. Clamp them to the king studs and nail them in place.

Making an arched header

1 LAY OUT THE ARCH

Cut two pieces of ¾-inch plywood long enough to reach across the opening and wide enough to reach from the top of the jack stud to the top plate. Drive a screw in the center near the bottom, and draw the arc you settled on in step one, page 189.

2 CUT THE ARCH

Cut along the line you drew with a jigsaw. For the sake of a smooth arc, pick one side of the line, and cut along the edge, especially if you used a wide marker to draw the line. Repeat on the second piece of plywood.

3 SMOOTH THE ARCH

Temporarily screw the arches together, and look for spots where the curves are slightly different. Remove the high spots with a Surform plane that has a round-bottomed blade.

WORK SMARTER

GET A TIGHT FIT

Test fit both pieces of plywood and the spacers in the opening, and check to see if the assembly is flush with the edge of the king stud. If it juts out, the drywall will too. Cut the spacers a bit narrower if necessary.

4 PUT THE FIRST ARCH IN PLACE

Cut two 3-inch-wide spacers. Rest one of the plywood arches on the jack studs and push it against the back wall. Put the spacers against the arch, and nail them to the king stud.

5 INSTALL THE SECOND ARCH

Put the second arch against the spacers, and nail or screw the arch to the spacers.

SAFETY ALERT

Wear eye protection and a dust mask when working with drywall. Wear hearing protection if using a drywall router.

5

GENERAL CARPENTRY

Making an arched header (continued)

WORK SMARTER

MINIMIZE TAPING
You can minimize the amount of taping you'll have to do by covering the opening with two sheets of drywall, one above the other. Put in the upper piece first, screw it in place, and then put in the lower piece.

6 INSTALL DRYWALL AND ROUT THE ARCH
Cover the opening with sheets of drywall and screw it in place. Guide a drywall router along the jack studs and along the plywood to cut out the arch. Rout out the arch on the other side of the wall too. Screw the drywall firmly to the jack studs and header on both sides of the wall.

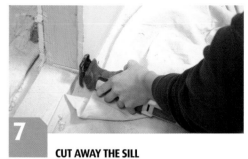

7 CUT AWAY THE SILL
Remove the sill from the old wall by cutting through it with a demolition blade in a reciprocating saw.

Drywalling the curve of the arch

Minimum bend

The minimum radius for wet bending drywall is between 20 inches and 30 inches, depending on whom you ask. You can make even tighter arches, however, by slicing through the back of the drywall, as explained in Making tight bends on page 193.

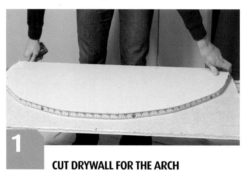

1 CUT DRYWALL FOR THE ARCH
Measure the cutout from the header to see how long the arch is and measure the width of the wall to see how thick it is. Cut strips about ¼ inch narrower than the wall and about 12 inches longer than the arch. If you're using the wet drywall method, you'll need two strips. If you're using the dry kerf method, see Making tight bends on page 193.

2 WET THE DRYWALL
Wet the face of the drywall that will be compressed—the face that will be exposed in this case—with water. You'll need about 30 ounces for an entire sheet of drywall, or just under ½ cup for a strip long enough to cover an arch with a 2-foot radius. Apply by dipping a clean paint roller into the water, and rolling it along the drywall.

3 STACK THE PIECES TO BE BENT
Stack the pieces you're bending together, wet face to wet face. Cover with plastic, and let them sit for at least an hour.

4 SCREW THE FIRST LAYER IN PLACE
When the pieces have sat for at least an hour, remove one. Push it gently into the arch, bending it to shape as you do. Screw the drywall into the plywood starting in the center of the arch and working toward the edges.

5

GENERAL CARPENTRY

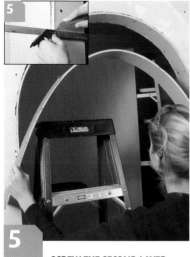

5

SCREW THE SECOND LAYER IN PLACE

Repeat with the second layer, screwing through the first layer and into the plywood. Put a combination square against the wall at the end of the arch. Guide a knife or drywall saw against it to cut through both layers of drywall.

6

SCREW THE LEGS IN PLACE

Measure the distance from the bottom of the arch to the floor, and cut two pieces of ½-inch drywall to this length. Screw both in place.

7

APPLY MESH TAPE AND BEAD

Tape over the seam between the arch and the legs with mesh tape, which is stronger than paper tape. Staple vinyl flex bead to the arch and adjoining wall surface. Nail metal corner bead to the straight section.

8

APPLY JOINT COMPOUND

Apply joint compound over both the arch and the legs. Mesh tape requires a "setting" compound that you mix from powder. Mix the powder with water, load a 6-inch drywall knife, and guide it over the bead to coat the entire surface of the arch and legs. If necessary, apply a second coat to smooth out the first.

Making tight bends

The archway shown in this project has a 40-inch diameter, which is about the tightest bend you can make by wetting ¼-inch drywall. It's also about the smallest opening you'd want for a doorway. If you're making a tighter bend for any reason, make it by cutting through the paper on the back of the drywall at 1-inch intervals, as shown in the picture on the left. The drywall will separate as it conforms to the arch. Screw it in place, and apply corner bead and joint compound as you would in a wet drywall application.

Installing a prehung interior door

Unless you're a master carpenter or a glutton for punishment, it's easiest to install a prehung door. Fitting a slab door into an existing jamb, as explained on page 204, is an involved process in which it's easy to make mistakes. A prehung door comes with all the precision work done for you: The door's hinges fit snugly into mortises in the jamb; the holes and mortises for the handle and for the strike are cut just right; and the jamb itself is neatly assembled. Once the rough opening has been prepared, the prehung door simply slips in.

There are two options when it comes to prehung interior doors—flat (or standard) and split jamb.

Flat doors are a single unit comprised of the door and side and top jambs. Standard interior doors come without the casing, leaving you free to choose the style of trim that suits your home most effectively.

Split-jamb doors are manufactured to be installed in extra-thick and uneven walls. Split-jamb doors usually come with their own casing.

Exterior prehung doors often come with the molding attached to one side.

The right swing

Make sure your new door will swing the way you want. When you pull (not push) open a door with a right-hand swing, the handle is on the right and the hinges on the left. A door with a left-hand swing has its handle on the left when you pull it open.

Fitting the right door

To find out the size of the door you need, measure the width of the existing door, not including the jamb, and take the measurements to the home center.

If it turns out that the existing door is not a stock size, remove the door trim and measure the opening. Check at the home center to see if they have a door that fits the rough opening and is close to the size of the original door. Measure to make sure that the new door and molding will fully cover the opening. If not, you'll either need to reframe the opening or order a custom door.

Most doors are 80 inches tall, but an older building may have taller doors. In that case you will need to special order a door to fit your opening or you'll have to lower the header to accommodate a standard size.

Installing a prehung door

1 REMOVE THE OLD DOOR AND JAMB

Open the door, and support it temporarily by wedging a few shims underneath the bottom. Use a pry bar and hammer to pop out the hinge pins, then pull the door away. Pry away the molding using a scrap of wood to keep from marring the wall. Use a reciprocating saw with an 8-inch utility blade to cut the nails holding the jamb in place.

2 PULL THE OLD JAMB OUT OF THE OPENING

Starting at the bottom, pry both the side jambs toward the middle of the opening. Pry the top jamb down and pull all three pieces out at the same time. Pull out or pound flush any nails that remain in the opening.

REAL WORLD

REMOVE THE PLASTIC BEFORE YOU INSTALL THE DOOR

More than one person has installed a door without removing the piece of plastic in the holes drilled for the door knob. The plastic, which holds the door shut during shipping, comes out pretty easily—unless the door is already in place. If you've hung the door without removing it, the only way to get the door open is to take the door back down.

3 PUT THE NEW DOOR INTO THE OPENING

Unpack the door, and remove the fastener that keeps the door shut. Slide the door into the opening, taking care to keep the jambs tight against the door as you position it. Make sure the door swings in the direction you want and center the door in the opening. Hold it in place by temporarily shimming between the framing and the top door jamb. After the shims are in place, level the top jamb as shown in step four.

WORK SMARTER

HANGING A PREHUNG DOOR— THE ORDER OF WORK

Attaching the jambs in the right order is essential if you want a door that swings easily and fits snugly in its frame. The hinge side is the most important because it has to be absolutely level and plumb, so that's where you begin. Once it's securely nailed in place, the balance of the job is making sure the latch side is level and plumb. Adjust the jamb until it encloses the door evenly from top to bottom before it's nailed into place. The top jamb does not need to be nailed.

GENERAL CARPENTRY

As you work, continually check to make sure that the jamb's edges are flush or close to flush with the wall surface. If the jamb sticks out beyond the wall on either side, you'll get gaps between the wall and the molding that will be hard to hide.

4

LEVEL THE HEAD JAMB
Put a 2-foot level across the head jamb at top of the door frame. Slip shims underneath the bottom of the door as needed until the head jamb is level.

5

PLUMB AND SHIM THE HINGE-SIDE JAMB
Slip shims from either side of the door between the bottom of the hinge jamb and the framing to bring the jamb into plumb. Hold a 4- or 6-foot level against the jamb and tap the shim gently until the level reads plumb.

Split-jamb doors

In some parts of the country, you can get a split-jamb door for dealing with extra-thick or uneven walls. The jamb is made of two pieces that slide together from opposite sides of the door and typically comes with molding attached to each side. To install the door, separate the two jamb pieces. Attach the half of the jamb with the hinges first, then slide in the other half until it is tight against the wall. Nail through the jamb into the framing.

6

NAIL THE THE HINGE-SIDE JAMB TO THE STUD
Drive a nail through the bottom of the jamb, into the shim, and partway into the framing. (Leave part of the nail exposed in case you have to remove it.)

7

INSTALL INTERMEDIATE SHIMS
Check again to see that the hinge jamb is plumb. Shim behind the hinges from both directions, sliding the shims in and out as needed to fill the space between the jamb and framing without flexing the jamb. Drive a nail through the shims into the stud, but don't set it until the jamb is plumb and flush.

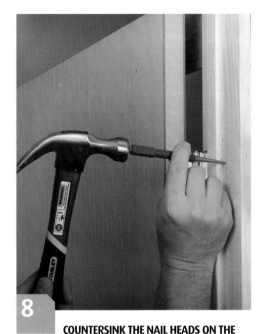

8 COUNTERSINK THE NAIL HEADS ON THE LATCH JAMB

Once you are sure the jamb is both plumb and flush with the wall surfaces, use a nail set to drive the nail heads just below the surface of the wood. Repeat on the latch-side jamb.

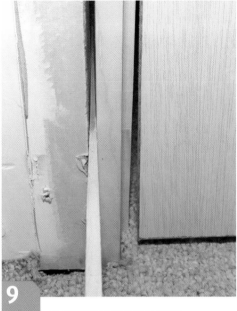

9 ATTACH THE LATCH-SIDE JAMB

Swing the door closed. Most likely, the gap between the door and the jamb is uneven, as shown above. Open the door, and slip in two shims, one on either side, every 16 inches or so.

10 ADJUST, NAIL, AND CUT THE SHIMS

Adjust shims so the jamb is plumb and the gap between the jamb and the door is a consistent ⅛ inch. Nail through the shims, check again for correct gap, and set the nails. Score the shims by running a utility knife along the edge of the jamb, and then pull on the end of the shims to snap them flush.

11 MOUNT THE HARDWARE AND APPLY TRIM

Install the door handle and the strike plate. Cut and install the door trim as explained on pages 102–105.

CLOSER LOOK

IF THE WALL IS TOO THICK
In an older home, the door opening may be wider than the jamb. (Jambs are typically is 4⅝ inches wide.) If so, install the door with the jambs flush with the wall on one side. Then measure and cut strips of wood, to be used as jamb extensions, to bring the other side flush with the wall. Nail the extension pieces to the edge of the jamb, then install the molding.

WORK SMARTER

FINISH THE FLOOR FIRST
Usually it is best to install new flooring—tile, hardwood, carpet, or laminate—before you install the door. If you do, you won't have to cut the new flooring to fit around the jamb, and you'll be sure that the door's bottom doesn't scrape against the flooring. If you can't install the flooring first, put scraps of the flooring under the jambs when you install the door. Remove the scraps and slip in real flooring when you install it.

5

GENERAL CARPENTRY

Installing an exterior door

PROJECT DETAILS

SKILLS: Measuring and layout; using power tools
PROJECT: Removing and replacing an exterior entry door

TIME TO COMPLETE

EXPERIENCED: 3 hrs.
HANDY: 4 hrs.
NOVICE: 5 hrs.

STUFF YOU'LL NEED

TOOLS: Pry bar; reciprocating saw; tape measure; 6-foot level; drill and bits; hammer and nail set; caulk gun; utility knife; screwdriver
MATERIALS: Shims; door; framing square; caulk; construction adhesive; 10d galvanized finish nails; insulation; #10 screws

When winter sets in, a lot of people find that their doors leak. Sometimes they've been limping along with an old wood door that's cracked with age or difficult to weather-strip. Sometimes the door's a contractor's special—special for the contractor, perhaps, but a bit drafty for the homeowner.

Replacement doors come in fiberglass and steel these days, and some are textured to look like wood. They come solid or with windows—clear windows, stained-glass Victorian windows, or Arts and Crafts windows. Sidelights—the rows of windows on either side of the door shown

here—also come in infinite varieties. But the best part is that while these doors look like they come from another era, they're all insulated and fully weather-stripped.

Exterior doors come prehung, and installing them is usually only a matter of taking out the old one and sliding in the new. You will have to put in a lockset, but you won't have to mortise hinges, or plane down any edges to the perfect bevel.

If you're interested in a new door, plan ahead. Some doors are in stock at your home center, but others are special order, and delivery may take up to six weeks.

1 REMOVE THE OLD DOOR

Remove the screen door, and take the door off its hinges. Remove the trim on the inside of the door, and then cut through the side jambs and pry them loose. If the top jamb doesn't come loose on its own accord, pry it loose and remove it. Wires for the doorbell are usually run between the door and the jack studs. Don't cut through them with the saw. The doorbell system is low-voltage so you won't risk a shock, but replacing the run can be difficult.

2 MAKE SURE THE OPENING IS SQUARE

An unsquare opening can force the door jambs out of alignment and haunt you later. If the opening is square, the diagonals will be equal. If the diagonals differ by more than ⅛ inch, check to see if the framing is plumb, and then test-fit the door.

3 MAKE SURE THE FRAMING IS PLUMB

Check the vertical framing to make sure it is plumb front to back and side to side. Check the subfloor to see if it's level. If either the jambs or the floor are out of alignment, put the door temporarily in its opening. Shim to see if there is enough room to bring the door into plumb. If so, you'll be able to install the door. If not, you will have to reframe the opening.

Applying construction adhesive

Some—but not all—doors require construction adhesive in addition to caulk. If you're installing a door with sidelights, look to see if the dividers between the door and sidelights go through the threshold. They don't on this door, but if they do on yours, apply construction adhesive to any parts of the door that will come in contact with the floor or subfloor. If you're installing a double door, put adhesive under the point where the doors meet at the center.

4

APPLY CAULK TO THE SUBFLOOR AND THRESHOLD
To keep rain from washing in under the door, you have to apply caulk to the subfloor and the underside of the threshold. Start with a healthy dab at each end, where water runs down the trim, then apply about half the tube in large beads along the subfloor. Apply the rest of the caulk along the bottom of the threshold.

CLOSER LOOK

WHY CENTER THE DOOR?
In may not seem important, but center the door in the opening as best you can. It not only gives you plenty of room to shim on each side, it won't leave you with a large gap on one side that forces you to use wider molding than you like.

5

REMOVE THE PACKING MATERIAL
Remove any packing material that will interfere with installing the door, but leave the clips in place that keep the door from opening.

6

PUT THE DOOR IN OPENING
Work with a helper to move the door and lift it into position, tilting it away from the opening to avoid scraping off caulk or adhesive. Center the door in the opening. Stand the door up, and push the threshold down into the caulk.

Follow the manufacturer's instructions for the proper amount of caulk and pattern of application.

GENERAL CARPENTRY

5

7

PLUMB THE HINGE SIDE

On a single door, hold a 6-foot level against the jamb that houses the hinges. On a door with sidelights, hold the level against the jamb on the hinge side. On a double door, hold the level against the jamb on the side of the door that is fixed, or passive. Make sure the door is plumb left to right and front to back, using just enough shims to hold it in place.

8

TEMPORARILY NAIL THE HINGE SIDE IN PLACE

Nail the jamb to the framing with 10d nails, locating them as directed by the manufacturer. On a single door, you usually drive the nails just below each hinge. On this door, you drive two nails at roughly the same height as the hinges. Do not drive nails all the way in.

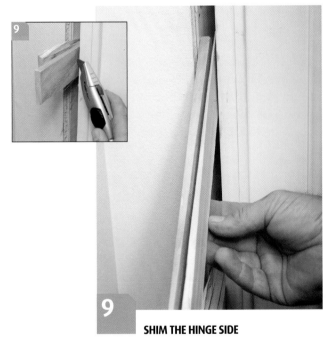

9

SHIM THE HINGE SIDE

Back on the interior side, shim as directed by the manufacturer. On a single door with no lights you usually shim behind each hinge, resting the shims on the nails your drove earlier. On this door you shim above each set of nails. Once the nails are set cut the shims flush with a utility knife.

10

DRIVE AND SET THE NAILS

Return to the outside side of the door, drive the nails all the way in, and set them.

11

SHIM THE LATCH SIDE OF THE DOOR

Go back inside the house. Look closely at the gap between the jamb and door. Shim near the top and bottom of the unfastened jamb to make the gap equal on the top and sides.

12

CHECK FOR PLUMB AND FASTEN THE JAMB

Return outside, and check to make sure the door compresses the weather stripping equally all around the door. If not, the door frame is twisted. Adjust the frame as needed until contact is equal on the sides and on the top. Check again for plumb, and make sure that the molding is tight against the house. Nail the unfastened jamb to the framing with 10d galvanized finishing nails.

13

ATTACH THE TOP JAMB

On some—but not all—doors you need to attach the top of the door jamb to the framing. On a door with sidelights, shim above the posts that separate the doors and jambs. Screw through the post into the framing. On double doors, screw through the top jamb where the doors meet, but do not shim. None of this is necessary on a single door with no sidelights.

Exceptions to the rule

On doors that don't have sidelights you have a couple of extra, but simple, steps. Once the door is in place you need to screw the hinges to the framing. A least one hole in each hinge will not have a screw in it. Drill pilot holes, and then drive the long screws provided by the manufacturer though the holes and into the framing.

The other thing you'll need to do is shim behind the lock. Open the door, put shims between the jamb and the latch plate, and nail through the jamb and into the framing. This gives you a nice, solid connection between the latch and the framing, making it harder to push the door open once it's locked.

5

GENERAL CARPENTRY

14
ADJUST OR ANCHOR THE THRESHOLD
Remove the clip that holds the door shut, following the directions supplied by the manufacturer. If the door has an adjustable sill, turn the screws to raise or lower the threshold so that it meets the weather stripping to the manufacturer's specs. If the threshold isn't adjustable, drive #10 screws through the threshold and into the subfloor.

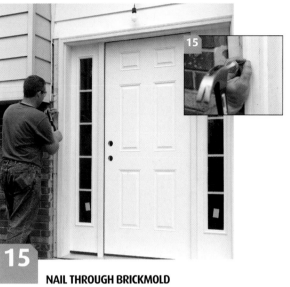

15
NAIL THROUGH BRICKMOLD
The molding around the outside of the door is called brickmold. Drive 10d nails through the brickmold and into the framing, spacing the nails as directed by the manufacturer. Caulk the seam between the brickmold and the house to keep water from working its way into the walls. Also caulk manufactured joints around the door frame at the top corners.

16
INSULATE BETWEEN THE FRAMING AND JAMB
The space between the framing and jamb is almost an open passageway for air leaks. Cut fiberglass insulation into strips with a utility knife, and stuff it into the openings with a shim.

17
APPLY TRIM TO THE INSIDE OF THE DOOR
Apply molding to the inside of the door. For more on trimming a door, see pages 102–105. Install the lockset as directed by the lockset manufacturer.

SAFETY ALERT
TREAT FIBERGLASS WITH RESPECT
Fiberglass is not only itchy and scratchy, repeated inhalation can cause cancer. Wear an approved dust mask when handling insulation. Wear gloves or push the fiberglass in place with another object to avoid irritating your hands.

5

GENERAL CARPENTRY

Hanging a slab door

PROJECT DETAILS

SKILLS: Measuring and layout; using power tools
PROJECT: Hanging a slab door in an existing opening

TIME TO COMPLETE

EXPERIENCED: 4 hrs.
HANDY: 6 hrs.
NOVICE: 8 hrs.

STUFF YOU'LL NEED

TOOLS: Router; router hinge template; door lock templates; hole saws; drill; block plane; tape measure; hammer; nail set; 2-foot level; 6-foot level; framing square; utility knife; safety glasses; hearing protection
MATERIALS: Door; hinges; screws; shims; lockset; door stop; molding

CLOSER LOOK

FOLLOW THE ARROWS
On the top of the door you'll find arrows pointing toward the side of the door that holds the lock block where the lockset and door handle are mounted.

When you buy or make a custom door, odds are it won't come prehung in factory-made doorjambs. You'll find yourself hanging a door the old-fashioned way—cutting the door to fit and mortising for the recesses that house the hinges in both the door and jamb. You won't be living entirely in the past, however: Inexpensive router jigs make it possible to cut the mortises quickly and minimize the chance of error.

Before you start routing, you will need to make two decisions: Will the hinges be on the left- or right-hand side of the door, and which room will the door open into?

Once you've made those decisions, things begin to fall in place. The hinge barrels face into the room that the door opens into, and the hinges are mounted so that the barrel is completely exposed. The latch side of the door is beveled, so that the leading edge of the door won't catch on the jamb as you close the door. When it comes time to cut the bevel, draw it on the top and bottom edges of the door so you cut the bevel in the right direction.

Before you cut anything check with the manufacturer to determine if there are any warranty restrictions that could affect your ability to return the door if there's a problem.

WORK SMARTER

DOOR JACKS
Carpenters make door jacks to hold the door securely on edge while they work. To make your own, cut 8-inch-long feet from a 2×4; cut two 36×4-inch platforms from ⅜-inch plywood, and four 8-inch blocks from a 2×6. Apply carpet to the inside faces of the blocks using brads; screw the feet and the blocks to the platform, leaving a gap slightly wider than the door. The plywood flexes under the weight of the door, causing the blocks to angle toward the door and hold it in place.

5

GENERAL CARPENTRY

1
MAKE SURE THE DOOR FITS
Measure the door opening, and lay out cuts on the door to make it ³⁄₁₆ inch narrower than the opening is wide. Check the height, and if necessary, cut the door to allow for a ³⁄₃₂-inch gap on top, and space at the bottom as recommended by the manufacturer. On modern doors, taking more than ½ inch from overall width or 2" from overall height will expose the joinery and ruin the appearance of the door.

2
CUT THE HINGE SIDE OF THE DOOR
The two edges of the door do not receive identical cuts. Most manufacturers suggest a bevel of 3 degrees on the latch side so that the leading corner won't catch on the jamb when you close it. The hinge side is square. Make a jig like the one described in Circular saws, page 53, and use it to cut along the hinge side of the door to size.

3
BEVEL THE LATCH SIDE OF THE DOOR
Set the saw to make a cut at 5 degrees. Guide it along the jig to cut a bevel on it, and then clamp the jig along the layout line on the door. Guide the saw along the jig to cut a bevel on the hinge side of the door.

4
LAY OUT THE HINGE ON THE JAMB
Mark the location of the hinges on the door, and measure the distance from the top of the door to the top of each hinge. To lay out the hinge on the door jamb, put a nickel between the ruler or tape measure and the top jamb, and mark the distances you measured on the side jamb. This will give you the proper gap between the top of the door and the jamb.

CLOSER LOOK

USE A DUTCHMAN
If you're reusing a door, you can reuse the hinge mortises as long as trimming the door to width doesn't eliminate them. Shim the door in place, make marks to show where the mortises meet the jamb, and rout mortises in the jamb. If the mortises are in the wrong place, cut patches (called Dutchmen in the trades) and glue them in place.

CLOSER LOOK

LAYING OUT THE HINGES
On a paneled door, the hinges align with the seam between the rails and the rest of the door. At the top, the top edge of hinge is in line with bottom of rail. At the bottom, the bottom edge of the hinge is in line with the top of the rail. The third hinge, if any, is centered between the two. On flush doors, the top hinge can be up to 9 inches from the top edge; the bottom hinge can be up to 13 inches from the bottom; the third hinge is centered between the two.

WORK SMARTER

SEAL THE EDGES
After you've trimmed the door to size, don't forget to seal the edges with paint or stain according to the manufacturer's recommendations.

5

GENERAL CARPENTRY

CLOSER LOOK

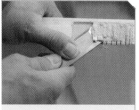

SQUARING THE OPENING WITH A CHISEL

New hinges have rounded corners to match the shape left by the router. If you're using square cornered hinges, rout them on the jig, then trace around them with a utility knife. Deepen the lines with a chisel, and come in from the side to remove the waste.

OLD vs. NEW

CUTTING MORTISES BY HAND

In the old days you cut a mortise with a knife, a chisel and a small backsaw called a dovetail saw. First you traced around the hinge with a knife to lay out the edges of the mortise, making repeated passes until the cut was as deep as the hinge leaf. Next, you made a series of cuts with the saw to remove much of the wood. Most of the wood that was left crumbled out of the way when you cleaned out the bottom of the mortise with a chisel.

5 ADJUST THE TEMPLATE

Put the template on top of the router, and the hinge on top of the template. Raise the router bit until the end of the bit is just flush with the top surface of the hinge. Adjust the size of the template opening, as necessary, following the manufacturer's directions.

6 NAIL TEMPLATE TO JAMB

Follow the manufacturer's directions to properly position the template on the jamb. On this template you line up the edge of a square cutout with the edge of the jamb.

7 ROUT OUT THE MORTISES

Turn on the router, and ease it onto the template, positioning it at first so that the bit doesn't hit the jamb. Move the router back and forth across the template to rout out the hinge mortise. Reposition the template and rout out the other jamb mortises based on the manufacturer's instructions.

8 INSTALL THE HINGE

Predrill holes for screws, and screw the hinges to the jamb.

9 MARK WHERE THE HINGES MEET THE DOOR

Put the door in place, and slip shims between it and the jamb until the door is jammed firmly in place. Put the head of an adjustable square against each hinge, and trace across each one to mark the location on the door. Remove the door from the opening.

10 ATTACH THE TEMPLATE TO THE DOOR

Align the template with marks on the door as directed by the manufacturer and nail the template in place.

11 ROUT OUT THE MORTISE

Turn on the router, and place it on the template so that it doesn't hit the door. Move the router back and forth to rout out the mortise. Repeat for each mortise on the door. Disassemble the hinge by removing the hinge pin. Screw the loose hinge leaves to the door.

12 HANG THE DOOR

Put the door in its opening, and slip the door hinge leaves over the jamb leaves. Shim the door in place or have a helper hold it while you put the hinge pins in the hinges.

13 INSTALL DOOR STOP MOLDING

Install the lockset, drilling a hole for it if necessary, as explained on page 208. Close the door, and hold door stop molding against it. Cut the stop to length, mitering the corner, but leaving the bottom end square. Nail the stop in place. Repeat on the other side. Miter a piece at both ends to fit across the top.

TOOL SAVVY

HINGE BITS

A tool sold as a hinge bit has a barrel that fits perfectly in the hinge's screw holes. The barrel is spring loaded so that when you push against the bit, the barrel retracts, exposing a drill bit that drives a perfectly placed screw hole every time.

WORK SMARTER

LOOSE LEAVES

If the hinge pin doesn't come out freely, knock it loose by driving a nail set against it from the bottom of the hinge.

5

GENERAL CARPENTRY

Installing a lockset

1

LAY OUT THE HANDLE

Most doors come with the holes for the handle predrilled. If yours doesn't, you'll drill a few holes, and then rout a recess, called a mortise, to house the hardware. Begin by laying out the door handle anywhere from 36 to 40 inches above the floor. Check your handle to see how far the center of the handle should be from the edge of the door. This is called the backset and is usually either 2⅜ or 2¾ inches.

2

DRILL A STARTER HOLE FOR THE HANDLE

Attach a jig, sold at most home centers, designed to guide a drill when drilling for handles. It usually screws in place; make sure you drill pilot holes to prevent splitting the edge of the door. The jig usually comes with hole saws sized to drill the proper size holes, and marks to help you locate it for the backset of your handle. When you drill for the handles, the wood will splinter as the hole saw exits the door. To prevent this, drill from one side until the pilot bit, which is in the center of the hole saw, and somewhat longer than the saw, exits the door.

3

BORE THE REST OF THE HOLES

Without using the jig, put the pilot bit in the exit hole on the other side of the door, and drill back toward the jig to complete the hole. Put the smaller hole saw in the drill, and use the jig to drill for the latch.

4

MORTISE THE DOOR

The latch plate is recessed, or mortised, into the door so that it won't stick out and hit the jamb. It's easiest to rout the recess using a commercially available jig. Nail the jig to the door, and guide the bearing around the jig to cut the mortise.

5

ATTACH THE HANDLE

Attach the handle, following the manufacturer's directions. Close the door, and mark where latch meets jamb. This will be the center of the strike plate that the latch fits into when the door is closed.

6

MORTISE FOR THE STRIKE PLATE

Rout a mortise in the jamb using the same jig you used to mortise the door. Drill a hole for the latch in the center, and then screw the strike plate in the door to finish the job.

5

GENERAL CARPENTRY

Installing a pocket door

GOOD IDEA

INSTALLING TWO POCKETS
Pocket doors are often installed in pairs, so that the two doors open and close like a curtain. This creates a dramatic effect in a formal living or dining area. This project shows how to install a single pocket door; to install two, simply double the width of the opening and add another door and track. You'll need a fairly large wall; however, two 36-inch pocket doors will require a wall slightly over 12 feet long.

B ecause half of the hardware that supports a pocket door is hidden inside the wall, it is virtually impossible to build a pocket door into an existing wall. The framing can be done with anything from 2×4s up. If you're removing a load-bearing wall and putting in a pocket door, however, you must install a header that will support the weight of whatever is resting above it. For more on installing doors in load-bearing walls, see pages 184–187.

When it comes to pocket door hardware, one size fits almost all. The most common kits are for doors 36 inches

and narrower. When you buy the hardware, make sure you're buying a kit that includes the split jambs as well as the pocket door header. There's often a similar (and cheaper) box on a nearby rack that includes only the header.

The pocket frame installed here comes with all the hardware you need, except for the door and the door handle. Any door that's within the width of the track will work; the knob should be recessed into the door. If your door is too wide or is thicker than 1⅜ inches, have a carpenter build a custom frame.

WORK SMARTER

TRY SCREW BLOCKS

If you'd rather not toenail the studs to the top plate, attach screw blocks to it before you nail it up. Mark the position of the studs and screw the blocks to one side of each stud location. Once the top plate is in the air, you can screw the studs directly to the blocks. Make sure the block nearest the opening for the pocket door is on the side of the stud away from the opening.

1

LAY OUT THE TOP PLATE

Put the top plate on the floor and lay out each of the pieces of framing that you'll nail into it. Start on the side that has the opening for the door. Lay out a 2×4 at the end of the plate. Follow the manufacturer's directions to lay out the next stud—in this case it should be twice width of the door, plus 1¼ inches from the first stud. Lay out from the rest of the studs 16 inches on center.

2

ATTACH THE TOP PLATE TO THE CEILING

Screw the top plate into joists in the ceiling with drywall screws—it's much easier to control the placement if you use screws instead of nails. Put a stud under one end of the top plate, plumb it, and nail or screw it in place. Repeat on the other side.

REAL WORLD

DON'T FRAME YOURSELF INTO A CORNER

If you're framing a closet, put drywall inside it before you hang the door. Once the door is in place, you may not have enough clearance to slip the drywall through the framing.

3

SCREW IN THE STUDS

Measure and cut studs for each one you drew on the top plate—the length of the studs may vary because of settling, so measure for each one. Toenail the studs in place or screw them to the screw blocks.

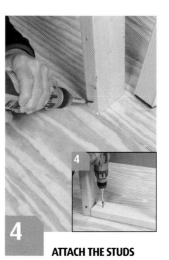

4

ATTACH THE STUDS TO THE FLOOR

Snap a chalk line between the end studs. Align a stud with the line, plumb it, and screw in place. Repeat on the remaining studs. Cut 2×4s to fit between the studs. Screw them to the floor or subfloor so that you'll have a surface to nail drywall and baseboard.

5

CUT THE SIDES OF THE HEADER

Measure the width of the door. Cut sides of the header, supplied with the pocket door hardware kit, along the preprinted lines that correspond with the width of the door.

6
CUT THE HEADER TO LENGTH

Remove the track and unscrew the bracket at the thin end of the header. Cut the end of the header along the line that corresponds to the width of the door.

7
CUT THE TRACK TO LENGTH

Cut the track 2 inches shorter than the distance between the end of the mounting bracket and the end of the header, or as directed by the manufacturer. You can make the cut with a hacksaw or with an old blade in the miter saw. Reinstall the track.

8
INSTALL THE UNATTACHED HEADER BRACKET

Draw a line on the studs at each end of the opening to show where the header will go. With this kit you draw a line marking the bottom of the bracket following a chart in the directions that come with the door. Attach the loose bracket to the stud farthest from the opening.

GOOD IDEA

TAKE THE FLOOR INTO ACCOUNT
This door framing is being installed on a subfloor. If you're going to install a finish floor after you install the door, hang the header high enough to account for it.

CLOSER LOOK

BE SURE IT'S LEVEL
Because the pocket door will glide smoothly and easily on its rollers, it's important that the header be level, or the door may open or close by itself.

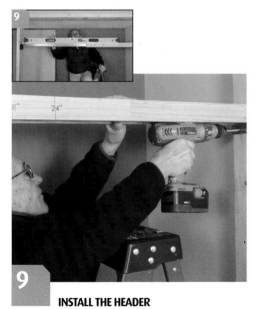

9
INSTALL THE HEADER

Rest one end of the header on the bracket, and screw the other bracket in place on the line you drew on the other side of the opening. Check to see if the header is level. Move the bracket as necessary, and screw it firmly to the stud and header.

10
ATTACH THE HANGERS

Screw the hangers to the top of the door, spacing them as directed by the manufacturer. Screw the bumper stop to the stud inside the pocket as shown in the inset.

11
HANG THE DOOR

Slip the roller carriage in the track as shown in the inset. Lift the door until the pins on the roller carriage snap into the brackets on the door.

5

GENERAL CARPENTRY

GOOD IDEA

USE A LEVER

Doors can be heavy, and jockeying one into position between the rollers can be tricky. Push the door into place on a lever made from a couple of scraps. You're hands will be free to maneuver the door into place.

CLOSER LOOK

REMOVING A DOOR

If you need to remove a pocket door, slide the tabs on the hanger plate to the side with a screwdriver and wiggle the door free.

12 INSTALL ONE OF THE SPLIT STUDS

The door kit comes with four thin studs wrapped in steel and with two brackets that hold them. Tap one of the brackets into one of the studs. Screw the other end into the header so that it is tight against the nailer.

13 SCREW THE BRACKET TO THE FLOOR

Plumb the stud and screw the bracket to the floor. Put the other split stud on the bracket, plumb it, and screw it to the header.

14 INSTALL THE DRYWALL

Remove the door. Brace the pocket with a piece of stock 2⅛ wide, put in place as shown. While this is optional, it stiffens the split studs while you hang the drywall. Install the drywall, and trim so it's flush with the opening. Remove the brace and drywall the interior.

Adjusting the door

The door should be plumb and the proper distance from the floor. If not, use the adjustment wrench supplied by the manufacturer to turn the hanger's bolt, raising or lowering the door.

WORK SMARTER

WAIT TO DRYWALL THE SECOND SIDE OF THE WALL

Don't drywall both sides of the wall—yet. Leave one side of the hardware accessible until you've hung the door and can slide it in its tracks. You'll often have to put an extra piece of wood between the bumper and framing order to get the door to stop exactly where you want it.

15 INSTALL THE HANDLE

The handles on pocket doors are recessed into either the face or edge of the door. The handle used here is set into the edge. Screw a board that you can use as an extra wide fence to the router's fence attachment, and hold the board against the door as you rout. Use a bit the same width as the handle. Set the fence so that it is the same distance to the center of the bit as it is from the face of the door to the center of the door.

16 REHANG THE DOOR AND INSTALL THE GUIDES

Drill a pilot hole and drive a screw to attach each of the bottom guides to the two split jambs so each guide is about 3/16 inch away from the door.

WORK SMARTER

USE THE RIGHT SCREWS

Drive screws instead of nails when attaching the drywall to the pocket frame to keep from shaking things apart. Use ½-inch drywall and 1-inch screws. Longer screws will poke through the pocket frame and could scratch the door.

17 INSTALL JAMBS AND DOOR STOPS

Nail a piece of 1× to the stud that the door rests against when closed. Cut pieces to fit against the split jambs and across the top of the opening. Apply door stops.

Installing a patio door

P atio doors can either be hinged or can slide. The door shown here is hinged—it's a regular door flanked by a stationary panel that looks like a door. Sliding doors, which travel back and forth in a track, open wider and usually have a broader expanse of glass.

A hinged door installs pretty much like any other exterior door. It's bigger and heavier, but it's still mounted on hinges inside a sturdy frame. Sliding doors, on the other hand, arrive disassembled. You screw the tracks together to form the frame, which you then install in much the same way you install a hinged door. Once the frame is in place, you put the doors in the track.

When you put in a door, take the time at the beginning to examine the home's framing. The opening for the door should be square, the sides should be plumb, and the floor or subfloor should be level. Rest assured, however, that this won't be the case. Framing is almost never perfect. That's why the opening a door fits into is always larger than the door. If something's slightly out of whack, there's room for correction. Before you despair because of a flaw in the framing, put the door temporarily in its opening. If you can shim it in place so that it's flush and plumb, you'll be able to install the door despite any irregularities in the home's framing.

REAL WORLD

If your jamb is wider than your wall is thick, it doesn't mean you've got the wrong door. On doors with installation jambs, a couple of inches of the jamb extends outside the wall. In fact, it's when your jamb isn't wider than your wall that you may have problems. But before you start tearing out floor to make room for a wider door, put the flange on the door and put the door in the opening. When the flange is against the house, the jamb should either be flush with the inside wall, or somewhat shy of it.

1 **REMOVE THE EXTERIOR TRIM**

Homes that have had siding applied after they were built often have aluminum that was custom-wrapped around the trim to protect it. You'll have to remove the wrapped aluminum to remove the door. It's only held in place with a few nails. Put on a pair of gloves, find a seam near a corner, pry the metal loose, and pull.

2 **REMOVE THE OLD DOOR**

Remove the interior trim and any screws holding the door to the floor or framing. On hinged doors at least one of the screws that goes through the hinges is long enough to go through the framing, so remove the screws and door before removing the frame.

Many doors have a flange around the edge that nests against the house, helping seal out wind and water. The flange is covered by a piece of thick molding; remove that before you pry the door out of its opening.

3 **MAKE ANY NECESSARY REPAIRS**

An old door often leaks, causing the surrounding wood to rot. On this door, leaks have caused the floor to rot. Cut out and replace any rotten surfaces.

4 **CHECK THE OPENING**

Check to make sure the jambs are plumb. Measure the diagonals of the opening. If they are within ⅛ inch of each other, the opening is square enough to accept the door. If the difference is greater than ⅛ inch, test-fit the door after you unpack it, then decide whether you need to reframe the opening.

5 **INSTALL THE FLANGE**

This door has a installation flange that needs to be installed (and that may not be needed on some walls). Attach the flange as directed by the manufacturer. In this case you put it in place, then seat it by holding a board against it and tapping.

6 **REMOVE THE FASTENER COVER**

There is usually a piece of trim that hides the screws used to attach the door to the framing. Remove the trim as directed by the manufacturer.

7   CAULK OPENING

On this door, you caulk both the rough sill and the section of wall that will be covered by the flange. Apply caulk as directed by the manufacturer of your door.

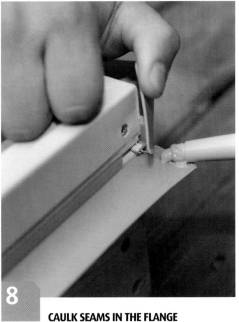

8   CAULK SEAMS IN THE FLANGE

The seam between strips of nailing flange at the top corners of the door will let water get into your wall unless you caulk it. Apply caulk along the seam, as shown.

9   PUT THE DOOR IN THE OPENING

With a helper lift the door into place as shown, and then roll it up into the opening.

10   PLUMB THE JAMB

Check the jamb with a level to see if it is plumb. If not, shim underneath the sill until it is.

 WORK SMARTER

TEST-FIT THE DOOR

The directions won't mention it, but this is a good time to put the door in the opening and look for problems. Make sure it fits, and shim as needed to see if you can bring the door into plumb. If you can, you'll be able to install the door in the opening. If you can't shim the door into plumb, however, you may have to reframe the opening before you go any further.

5

GENERAL CARPENTRY

11
MAKE SURE THE ASSEMBLY IS SQUARE
If the door assembly is square, the diagonals will measure the same. If not, shim to correct the problem.

12
SHIM THE DOOR IN PLACE
Shims keep the screws that hold the door in place from bending the frame. Working from inside the house, shim above and below the hinges and near the screw holes in the jambs. Try to put two shims at each location—use the thick end of one shim and the thin end of another, sliding them back and forth or trimming them until you get a snug fit. Double-check for plumb and square and make any corrections needed.

OLD vs. NEW

PRESSURE-TREATED LUMBER
If the framing you're screwing into is made of new pressure-treated lumber, screw the door in place with stainless-steel screws. It wasn't an issue with the old pressure-treated wood, but the chemicals in the newer pressure-treated woods corrode regular screws and may eat through them completely.

Shimming the head jamb
Not all doors require shims between the head jamb and framing, but some do. Follow the directions that came with your door.

13
SCREW THE DOOR IN PLACE
Screw the door to the framing, placing the screws as directed. Check to make sure the door is working before you tighten the screws completely. Hide the screws by reattaching the cover you removed in step six. (On some doors, the door is held in place by long hinge screws and no cover is necessary.) Use a pry bar to remove the clips—if any—that held the door in place during installation.

CLOSER LOOK

Check operation of the door. Open and close the door to make sure it swings and closes freely. Expect the weather stripping to cause some stiffness as you close the door. The stiffness goes away with use. If there is a problem with the door, remove the screws, and shim to correct them.

14 APPLY FLASHING

The top of the door needs to be flashed to prevent rain from working its way into the house. Use a piece of flashing drip cap which is designed to be applied on the lower edge of the roof when roofing. Cut it to length with tinsnips, apply a bead of caulk along the top, and slide it under the siding as shown.

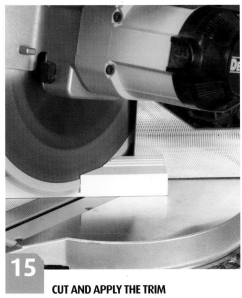

15 CUT AND APPLY THE TRIM

The trim put around doors and windows is called brickmold. Cut and apply it the same way you would if you were applying trim to the inside of a door.

16 POSITION THE FLASHING

Apply a bead of caulk along the top of the molding, and slide the flashing down over the molding as shown, to protect it from weathering. On this door, side flashing was installed too. If you install side flashing, put it in before the brickmold and caulk the joints between the top and side pieces of flashing.

5

GENERAL CARPENTRY

Framing a window

PROJECT DETAILS

SKILLS: Measuring and layout; using power tools

PROJECT: Framing a window in an existing wall

TIME TO COMPLETE

EXPERIENCED: 6 hrs.
HANDY: 6 hrs.
NOVICE: 8 hrs.

STUFF YOU'LL NEED

TOOLS: Tape measure; level; combination square; straightedge; hammer; pry bar; utility knife; 3-lb. sledgehammer; reciprocating saw; end nippers; clamp; drill with screwdriver bit and drill bit; vinyl siding removal tool; chalk line; circular saw; drywall router; drywall knives; work gloves; safety glasses; dust mask; hearing protection

MATERIALS: 2×4 studs; 2×6, 8, 10, or 12s for header; ½-inch plywood for header; 8d, 10, and 16d nails; drywall; joint tape; joint compound; and replacement siding if some is damaged during installation

SAFETY ALERT

INSTALL THE PROPER SIZE HEADER
Make sure the header you install is sufficient to support the weight of the structure above it. Consult with a building engineer to ensure a safe installation. Also check local building codes to get guidelines for proper installation in your area.

I nstalling a window is a bit more complicated than cutting a hole in the side of the house. Unless you want your house to start sagging, you'll need to replace the structural pieces—the studs—that you cut through. And you'll need to build structure—sills and more studs—to support the window.

All of this necessitates cutting a hole in the drywall that is quite a bit bigger than the window—think floor to ceiling and all the way to the first studs on either side of the window. The drywall you remove will make it look like you're installing a door, and in fact the jobs are similar.

You cut the opening, and then put in studs, called king studs, that run from floor plate to top plate. You nail slightly shorter studs, called jack studs, to the king studs, and set a built-up beam, called a header, on top. At this point you've built a structure to support what you've removed, and the job has been exactly like framing a door.

Once the header is in place, however, you need to put in a rough sill that the window will sit on. The sill sits on short studs, spaced every 16 inches on center, that keep the window from sagging over time.

The opening you create in the wall with all this framing is called the rough opening. It's almost always ½ inch wider than the window on each side and ½ inch taller, but check the manufacturer's specs. Work carefully to make sure the sides of the opening are plumb and that the sill and header are level.

Working with headers

The header sizes given on page 221 reflect common building practice, but don't apply in all situations. They assume, for example, that the house was properly built in the first place, and that no modifications have been made since the house was built. The addition of a slate roof, a hot tub, or any significant amount of weight can turn a non-load-bearing wall into a load-bearing one, or require an oversize header in a load-bearing wall.

Poorly done alterations made before you begin the job could have robbed a load-bearing wall of its load-bearing capacity, or put an improper amount of weight on a wall not built to support it. Any of these situations could result in the collapse of the wall you're working on. When you're removing studs in a load-bearing wall, it isn't safe to assume anything. Have a structural engineer look at the house, and advise you about installing proper support during construction and about proper header construction.

Cutting the opening

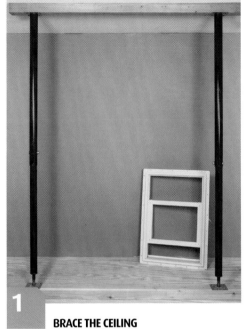

1 **BRACE THE CEILING**

Exterior walls support the roof. When you're adding and removing studs as part of installing a window, brace the wall to keep it from sagging and possibly collapsing. Protect the ceiling and floor with 2×4s or 4×4s, and install adjustable basement posts to provide temporary support.

2 **REMOVE THE BASEBOARD**

Pry the baseboard loose from the wall using a hammer and pry bar. Protect the walls from damage by prying against a piece of scrap wood.

3 **FIND THE STUDS AND MARK THEM ON THE WALL**

Use a stud finder to locate the studs that you'll have to remove to install the window, then find the first stud on each side of the window. Stud finders are often only approximate, so double-check the location by driving nails to find the exact edge of the two outside studs. Mark the middle of the stud, and draw a line along it with the help of a level.

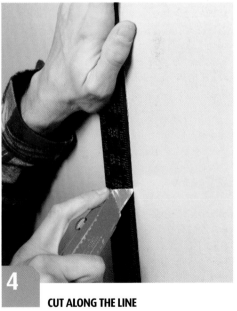

4 **CUT ALONG THE LINE**

Guide a utility knife along the line with the help of a straightedge. Make repeated cuts—you won't need the straightedge after the first few passes—until you've cut all the way through the drywall.

5

GENERAL CARPENTRY

Removing nails

Once you remove the studs, the nails that held them will be sticking out all over the place. Remove them with a pair of end nippers. Grab the base of the nail with the nippers, and then roll the nippers sideways to pull out the nail.

5

REMOVE DRYWALL

Punch a hole through the drywall with a hammer, and then pull the drywall loose. The drywall is probably still held in place by at least one stud, so you'll have to break the drywall off in pieces. Remove any insulation in the wall.

6

REMOVE UNNEEDED STUDS

Remove any studs within the rough opening. Start by cutting through the middle of the stud with a reciprocating saw. Hit the studs with a 3-pound sledge, and then pry gently to remove the studs from the nails attaching them to the sheathing. Do not remove the two outer studs.

Framing the opening

Kings, jack

A king stud is a stud that runs from floor to ceiling as part of a door or window opening. A jack stud is shorter, and runs from floor to the header that you'll install across the top of the door for support. It's installed right next to the king stud and nailed to it.

1

LAY OUT THE KING AND JACK STUDS

Draw a line on the floor plate, marking one edge of the rough opening. Draw a second line 1½ inches toward the outside of the opening. The jack stud will go between these lines. Draw a third line another 1½ inches toward the outside of the opening. This marks the outside edge of the king stud. Draw an "x" between the lines to show where the king and jack studs go. Repeat on the other side of the opening.

2

INSTALL THE KING STUDS

Put the king stud on the "x" that marks its location on the floor plate. Toenail it in place, driving a nail through the front edge first to hold it in place; then toenail in from the side. Make sure the stud is straight up and down, and then nail the top in place too. On this window, the stud to the left of the opening falls almost exactly where the king stud should go, so it substitutes for the king stud.

3 INSTALL THE JACK STUDS

Make a mark on the king stud showing where the top of the window will be, making sure you allow room for the header. (See the Header size chart.) Measure from the mark to the floor. Cut the jack studs to this length. Clamp and then nail them to the king studs.

4 MEASURE AND CUT THE HEADER

The header is a piece of ½-inch plywood sandwiched between two pieces of 2×. Measure the opening and choose the width for the 2× recommended in Header size, below. You can build a header larger than recommended, but don't build one smaller. Cut the 2× to length, cut the plywood to width and length, and nail them together.

Laying out the top of the window

You can put the window almost anywhere you want, with one limitation. There has to be enough room between the top of the rough opening and the top plate for a header. A header is a sandwich of 2× stock and plywood that bridges the top of the window and replaces the support once provided by the studs you cut away. The size of the 2× sandwich depends on the load above and the width of the opening. The chart below will tell you what size to use. But it's also important to check with a structural engineer if you have any concerns about the weight of the load above.

5 INSTALL THE HEADER

Install the header. Rest the header on the jack studs, and toenail a 16d nail through the header and into the king studs to fasten it. The number of nails depends on the size of the header: Divide it into imaginary 2x3s and drive a single nail into each. A header made of two 2x6s requires four nails at each end.

Figuring header size for load-bearing walls

Headers are put in place across the top of an opening in a structural wall. They are essentially beams built up from pieces of thinner wood, and provide the support once provided by the studs removed to make room for the window. If you're putting an opening in a load-bearing wall, you'll need to build a load-bearing header. The header is a layer of ½-inch plywood sandwiched between two 2×s. The exact size of the header depends on the size of the opening. The chart below gives you standard header sizes, but codes vary, so check with your local building authority and bring in a structural engineer to inspect the structure and provide you with specifications for the header that will guarantee a safe installation that meets building codes. See the introduction to this project on page 218 for more information on dealing with load-bearing walls.

	MAXIMUM OPENING	
	HEADER SUPPORTS	HEADER SUPPORTS
HEADER	FLOOR, CEILING,	CEILING AND
MATERIAL	AND ROOF	ROOF ONLY
2×4 and ½ ply	3'	3'6"
2×6 and ½ ply	5'	6'
2×8 and ½ ply	7'	8'
2×10 and ½ ply	8'	10'
2×12 and ½ ply	9'	12'

Framing the opening *(continued)*

6
INSTALL THE CRIPPLE STUDS
Cut short studs, called cripples, to fill the opening between the header and top plate. Put one on each side of the opening, and space them 16 inches on center throughout the opening.

On center

2×4 studs are placed every 16 inches "on center," meaning the centers of the studs are 16 inches apart. Spacing the studs on center simplifies layout and ensures that the centers of the weight-bearing studs are uniformly spaced, even if the thickness of the stud varies.

7
LAY OUT THE TOP OF THE SILL
Measure down from the header by the height of the rough opening, and make a mark on the stud. This will be the top of the rough sill. Lay out the sill below that, and a second sill below the first. Structurally, you only need one sill, but putting in a double sill gives you more surface to nail the trim to.

8
INSTALL THE OUTSIDE JACKS
The short studs that support the sill are called sill jacks. Measure to the line marking the bottom of the double sill and cut sill jacks to this size. Cut one jack for each side of the opening, and one for every 16 inches on center throughout the opening.

9
INSTALL THE LOWER SILL
After installing the two outer sill jacks with 10d nails (16d are longer than the depth of two 2×4s), cut a sill to fit on top of them, and nail it in place with 16d nails. Nail the remaining sill jacks in place as shown in the inset.

10
NAIL IN THE UPPER SILL
Place the upper sill on the lower sill and check to see if it's level. If not, shim between the two sills to level it, as shown in the inset. Nail the top sill to the lower sill with 10d nails.

Cutting the opening

1   REPLACE THE DRYWALL
Cut a piece of drywall to fit over the entire section and screw it in place. Guide a drywall router along the new framing to create an opening for the window. For more on drywall work, see Installing drywall, pages 236–246.

2   DRILL THROUGH THE WALL
You will have to cut the opening for the window from outside the house, where the studs won't interfere with your work. Drill a hole in each of the four corners of the rough opening so that you can see where they are from the outside.

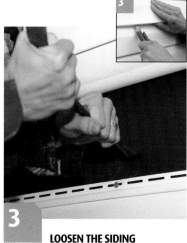

3   LOOSEN THE SIDING
Remove vinyl siding by wedging a siding removal tool between two pieces of siding. Make sure you've actually wedged the tool into a seam: Each piece of siding looks to be two or three clapboards wide, but you'll see the seam if you look for it. Roll up the piece above the seam, and free up the piece below it by prying out the nails. Set the piece aside and work your way down the wall.

4   LAY OUT THE OPENING
Snap chalk lines between the outside edges of the four holes.

5   CUT ALONG THE LINES WITH A CIRCULAR SAW
As you finish each side, drive a screw into the kerf left by the saw. The screw helps to keep the scrap from flopping around as you cut.

6   REMOVE THE SCRAP
Remove the screws you drove to keep the scrap from flopping and remove the scrap from the opening.

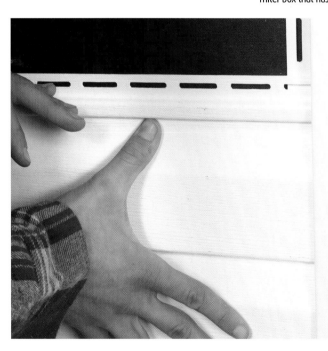

Unlike wood siding, vinyl doesn't simply butt against a piece of molding. It fits inside a piece of trim called J-channel. The molding itself is simple to install—you snug it up against the window and then nail it in place. The corners, though, require special attention. Cut them to the shapes shown with straight-cutting tin snips. Start by cutting a miter in the front face of the piece that goes across the top of the window; then make parallel cuts to create a flap across the bottom. On the side piece, trim away the back piece and the neighboring surface. Leave the front piece alone, and tuck it under the miter when you assemble the two pieces.

Installing the window

1
PUT IN THE WINDOW
Install the window as directed by the manufacturer, and nail the trim in place. For more on installing windows, see Installing windows, pages 225–228.

2
CUT THE OLD SIDING TO FIT
Cut the pieces of siding you removed so that they will fit against the window or window trim. Cut aluminum with tin snips; cut wood with a circular saw or power miter box. You can avoid chipping vinyl by cutting it with a circular saw or miter box that has the blade in backward.

3
INSTALL THE SIDING
Nail the siding against the trim. Wood siding will butt against the trim, which is usually a molding called brickmold. The trim when installing vinyl is a channel, called J-channel, that houses the siding. You can use the same channel as trim for aluminum siding, or you can purchase the aluminum counterpart from a supply house. Use galvanized roofing nails and don't nail them tightly; there should be ⅛-inch play to prevent damage as the siding expands or contracts with the seasons.

5

GENERAL CARPENTRY

Installing windows

PROJECT DETAILS

SKILLS: Measuring and layout; using power tools
PROJECT: Installing a window

TIME TO COMPLETE

EXPERIENCED: 1 hr.
HANDY: 2 hrs.
NOVICE: 4 hrs.
Time does not include cutting and framing an opening, or installing trim.

STUFF YOU'LL NEED

TOOLS: Hammer or pneumatic nailer; nail set; level; square; tape measure; caulk gun; safety glasses; work gloves; miter saw (for framing half-circle window)
MATERIALS: Window; extension jambs; 1¾-inch roofing nails; flashing tape; 10d finishing nails; insulation; 3½-inch finishing screws; caulk; shims; backer rod; insulation

BUYER'S GUIDE

GETTING A WINDOW THAT FITS

Windows fit in a level and plumb opening—called the rough opening— generally ½ inch wider than the window on each side and ½ inch taller at the top than the overall size of the window itself. But don't assume anything. Work with the staff at the home center to get the right size. If you're filling an existing opening, remove the trim, measure the size of the rough opening, and ask for a window that fits. If you're putting in a new window, have the store help you choose the right size. Ask what size the rough opening should be, and note it. Often the directions that come with the window don't include the size of the rough opening.

This window unit is actually four windows—three regular double-hung windows with a circle-top window above them. The windows, including the circle-top, can either be installed separately or can come as a single unit. Joining multiple windows in this fashion is called mulling. You'll see how to install a double-hung window first. Installing the circle-top is covered on page 228. The windows in the following project were installed in a carriage house undergoing renovation. As a result the framing for the window is unique, but framing aside, installing one window is like installing another. For step-by-step directions on traditional framing see Framing a window, pages 218–224.

Most carpenters agree that installing a window is easier than installing a door. To begin with a window is usually smaller. Better yet the jambs and sill wrap around all four sides of the window and help keep the assembly square. Still it pays to check and double-check your work. To begin with there is the visual aspect—you don't want your windows to slope. And then there are the laws of physics. An out-of-square window can be impossible to open and close; an out-of-plumb window travels on a diagonal and can seem harder to open than it actually is.

When you're done with the installation, don't forget that the window is only part of the system that keeps out the weather. Don't forget to caulk, insulate, and put flashing tape around the window.

Installing a double-hung window

1 REMOVE THE OLD WINDOW

The window is held in place by nails that run through the jambs and into the framing. Cut through them with a reciprocating saw, and then remove the window from the outside.

2 PREPARE THE OPENING

Check to make sure the rough opening is the right size, is plumb and level, and was square. If necessary, frame a new opening. Because the window won't interrupt any weight-bearing framing on this job, no headers were required. The opening was a bit narrower than the old opening, however, so there is new framing to support both the window and the edge of the siding. Aside from this window, almost all windows require a header. For more on headers and framing a window opening, see pages 218–224.

3 PREPARE THE WINDOW

If the wall is thicker than 4½ inches, as this one is, the jambs on the new window may not be wide enough. If so, buy extension jambs. Rip them to width so that they will be flush with the drywall when installed. Cut the jambs to length, and put the extension's tongues in the groove around the window. Screw the extensions to the window with trim screws or as directed by the manufacturer. Nail the extensions together at the corner.

4 PUT IN THE WINDOW

Apply a bead of silicone caulk all along the installation flange. Put the window in its opening, lifting it in place from the outside.

5 LEVEL THE WINDOW WITH SHIMS

Have someone hold the window in place from the outside while you work from the inside. Center the window in the opening. Slip shims under the corners, and adjust until the sill is level. From the outside of the window, nail one—and only one— of the top corners in place to help hold the window in position.

6 CHECK FOR SQUARE

Measure diagonally from outside corner to outside corner of the window. The window is square if the measurements are equal. If not, adjust the shims until it is. (Usually you'll push in the shim under the lower corner of the long dimension.) Recheck for level, and adjust shims until the frame is both square and level.

GENERAL CARPENTRY

5

7 **NAIL IN THE REMAINING CORNERS**

Once the window is level and square, nail in the remaining corners. Do not drive nails along the rest of the flange yet.

In some cases the flange (or fin) is only for holding the window in place temporarily. Follow the manufacturer's installation procedures.

8 **MAKE THE SIDES PARALLEL**

Measure the width of the window at the top, bottom, and middle. The measurements should be equal. If the middle measurements are more than those at the top and bottom, drive shims to push the middle in. If the middle is narrower, drive a drywall screw through the middle and tighten it to remove the problem.

9 **FINISH NAILING**

Check and double-check for square and to make sure the width of the window is still constant. When everything is in place, nail the rest of the flange to the house, driving nails through every other hole.

10 **APPLY FLASHING TAPE**

Unless the window is properly sealed, water can leak in. Apply flashing tape across the bottom of the unit, then along the along the sides, and finally at the top. Working in this order helps ensure that the seams are watertight.

11 **INSULATE**

Stuff fiberglass insulation between the jamb and framing. Overstuffing can cause the jamb to bow, making it difficult to operate the window. When you're done use the level as a straightedge to make sure the jamb is still flat, and remove insulation if necessary.

Nailing

Until you're sure everything is as it should be, leave about ⅛ inch of the top of the nail exposed. It makes the nail easier to remove if there's a problem.

⊘ SAFETY ALERT

Wear gloves, safety glasses, and a dust mask when handling fiberglass.

Check for plumb — again?

Check and recheck for plumb, and don't believe anything stays the way you put it until all the nails are in place. Don't think that because the sill is level the sides are plumb. They may be—if all four corners of the window meet at 90 degrees, if the sides are parallel, and if nothing is bowed. Spend an extra 30 seconds with the level to make sure.

5

GENERAL CARPENTRY

Attaching the top

1 ATTACH 2×4S

The top of the window needs to be protected from the weather. If the top of the window is exposed to the weather, build a roof as shown in Bay window roofs below. If the window is under an existing roof, like this porch roof, bridge the gap with siding. Start by cutting 2×4s to lay flat along the outside edge of the window. Nail them to the plywood on the top of the window.

2 INSULATE THE TOP

Cut insulation to fit on the top of the window and put it in place.

Bay window roofs

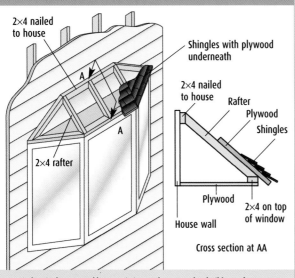

2×4 nailed to house

Shingles with plywood underneath

2×4 nailed to house

Rafter

Plywood

Shingles

2×4 rafter

Plywood

2×4 on top of window

House wall

Cross section at AA

If your window isn't protected by an existing roof, you need to build one that protects it. Frame it as shown in the drawing. Start by cutting 2×4s to lay flat along the outside edge of the window. Nail them to the plywood on the top of the window. Nail a 2×4 header to the wall, positioned so that the distance from the top of the header to the top of the window is the same as the distance from the wall to the outside edge of the window. Cut 2×4s with 45-degree angles on the end to act as rafters. Draw a line along the wall connecting the end of the header with the window and cut a 2×4 to fit along it. Cover with plywood, install flashing, and apply 30-pound tarpaper and shingles.

3 ADD FRAMING FOR THE TOP SIDING

Cut scrap plywood to fit between the top of the window and the ceiling. Rest it on top of the window and trace along it to mark where you'll need to put 2×4s on the ceiling to secure the siding. Screw the 2×4s to the joists.

4 NAIL THE SIDING IN PLACE

Put the siding in place and make marks to show where it needs to be cut. Cut and nail in place with galvanized finishing nails.

5

GENERAL CARPENTRY

Insulating the bottom

1 BUILD A SKIRT

Keep cold air from working its way in by building a skirt that goes below the window and then insulating it. Start by cutting a 2×4 that fits under the window against the house. Tack it in place, and then lay out the other pieces as shown in the inset. Remove the board you tacked to the house, and screw the skirt together.

2 INSTALL JOISTS

Cut joists to fit in the skirt and trace around the skirt to lay out a plywood bottom. You'll install the bottom later, once everything is in place.

3 INSTALL THE SKIRT

Slip the skirt in place, and nail the back piece to the house. Nail into the framing rather than just the sheathing.

4 INSULATE AND NAIL THE BOTTOM IN PLACE

Cut insulation to shape and put it in between joists. Mark and measure the position of the nuts and drill a hole in the plywood bottom so that you can tighten the nuts on the cables if necessary. Nail the bottom in place.

5 NAIL ON VINYL TRIM

Cut pieces of vinyl trim to fit around the skirt and nail them in place. You can buy special trim from the window manufacturer or use stock trim available at the home center.

Installing the ceiling

DIMPLES

Hang ½- and ⅝-inch-thick drywall with 1¼-inch drywall screws spaced at 16-inch intervals. Use Type W for wood framing and Type S for steel framing. Drive the screws so they make a small dimple in the drywall paper without ripping it. Keep screws ⅜ inch from the ends and edges of the panel.

When installing drywall the ceiling goes in first, in part so that the drywall on the walls will support the edges, and in part to ensure a tight seam at the edges of the room. Apply the drywall in several rows, each made of the longest pieces you can handle. Half-inch drywall comes in lengths of 8, 10, 12, 14, and 16 feet. In the best of all possible worlds, you can use a sheet as long as the room, but unless you're experienced and have lots of helpers the sheet may be too hard to handle. The professional drywallers shown here tripled up to handle a 12-foot sheet. Install the drywall so that the short edges of the sheet will meet in the center of a joist. Generally speaking you can cover utility boxes and vents when you install the sheet and then cut them out once the sheet is in place. Sometimes, however, you'll need to make a cutout before you install the sheet.

1 **SET UP THE ROOM**

Rent or buy platforms or scaffolding so that you can reach the ceiling easily. If you can't cover the length of the room in a single sheet, the ends (but not the sides) of adjoining pieces have to meet over a joist. Measure to find the middle of the joist you'll use. Measure for any cutouts in the edge of the sheet, and for other obstructions such as an air vent, which sticks out and would bend if you tried to cover it.

2 **CUT THE SHEET**

Measure and cut the sheet to length, guiding a utility knife along a drywall T-square. Lay out any cuts you'll have to make for obstructions. If there are openings along the edge, like the one in the corner of this sheet, cut along the lines with a drywall saw.

MAKING CUTOUTS

Instead of making cutouts for windows, doors, and electrical outlets before you hang the sheets, put the panel in place over the opening, and mark its location. Drive just enough screws to hold the panel in place. Use a drywall router—a small router that uses a drywall bit—to poke a hole in the drywall near the center of the opening you want to make. Guide the bit around the box or framing to make the cutout, and then finish screwing the panel in place.

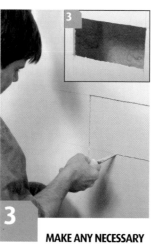

3 **MAKE ANY NECESSARY INTERIOR CUTOUTS**

Most cutouts on the interior of the sheet are made after the drywall is in place. The air vent in this room, however, extends through the drywall and would bend if you try to cover it without making a cutout. Lay out the cut, punch the nose of a drywall saw through the sheet to start the cut, and then cut along the lines.

4 **APPLY ADHESIVE**

Adhesive helps hold the panels in place. Put a tube of drywall adhesive in a caulk gun. Cut off the tip, puncture the seal with a screwdriver or nail, and spread a ⅜-inch bead of drywall adhesive along the ceiling joists.

5 **PUT THE PANEL IN PLACE**

Work with some helpers to put the panel in place so that it's tight against the studs along both corners. Cover electrical boxes that are mounted on the ceiling. You'll cut them out later. Screw the panel to the joists with 1¼-inch drywall screws.

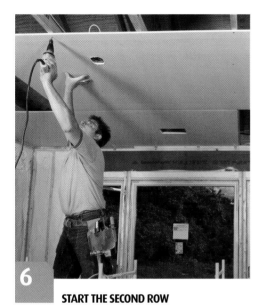

6 START THE SECOND ROW

Start the second row before you finish the first row. Start at the end of the room opposite from where you began, and put up a full sheet. This automatically offsets the short seams from row to row, creating a stronger surface. It also keeps an out-of-square corner from creating a zigzag row that makes subsequent rows hard to hang.

7 FINISH THE FIRST AND SECOND ROWS

Measure and cut pieces to fit in the openings at the end of the first and second rows. Apply adhesive, and screw the panels in place. Continue installing full-width rows, alternating between ends of the room as you start each row.

CLOSER LOOK

COVERING LARGE CEILINGS

A very large room may be more than two sheets of drywall long. It may also be a long way out of square. To avoid problems apply the first sheet of the first row, and work your way along the wall until you can't apply any more full sheets. Then start the second row at the end of the room opposite where you started the first row, nesting the edge of the sheet against the edge of the last sheet of the first row. Install the second row, working toward the opposite end until you can't install any more full sheets. Cut the last pieces of the first and second rows to fit—the corners may not be square on these two pieces, but the seams between the rows will be straight, making it easy to quickly lay one row against another.

8 CUT PIECES FOR THE FINAL ROW

The fourth row is the final row in this room, and the pieces are about 22 inches wide. To cut the pieces to width, you can measure and draw a line, or you can guide the knife along a tape measure as shown. For more on cutting with the tape measure as a guide, see Cutting long drywall sheets to length, page 237.

9 INSTALL THE LAST ROW

Put up adhesive, and screw the last pieces in place.

5

GENERAL CARPENTRY

Hanging drywall on the walls

It may not make sense at first glance, but you install drywall from the top of the wall down, and place it so the seams are horizontal. Starting at the top ensures a nice tight seam between the wall and ceiling; any gap that occurs will be at the floor where it gets covered by baseboard. Horizontal seams can result in fewer linear feet of seams per room because you can use longer sheets of drywall.

TIME SAVER

MARK THE OPENINGS
Once you cover a window it can be hard to find again. Before you cover it completely, make a couple of saw marks along the edge of the drywall so you'll be able to find it when you rout the opening, as shown on the opposite page.

1 MEASURE TO FIND THE LENGTH OF THE SHEET
The shorts ends of adjoining sheets must meet over the center of a joist. Measure to find the middle of a stud that the sheet will reach, and cut the sheet to this length.

2 INSTALL THE TOP ROW
Apply adhesive to the studs and screw the sheet along the top of the wall. Cover any openings, such as the window in this wall. Measure for the next piece, cut it to size, put it in place, and continue until you complete the top row.

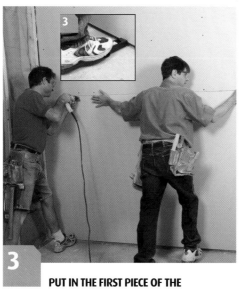

3 PUT IN THE FIRST PIECE OF THE BOTTOM ROW
The vertical seam between panels in this wall is interrupted by the window. If it wasn't you would start the bottom of the first row with a half panel in order to offset seams between rows and create a stronger wall. Cut the panel to size, and apply adhesive. Put the panel on a roll lifter, as shown in the inset, and push the top edge gently against the edge of the sheet already in place. Screw the panel in place.

4 PUT IN THE REMAINING PIECES
Install any remaining pieces, cutting the last ones in each row to fit. Rout out windows and electrical boxes with a drywall router; cut out doors with a drywall saw. For more on routing openings, see Making cutouts, page 238.

5

GENERAL CARPENTRY

Working around doors

1

COVER THE DOOR OPENING WITH DRYWALL

Cover the opening for the door as if it weren't there, screwing the panel into the studs and the framing around the door.

2

CUT OUT THE OPENING

Guide a drywall panel saw along the framing to cut out the edges of the opening. Run a utility knife across the back of the piece of drywall along the top of the opening.

3

REMOVE THE SCRAP

Pull the section covering the door forward until you crease the paper at the top of the drywall opening. Score along the crease with a knife and pull the scrap free.

Working around windows

Cover windows the same way you cover doors. Mark the edge of the opening with a couple of passes with the drywall saw so that you'll know where it is.

Cut out the drywall with a drywall router—a specialty tool that looks like a small handheld router.

Finishing drywall

The drywall may be up, but it's not done. Seams with beveled edges get a strip of paper reinforcing tape and three coats of joint compound. Each coat is slightly wider the previous coat, and the final coat is 12 inches wide. Butt joints get much the same treatment, but end up somewhere around 24 inches wide by the time all is said and done. Outside corners are a snap—three simple coats and no tape. Inside corners are slower—once the first coat and tape is up, you work on one wall, let it dry, and then work on the other, until you've built up a total of three coats on each wall. No coat is perfect, so when you're done every bit of joint compound gets sanded.

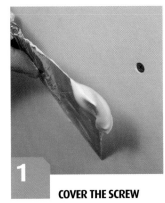

1

COVER THE SCREW HEADS

Dip a 6-inch knife in the mud pan, and load it with joint compound. Apply the compound over a screw head, filling the dimple. Make a few more passes, holding the knife at a shallow angle to the wall to pick up any excess. Fill all the holes. The compound shrinks as it dries, so let the compound dry overnight and apply a second coat to fill any depressions. Apply a third coat once the second coat has dried.

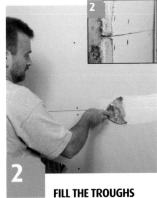

2

FILL THE TROUGHS ALONG THE SHEET EDGES

The long edge of each sheet is beveled—purposely made thinner than the rest of the sheet. This creates a trough when the edges are put together, as shown in the inset. Build up about an inch of joint compound on a 6-inch knife, and fill the trough with compound.

3 **PUT TAPE IN THE TROUGH**

Put paper drywall tape in the compound in the trough, pushing it in every foot or so to hold it in place.

4 **PULL THE KNIFE ALONG TAPE**

Pull the knife along the tape, embedding it in the mud. If you start in the corner, and work toward the middle of the room, the tape will pull loose. Start in the middle and work toward the corners, at least until you have the ends embedded in the compound.

5

GENERAL CARPENTRY

5 APPLY A SECOND COAT

Let the compound dry overnight, and apply a second coat of compound with a 10-inch knife. Let it dry overnight.

6 APPLY A THIRD COAT

Thin the joint compound with water to the consistency of mayonnaise before you apply the third coat. The thinner compound goes on more easily, fills irregularities, and is less likely to leave small pinholes as you spread it. Apply the compound with a 12-inch knife.

TOOL SAVVY

GET THE DUST OUT

Sanding drywall compound raises a huge amount of fine, white dust. You can avoid the mess by smoothing the surface with a damp sponge instead of sanding. Wet the sponge, wring it out, and then wipe all the seams with it, dissolving the compound and smoothing it out as you go. Rinse frequently. The thicker the sponge, the easier it is to handle.

7 SANDING

No coat of joint compound goes on perfectly. Let the third coat dry overnight, and sand the surface smooth using a pole sander and 120-grit paper. Start by folding the paper around the ends of the pads and tightening the wing nuts on the back to clamp it in place. Run the pole over the joints until you get a smooth surface with no steps between the edge of the compound and the drywall and with no ridges or pinholes elsewhere in the compound.

CLOSER LOOK

FEATHERING THE EDGES

The second and third coats of drywall compound go on in several passes. The first pass gets the compound on the wall; a second pass smooths it out. After that you feather the edges. Tilt the knife slightly, so that one end runs along the wall, and the other skims along the center of the wet joint compound. This creates a bed that is thicker in the center, where it needs to be strong, and feather thin along the edge, where it is indistinguishable from the rest of the wall.

5

GENERAL CARPENTRY

Taping butt joints

Butt joints occur along the short ends of the sheet, where the edge is square instead of beveled. It's like any other joint in that you embed drywall tape in joint compound, and then apply two more coats over it. Because there are no bevels to create troughs that house the joints, however, everything sits above the surface of the drywall. As a result drywallers make the joint very wide in order to camouflage it. Start by embedding the tape in joint compound with a 6-inch knife, and then let it dry. Apply the next coat with an 8- or 10-inch knife, in two side-by-side passes, creating a bed of compound 16 to 20 inches wide. Finish with a 12-inch knife, creating a 24-inch-wide bed.

1

APPLY THE FIRST COAT OF COMPOUND AND TAPE
Put a bed of joint compound across the joint with a 6-inch knife. Put drywall tape in the bed, and embed it with a pass of the knife. Let it dry overnight.

2

APPLY THE SECOND COAT OF JOINT COMPOUND
Load the knife up with compound, and make a pass along one side of the tape with one edge of the knife centered over the tape or slightly overlapping the center. Put more compound on your knife, then make a second pass—parallel to the first with one edge of the blade slightly overlapping the first pass. Leave a small ridge in the center—you'll sand it out later. Feather the edges, as shown here.

3

APPLY THE THIRD COAT OF JOINT COMPOUND
The third coat is just like the second, only wider. Make a pass with the 12-inch knife with one edge of the knife roughly centered over the joint. Make a second pass, parallel to the first and on the other side of the seam. Feather the edges and let the compound dry. Sand out the ridge in the middle, and sand out any imperfections along the edges.

5

GENERAL CARPENTRY

Taping inside corners

Inside corners go slowly. Once the first coat is up, any work you do on one wall will spoil the work you've done on the other wall. The best approach—one manufacturers recommend and most pros use—is to do one wall, let it dry, and then do the other. And while corner shaped drywall tools you see hanging next to the knife may speed up the job, they don't simplify it. Most pros say that they leave a pretty messy edge, one that requires a lot of sanding. Their best advice: Use a regular knife and a bit of patience.

1 APPLY COMPOUND AND TAPE TO THE CORNER
Coat both walls of the corner with drywall compound using a 6-inch knife. Fill any gaps between the two walls.

2 FOLD THE DRYWALL TAPE
Unroll a length of drywall tape—the longer the better, but experiment to find a length that is easy to work with. You can cover the corner in several strips, overlapping the ends. Fold the tape in half, as shown, along the crease made by the manufacturer.

3 PUT THE TAPE IN THE COMPOUND
Stick the tape in the joint compound, pushing it in place every 12 inches or so. Draw a knife along each wall to press the tape into the compound and remove excess mud. Let the compound dry overnight.

4 APPLY COMPOUND TO ONE SIDE
Apply joint compound to one side of the corner with a 6-inch knife. Feather the outside edge, and let it dry overnight.

5 APPLY COMPOUND TO THE SECOND SIDE OF THE CORNER
When the first side of the corner is dry—it usually takes overnight—apply compound to the other side. Smooth it, feather it, and let it dry. Repeat the process, still using a 6-inch knife to apply a third coat on one wall at a time. Let it dry, and then sand smooth.

5

GENERAL CARPENTRY

Drywalling outside corners

Outside corners, like the rest of the room, get three coats of joint compound. Start by dipping an 8-inch knife into the mud pan, and pick up about 1 inch of joint compound. Put the knife against one wall of the corner, with one end of the knife against the corner bead and the other end against the wall. Pull the knife along the corner bead and wall.

Because outside corners have a metal bead instead of tape, they're probably the easiest section of wall to cover. Just run one side of the knife along the edge of the bead, and the other side against the wall, and it all happens pretty much automatically.

1

APPLY THE DRYWALL

Apply drywall over one side of the corner and then the other, using adhesive and screws.

2

CUT THE CORNER BEAD

Measure the length of the corner, and cut the bead to length with a pair of tin snips. The metal is thin and easy to cut—cut from one edge toward the bead in the center, and then cut from the other edge toward the center.

3

NAIL THE BEAD TO THE WALL

Nail the bead to the wall. Drywall bead is nailed to the wall instead of screwed because the screws tend to bend the metal. Drive a 1½-inch drywall nail every 9 inches into the holes along the edge of the bead.

4

APPLY THE FIRST COAT

Dip the knife in drywall compound and pick up about an inch of compound. Rest one edge of the knife against the wall, and the other against the bead. Pull the knife along the bead to apply the compound. Repeat on the other side of the corner.

5

APPLY THE SECOND COAT

Let the first coat dry overnight, and apply the second coat exactly the same way as the first, using a 10-inch knife.

6

APPLY THE THIRD COAT

Apply the third coat like the second, using a 12-inch knife.

Applying sheet paneling

PROJECT DETAILS

SKILLS: Measuring and layout; using power tools
PROJECT: Installing sheet paneling on existing walls

TIME TO COMPLETE

EXPERIENCED: 1 day
HANDY: 1½ days
NOVICE: 2 days

STUFF YOU'LL NEED

TOOLS: Tape measure; level; straightedge; stud finder; drill; paintbrush; compass; circular saw; jigsaw; hammer and nail set; chalk line; drill; safety glasses; miter box
MATERIALS: Paneling; electrical box extenders; baseboard; ceiling molding; caulk; paint

GOOD IDEA

ACCLIMATE THE SHEETS
Manufacturers say you should put the panels in the room you're installing and let them acclimate for 48 hours, stacking them on the floor or leaning them against the wall with spacers between the sheets. This brings the sheets to roughly the same moisture content as the air in the room, so they won't change size immediately after installation, leaving gaps between sheets or causing them to buckle.

Paneling that comes in 4×8 sheets installs quickly and easily. As long as you plan the job carefully and install the first sheet accurately, the rest of the job should go smoothly.

Choose paneling that looks good and is strong enough for your purposes. The least expensive paneling is made of ⁵⁄₃₂-inch medium density fiberboard (MDF) with a printed-paper facing but is not as durable as paneling made of plywood or oriented strand board (OSB) topped with ¼ inch of real hardwood veneer.

Choose moldings along with the paneling. There's a pretty good selection of vinyl or foam moldings that match the paneling; for a custom look, you can stain regular molding to match.

Installing paneling

CHECK THE WALLS
Use a straightedge, such as a 4-foot level, to check the walls for waves. If you find dips or bulges greater than ⅜ inch, they'll be noticeable if you apply the paneling without corrective action. Trowel on joint compound to create a smooth surface.

1 LAY OUT THE EDGES OF THE PANELS
Start in the corner, and make a mark every 4 feet to mark where the edges of the panels will be. In this case the edges of the drywall panels are good indicators, but if the wall has been finished you will need to make the marks. Draw vertical lines with the help of a level.

2 PAINT ALONG THE JOINTS
Panels need to be spaced a minimum of 1/16 inch apart to allow for expansion in humid weather. (Check the manufacturer's directions to see if the gap needs to be even wider.) Paint the wall at each joint location, using a color that matches the panel so that gaps will not be noticeable.

GOOD IDEA

GET A PERFECT MATCH
Most stores now have computer scanners that can re-create any color sample they scan, from paint swatches to strawberry jam. Have them scan one of the panels you're using to get a color that matches, and use it to paint the walls along the edge of the panels.

3 FIND AND MARK THE STUDS
Mark the wall to show where an electronic stud finder says the studs are. Double-check by drilling holes near the mark until you hit a stud. Draw lines along the wall to show the location of each stud. Continue the lines onto the floor and ceiling so that you'll be able to find them once you've covered the walls with paneling.

4 CUT TO LENGTH
Manufacturers say paneling needs a ¼-inch gap at the floor and ceiling to allow for expansion. Measure and mark the panel, taking the combined size of the gap off one of the edges. Because this cut will be covered by molding, you can cut more than one sheet at a time, and can cut the paneling from either the front or the back. On edges that will be visible, cut one sheet at a time.

CUT THE FIRST PANEL TO FIT

Put the first panel in a corner, and plumb it with a level. If there are gaps between the panel and the wall, set a compass to the width of the gap, and guide it along the wall to mark the paneling. Cut along the line with a jigsaw for a panel that will fit snugly in the corner.

APPLY PANEL ADHESIVE

Panels should be held in place with both nails and panel adhesive. Once you are sure the panel will fit, apply zigzag-shape beads of adhesive to the wall area that will be covered by the panel. Also apply adhesive along the perimeter on the back of the sheet.

CLOSER LOOK

CUTTING PANELING

Paneling is covered with a facing, either veneer or paper, that will splinter when cut. To minimize splintering you need the right tools, and you need to use them correctly. Use a plywood blade in a circular saw, and cut from the back, so that any splintering will occur there. When cutting with a jigsaw use a veneer blade, which cuts on the downstroke, and cut from the front.

NAIL THE FIRST PIECE IN PLACE

Set the first sheet in place, using a spacer to keep it ¼ inch above the floor. Double-check to make sure that it is plumb. Look at the marks you made on the ceiling and floor, and find a groove that lies over them. Drive colored paneling nails, at least 1½ inches long, every 12 inches into the studs. Along the edges drive the nails every 6 inches.

INSTALL THE REMAINING PANELS

To prevent buckling when the panels expand in humid weather, install the panels with a ¹⁄₁₆-inch gap between the sheets. (Some paneling requires larger spaces. Check the manufacturer's directions.) For a ¹⁄₁₆-inch gap, use the head of an 8d finishing nail or a dime as a spacer.

TOOL SAVVY

INDUSTRIAL-STRENGTH CAULK GUNS

A standard tube of panel adhesive contains enough glue for only two sheets or so. If you have lots of paneling to install, invest in a professional-sized caulk gun, which uses tubes that hold a full quart.

5

GENERAL CARPENTRY

REAL WORLD

WHEN THE STUDS DON'T ALIGN

Every now and then you'll discover the studs don't fall along the lines in the panel. If this happens, it's usually because of the amount you had to remove to fit the panel in the corner. Measure for a second cut to see how much you'll have to remove in the corner to realign the grooves and studs. Cut 1½ inches less than measured off the edge that goes in the corner. Put the panel in place and set the compass to 1½ inches. Trace along the wall, as before, to draw a line on the panel. Cut along the line for a panel with grooves that fall over the studs.

SAFETY ALERT

SHUT OFF THE POWER

A switch or receptacle must be disconnected and removed before installing the panel. Shut off power at the service panel (circuit-breaker panel or fuse box) before you do this.

Reinstalling the switch or outlet

Install the panel, then replace the switch or receptacle. Because the cut ends of the panel will be exposed around the electrical box, code requires you to install a box extender before reinstalling the wiring. The extender slips inside the existing box and screws in place with screws that come with it.

9

LAY OUT THE SIDES OF AN ELECTRICAL BOX

Use a level to mark the floor showing where the edge of the box is. Put the panel in place and use the level to transfer the marks from the floor back to the paneling.

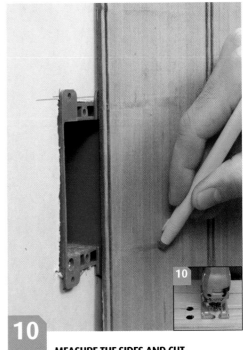

10

MEASURE THE SIDES AND CUT

Mark the paneling with a grease pencil at the top and bottom of the switch box. Connect the marks with a pencil and square, drill holes in the corners, and cut along the lines with a jigsaw.

11

APPLY MOLDING

Apply molding to cover the gaps at the top and bottom of the paneling; some installers like to install a cove molding in the corners too.

Installing paneling around doors and windows

Expansion and contraction of the panels and trim around doors and windows means you need to leave a gap between the trim and the paneling. The gap is much larger than the one between panels—manufacturers recommend a gap as large as ⅜ inch. Measuring to find where to cut assumes that everything is plumb and square—a dangerous assumption. Instead, draw some lines on the wall that are based on where the trim is, and transfer the lines to the paneling. Offset the line by the required expansion gap, and cut along the lines. Installing around windows is much the same, except you will have to lay out the bottom of the window too. Once you've made the cuts, scribe around the sill, if necessary.

1 MARK WHERE THE TRIM WOULD MEET THE CEILING
Lay a straightedge along the side of the trim, and draw a line connecting the edge of the trim with the ceiling. Mark the ceiling to show where the line is. Make a mark on the floor, too, to show where the trim meets the floor.

2 MARK WHERE THE TRIM WOULD MEET THE NEXT PANEL
Use the straightedge to extend the line along the top of the trim. Continue the line until it meets the adjoining panel, or in this case the corner.

3 TRANSFER THE LINES TO THE PANEL
Put the panel in place, and make four marks. Mark where the panel meets the top trim. Mark where the panel meets the line you extended to the corner or neighboring panel. Make marks where the marks you made on the ceiling and the floor meet the panel.

4 CONNECT THE DOTS AND CUT OUT FOR THE DOOR
Transfer the marks you made to the edge of the panel, and from there to the back of the panel. Draw lines connecting the marks that are on opposite edges of the panels. Mark the section you'll cut out with a series of scribbles, and then draw a second set of lines parallel to the first lines and ⅜ inch away from the cutout. Cut along the lines to make the cutout for the door.

5 PUT THE PANEL IN PLACE AND REPEAT ON THE OTHER SIDE
Nail the panel in place like any other panel, and repeat on the other side of the door. Caulk the gap between the panel and the door.

TOOL SAVVY
Instead of drawing a second set of lines parallel to the first, you can use the cutting guide on your saw. Find the mark that shows where the blade will cut. Measure over by the amount of the required expansion gap on each side of the line (⅜ inch in this case) and make a mark or apply a piece of tape. Line up the original layout lines with the mark, and make your cut. Double-check to make sure the piece of tape you're using as a guide will make the cut wider than drawn. You'll use one mark for the first cut, and the other mark for the second.

Apron. A piece of molding applied to the wall below the window sill.

Base cap. A molding applied to the top of a plain board to create a baseboard. WM167 is a common choice, as are other moldings in the WM160 range. You can, however, create a baseboard with any molding you want.

Bead. A detail in a piece of molding that looks like a half circle when viewed from the end.

Bevel. An angle cut in the end of a board.

Bottom plate. The 2×4 that the studs sit on in framing.

Casing. Molding around a door or window.

Chamfer. An angle cut on the edge of a board.

Clearance hole. A hole for a screw that is slightly larger than the screw shank. When screwing two pieces of wood together, a clearance hole keeps the threads from grabbing both pieces of wood simultaneously and forcing them apart.

Cope joint. A nesting corner joint, in which you cut the profile of a molding into the face of its neighbor. When assembled on the wall, the joint looks like a miter, but it is much sturdier.

Countersink. A cone-shaped recess in a piece of wood that houses the head of the screw. Drill countersinks with either a combination bit, which drills pilot, clearance, and countersink in one pass, or with a countersink, which drills only the recess.

Cove. Any of several concave moldings used in trim work.

Cripple. A short stud installed between the header and top plate.

Crosscut. To cut across the grain.

Crown molding. Molding applied along the top of the room.

Dado head. A blade or a group of table saw blades used to cut grooves. It takes its name from the term dado, which is any groove you cut across the grain.

Flashing. A metal or asphalt-based strip applied to keep rain from coming in around windows and doors.

Glazing putty. The putty that holds glass in place in older windows. Excellent for filling nail holes in molding that will be painted.

Header. A beam built up from framing lumber and plywood to provide support across openings for windows and exterior doors. Headers are also needed above interior doors in load-bearing walls.

Jack stud. A stud nailed to the king stud, but cut shorter to provide support for the header.

Jamb. The piece of wood applied over the framing to create the edge of a doorway or window opening.

Jamb extensions. Windows and doors are manufactured to match standard wall thicknesses. Jamb extensions are applied on the edge of a jamb to build the jamb up to the proper width in a nonstandard wall.

Joist. The framing that supports the floor or ceiling.

King stud. In framing a window or door, the king stud is the last full-length stud before the window opening. The shorter jack stud is nailed to it to create the rough opening.

Level. Flat with no slope.

Load-bearing wall. A wall that supports the floors above it and ultimately the roof. All exterior doors are load bearing, as are some interior walls. Load-bearing interior walls will have walls above them up to the attic and sit on other walls or on a beam. Any wall with a double top plate is a load-bearing wall.

Medium Density Fiberboard (MDF). This is made by pressing sawdust and glue together. The surface is very smooth and takes paint well. It comes in 4×8 foot sheets and as molding.

Miter joint. A joint in which each of the neighboring pieces is cut at an angle and then fit together to form either a corner or a straight line. In a 90-degree corner typical of most rooms, each piece has a 45-degree angle on it.

On Center (OC). The spacing between framing pieces, such as studs, is "on center," meaning the carpenter lays out the studs so that the center of each is 16 inches from the center of its neighbors. This helps eliminate errors caused by variations in the thickness of framing lumber.

Pilot hole. A hole for a screw that is slightly smaller than the screw shank. The screw goes into the pilot and the threads grab the surrounding wood.

Piloted bit. A type of router bit. The pilot is a bearing, usually on the end of the bit, that you guide along the wood to control depth of cut.

Plumb. Straight up and down.

Quarter round. A molding, which, when viewed from the end, looks like a quarter of a circle. It comes in several sizes.

Rabbet. A groove cut in the edge of a board.

Rip. To cut parallel with the grain.

Rough opening. The opening for a door or window is slightly larger than the outside dimensions of the door or window. This larger opening makes it easier to put the door or window in place and is called the rough opening.

Rough sill. The bottom of the rough opening for a window.

Sheathing. Wood, plywood, or sheet materials applied to the exterior studs to reinforce the framing and serve as a surface for the siding.

Shoe mold. A molding applied to the front of baseboard to hide any gaps between the floor and baseboard. Carpenters often simply use quarter round, but there are slightly thinner moldings sold as base shoes.

Splice. A joint used to piece two lengths of molding together to make a long piece. The simplest splice consists of cutting the adjoining ends square and butting them. A stronger splice, and one that is less likely to become visible over time, consists of mating 45-degree miters cut in adjoining ends.

Square. 90 degrees. The end of a piece of wood cut at exactly 90 degrees is said to be square. Two pieces of wood that come together at exactly 90 degrees are also said to be square.

Studs. The vertical pieces of framing that make up a wall. Studs are usually spaced 16 inches on center, meaning that it is 16 inches from the center of one stud to the next.

Top plate. The 2×4 that runs along the top of the studs in wall framing. If the wall is load bearing, there will be two top plates. If not, there is only one.

Trim. Molding.

Trimmer stud. Same as a jack stud.

WM number. WM, followed by a number, designates one of several hundred standard wood moldings.

RESOURCES

Andersen Corporation
100 Fourth Avenue North
Bayport, MN 55003-1096
651/264-5150
www.andersenwindows.com

Asteak & DeWalt Law Office
8 N. Main Street
Nazareth, PA 18064

Aunt Daisy's
5412 Shimerville Road
Emmaus, PA 18049
610/967-0522
www.auntdaisys.com

The Bucksville House
4501 Durham Road
Kintnersville, PA 18930-1610
610/847-8948
www.bucksvillehouse.com

Cecil Baker & Associates
1107 Walnut Street, 2nd Floor
Philadelphia, PA 19107
215/928-0202
www.cbaarch.com

David Hornung Architect Planner, Inc.
215½ N. 7th Street
Allentown, PA 18104
610/434-6205

DEWALT Industrial Tool Co.
701 E. Joppa Road, TW425
Baltimore, MD 21286
800/4-DEWALT (800/433-9258)
www.dewalt.com

Heritage House Bed and Breakfast
500 Chestnut Street
Emmaus, PA 18049
610/965-6100

Leverne Hendricks Builders, Inc.
712 Godshall Road
Telford, PA 18969
215/723-5492

The Morning Star Inn
72 E. Market Street
Bethlehem, PA 18018
610/867-2300
www.morningstarinn.com

RIDGID Tools
One World Technologies, Inc.
Highway 8
Pickens, SC 29671
800/4-RIDGID (800/474-3443)
www.ridgid.com

Robert Bosch Tool Corporation
1800 W. Central Road
Mt. Prospect, IL 60056-2230
877/BOSCH-99 (877/267-2499)
www.boschtools.com

Ryobi Technologies, Inc.
1428 Pearman Dairy Road
Anderson, SC 29625
800/323-4615
www.ryobitools.com

The Sayre Mansion Inn
250 Wyandotte Street
Bethlehem, PA 18015
610/882-2100
www.sayremansion.com

Stephen Varenhost Architects
Conshohocken, PA 19428
610/940-0855

Strictly Mission
3946 Lanark Road
Coopersburg, PA 18036
866/MISSION (866/647-7466)
www.strictlymission.com

Waddell Manufacturing Co.
1676 Commerce Drive
Stow, OH 44224
800/433-1737
www.waddellmfg.com

INDEX

INDEX

Metric conversions

U.S. Units to Metric Equivalents

To convert from	Multiply by	To Get
Inches	25.4	Millimeters
Inches	2.54	Centimeters
Feet	30.48	Centimeters
Feet	.03048	Meters
Yards	.9144	Meters
Miles	1.6093	Kilometers
Square inches	6.4516	Square centimeters
Square feet	0.0929	Square meters
Square yards	0.8361	Square meters
Acres	0.4047	Hectares
Square miles	2.5899	Square kilometers
Cubic inches	16.387	Cubic centimeters
Cubic feet	0.0283	Cubic meters
Cubic feet	28.316	Liters
Cubic yards	0.7646	Cubic meters
Cubic yards	764.55	Liters

To convert from degrees Fahrenheit (F) to degrees Celsius (C), first subtract 32, then multiply by ⅝.

Metric Units to U.S. Equivalents

To convert from	Multiply by	To Get
Millimeters	0.0394	Inches
Centimeters	0.3937	Inches
Centimeters	0.0328	Feet
Meters	3.2808	Feet
Meters	1.0936	Yards
Kilometers	0.6214	Miles
Square centimeters	0.1550	Square inches
Square meters	10.764	Square feet
Square meters	1.1960	Square yards
Hectares	2.4711	Acres
Square kilometers	0.3861	Square miles
Cubic centimeters	0.0610	Cubic inches
Cubic meters	35.315	Cubic feet
Liters	0.0353	Cubic feet
Cubic meters	1.038U	Cubic yards
Liters	0.0013	Cubic yards

To convert from degrees Celsius to degrees Fahrenheit, multiply by ⅝, then add 32.

Toolbox essentials: nuts-and-bolts books for do-it-yourself success.

Save money, get great results, and take the guesswork out of home improvement projects with a growing library of step-by-step books from the experts at The Home Depot®.

Packed with lots of projects and practical tips, these books help you design, remodel, decorate, and repair your home or garden. Easy-to-follow, step-by-step instructions and colorful photographs ensure success. Projects even estimate time, skills, materials needed, and tools required.

**You can do it.
We can help.**℠

**Look for the books that help you say "I can do that!"
at The Home Depot® www.meredithbooks.com,
or wherever quality books are sold.**